FUNDAMENTAL QUESTIONS
OF PHILOSOPHY

by

A. C. EWING

ROUTLEDGE & KEGAN PAUL
London, Boston, Melbourne and Henley

First published in 1951
BY ROUTLEDGE & KEGAN PAUL PLC
14 Leicester Square, London WC2H 7PH, England

9 Park Street, Boston, Mass. 02108, USA

464 St Kilda Road, Melbourne,
Victoria 3004, Australia and

Broadway House, Newtown Road,
Henley on Thames, Oxon RG9 1EN, England

Printed in Great Britain
by T. J. Press (Padstow) Ltd.,
Padstow, Cornwall

Second impression 1952
Third impression 1953
First published as a paperback in 1985

British Library Cataloguing in Publication Data
Ewing, A.C.
The fundamental questions of philosophy.
1. Philosophy, Modern—20th century
190'.9'04   B804
ISBN 0-7100-0586-5

CONTENTS

PREFACE

THERE are two classes of readers for whom this book is specially intended, first, university students who have just begun the study of philosophy, and, secondly, those who, without having had the advantage of being at a university, wish to acquire by private reading some idea of what philosophy is and of the great topics with which it deals. I have tried very hard to make the book clear for both these classes, but it is best to realize at the start that it is not possible for a man to enter on the study of philosophy without real hard mental work, however much is done to make his task easier. Many philosophers, whose ranks I hope I have not joined, have been and are very much to blame for making the subject unnecessarily obscure by their manner of presentation, but the nature of the subject-matter is such as to forbid the sort of effortless understanding we may have of a novel.

Professor Dorothy Emmet and Mr. G. E. Hughes have kindly helped me by reading the last chapter and making valuable criticisms. My indirect debts to those whose books I have read on philosophy or who have had verbal discussions with me in the past are naturally in the case of a book of this kind too numerous to recount.

A. C. EWING

Trinity Hall
Cambridge

Chapter One

WHAT PHILOSOPHY IS
AND WHY IT IS WORTH STUDYING

INTRODUCTORY. ORIGIN OF THE TERM
'PHILOSOPHY'

A precise definition of the term 'philosophy' is not practicable and to attempt it, at least at the beginning, would be misleading. A sarcastic person might define it as 'everything and/or nothing'. That is, it differs from the special sciences in that it attempts to give a picture of human thought as a whole, and even of Reality in so far as it is held that this can be done; but in practice the content of real information given by philosophy over and above the special sciences tends to evaporate till it seems to some that there is nothing left. This appearance is, I think, misleading; but it must be admitted that philosophy has so far failed to live up to its great claims and that it can produce no body of agreed knowledge comparable with that of the sciences. This is partly, though not wholly, because where agreed knowledge is attained in answer to any question, the question is said to belong to science and not to philosophy. The term 'philosopher' originally meant 'lover of wisdom', and took its origin from a famous retort which Pythagoras made when he was called 'wise'. He said that his wisdom only consisted in knowing that he was ignorant, and that he should therefore not be called 'wise', but 'a lover of wisdom'. 'Wisdom' here is not restricted to any particular part of thought, and 'philosophy' used to be understood as including what we now call the 'sciences'. This usage still survives in such phrases as 'Chair of Natural Philosophy'. As a great mass of specialized knowledge came to be acquired in a given field, the study of that field broke off from philosophy and came to be an independent discipline. The last sciences to do that have been Psychology and Sociology. Thus there is a tendency for the sphere of philosophy to contract as knowledge advances. We refuse to regard as philosophical those questions the answer to which can be given empirically. But this does not mean that philosophy will eventually shrink to nothing. The fundamental concepts of the sciences and the general picture of human experience, and of reality in so far as we form justified beliefs about it, remain within the purview of philosophy, since they cannot from the nature of the case be determined by the methods of any of the special sciences. It is discouraging that philosophers have not succeeded in attaining more agreement in regard to these matters, but we must not conclude that, where there is no agreed result, the effort has been wasted. Two philosophers who disagree may well each be contributing something of great value, though they are not yet in a position to disentangle it completely from error, and their rival accounts may be taken as supplementing each other. The fact that different philosophers are thus needed to supplement each other brings out the point that philosophizing is not only an individual but a social process. One of the cases of useful division of labour is the emphasis by different people of different sides of a question. Very much philosophy is, however, concerned rather with the way we know things than with the things known, and this is another reason why it may seem lacking in content. But discussions as to the ultimate criteria of truth may eventually determine in their application which propositions we decide in practice to be true. Philosophical discussions of the theory of knowledge have had indirectly an important effect on the sciences.

THE USE OF PHILOSOPHY

The question which many people will first ask when hearing of the subject, philosophy, is—What is the use of it? Now it cannot be expected to help directly in the production of material wealth. But unless we suppose that material wealth is the only thing of value, the inability of philosophy to contribute to this would not mean that it was of no practical value. We value material wealth not for itself—a pile of the paper we call banknotes is not good in itself—but for its contribution to happiness. Now there is no doubt that one of the most important sources of happiness for those who can enjoy it at all is the search for truth and the contemplation of reality, and this is the aim of the philosopher. Further, those who do not in the interests of a theory rate all pleasures as equally valuable and who have experienced this pleasure at all, regard it as a pleasure superior in quality to most. Since almost all the goods which industry produces other than sheer necessities have value only as sources of pleasure, philosophy can well compete with most industries in utility, when we think how few people have whole-time employment as philosophers. It would be unfitting to grudge such a small expenditure of man-power to the subject even if we thought of it only as a source of innocent pleasure of a particularly valuable kind in itself (not only of course for the philosophers themselves alone but for the people they teach and influence).

But this is not all that can be said on behalf of philosophy. For, apart from any value that belongs to it in itself over and above its effects, it has constantly had, overlook this though we may, a very important indirect influence on the lives even of those who have never heard of the subject. For indirectly it filters down through sermons, literature, newspapers and oral tradition and affects the whole general outlook on the world. The Christian religion was made what it is to a considerable extent through the influence of philosophy. Ideas which have played such a potent part in general thought even at the popular level as the idea that no man should be treated only as a means or that government should depend on the consent of the governed we owe originally to philosophers. In the political sphere the influence of philosophical conceptions has been especially great. For instance, the American constitution is to a very considerable extent an application of the political ideas of the philosopher, John Locke, with a president substituted for an hereditary king, and the ideas of Rousseau are admitted to have played an enormous part in the French Revolution of 1789. No doubt the influence of philosophy on politics is sometimes bad: the German philosophers of the nineteenth century have to bear some part of the blame for the development of that exaggerated nationalism which eventually took such perverted forms, though the extent to which they are to blame has no doubt very often been much exaggerated and is difficult to determine exactly owing to their obscurity. But, if bad philosophy can have a bad influence on politics, good philosophy can have a good. We cannot in any case prevent politics being influenced by some philosophical conceptions, and therefore it is very desirable to devote careful attention to philosophy in order to see that the conceptions which do wield an influence are good rather than bad. What horrors would the world have been spared if the Germans had come under the influence of a better philosophy instead of that of the Nazis!

I must, therefore, now take back the suggestion that philosophy can have no value even as regards material wealth. A good philosophy by influencing politics favourably might well help even to make us wealthier than if we had a bad one. Again, the enormous development of science with its consequent practical benefits depended for its possibility a good deal on its philosophical background. It has even been said (though no doubt exaggeratedly) that the whole development of civilization could be traced to changes in the idea of causation, i.e. from the magical to the scientific, and the idea of causation certainly belongs to the subject-matter of philosophy. The 'scientific outlook' is itself a philosophy and was brought into being initially to a large extent by philosophers.

But we should certainly not be in the best mood for a profitable study of philosophy if we looked on it mainly as an indirect means to material wealth. Its chief contribution is to that intangible intellectual background on which the emotional mood and outlook of a civilization so much depend. A still more ambitious claim is sometimes advanced. Whitehead, one of the greatest and most respected thinkers of modern times, describes the gifts of philosophy as 'insight and foresight, and a sense of the worth of life, in short, that sense of importance which nerves all civilized effort'.[1] He adds 'that when civilization culminates, the absence of a co-ordinating philosophy of life, spread throughout the community, spells decadence, boredom, and the slackening of effort'. The importance of philosophy is based for him on the fact that it

[1] *Adventures of Ideas*, p. 125.

is 'an attempt to clarify those fundamental beliefs which finally determine the emphasis of attention that lies at the basis of character'. However that may be, it is certain that the character of a civilization is greatly influenced by its general view of life and reality. This till recently has been provided for most people by religious teaching, but religious views themselves have been greatly influenced by philosophic thought. Further, experience shows that religious views are apt to end in folly unless subject to constant review by reason. As for those who discard all religious views, they should be all the more concerned to work out a new view, if they can, to take the place of religious belief, and to work out such a new view is to engage in philosophy.

Science cannot take the place of philosophy, but itself raises philosophical problems. For science itself cannot possibly tell us what place in the whole scheme of things is held by the realm of facts with which it deals or even how they are related to the human minds which observe them. It cannot even demonstrate, though it must assume, the existence of the physical world, or the legitimacy of using the ordinary principles of induction to predict what will probably happen or to pass in any way beyond what has actually been observed. No scientific laboratory can demonstrate in what sense human beings have souls, whether or not the universe has a purpose, whether and in what sense we are free, and so on. I do not say that philosophy can solve these problems, but if it cannot nothing else can do so, and it is certainly worth while at least trying to see whether they are soluble. Science itself, as we shall see, is all the while presupposing concepts which fall within the subject matter of philosophy. And, while we cannot even start science without tacitly assuming answers to some philosophical questions, we certainly cannot make adequate mental use of it for our intellectual development without having a more or less coherent world-view. The successes of modern science would themselves have probably never been achieved if the scientist had not taken from great original philosophers certain assumptions on which he based his whole procedure. The 'mechanistic' view of the universe characteristic of science during the last three centuries is derived chiefly from the philosopher Descartes. This mechanistic scheme has achieved such wonderful results that it must be partly true, but it is also partly breaking down, and the scientist may have to look to the philosopher to help him build up a new one in its place.

Another very valuable service of philosophy (this time especially 'critical philosophy') lies in the habit it forms of attempting an impartial judgment of all sides and the idea it gives of what evidence is and what one should look for and expect in a proof. This should be an important check on emotional bias and hasty conclusions and is specially needed and often specially lacking in political controversies. If both sides looked at political questions in the philosophical spirit, it is difficult to see how there could ever be a war between them. The success of democracy depends very much on the ability of the citizen to distinguish good and bad arguments and not to be misled by confusions. Critical philosophy sets up an ideal of good thinking and trains one in removing confusions. This is perhaps why Whitehead in the passage just quoted says that 'there can be no successful democratic society till general education conveys a philosophic outlook'.

While one should be careful to avoid assuming that men will necessarily live up to the philosophy in which they believe, and while we should attribute a larger part of human wrongdoing to the lack of will to live up to the best ideas we have than to sheer ignorance and error, we cannot deny that general beliefs about the nature of the universe and of good play a very large part in determining human progress or degeneration. Some parts of philosophy no doubt have more practical influence than others, but we must not make the mistake of assuming that, because some study has no apparent practical bearing, it will necessarily be of no practical value to study it. It is reported that a scientist who rather prided himself on despising the practical viewpoint said of some research: 'The best thing about it is that it cannot possibly be of any practical use to anybody', yet that very line of research turned out to lead to the discovery of electricity. Studies in philosophy which are apparently practically useless and quite academic may eventually come to have all sorts of influence on the world outlook, ultimately affecting our ethics and our religion. For the different parts of philosophy, the different elements in our world-outlook, should all hang together. At least this is the aim—not always attainable—of a good philosophy. That being so, concepts apparently the most remote from practical interests may vitally affect others which touch ordinary life far more nearly.

So philosophy need not fear the question—What is its practical value? At the same time a purely pragmatic view of philosophy is one which I by no means approve. Philosophy is not to be valued only for its indirect practical effects but for itself; and the best way of securing these good practical effects is to pursue philosophy for its own sake. In order to find truth we must aim at it disinterestedly. It may be practically useful when found, but premature concern about its practical effects will only handicap us in trying to find out what is really true. Still less can we make its practical effects the criterion of its truth. Beliefs are useful because they are true, not true because they are useful.[1]

MAIN DIVISIONS OF PHILOSOPHY

The following are commonly recognized sub-classes of the subject, philosophy.

(1) Metaphysics.[2] This is conceived as the study of the nature of reality in its most general aspects in so far as this can be achieved by us. It deals with such questions as—What is the relation between matter and mind? Which is primary? Are men free? Is the self a substance or only a series of experiences? Is the universe infinite? Does God exist? How far is the universe a unity and how far a diversity? How far, if at all, is it a rational system?

(2) To metaphysics (or speculative philosophy, as it is sometimes called) there has recently been very often opposed '*Critical Philosophy*'. This consists in an analysis and criticism of the concepts of common sense and the sciences. The sciences presuppose certain concepts which are not themselves susceptible of investigation by scientific methods and therefore fall in the province of philosophy. Thus all sciences except mathematics presuppose in some form the conception of natural law, and to examine this is

---

[1] For my criticism of the 'pragmatist' attitude *vide* below, pp. 56-7, 66-7.

[2] The term owes its origin to the fact that it was discussed in the work of Aristotle which was put next in order after (*meta*) his work on Physics.

15

the business of philosophy and not of any particular science. Similarly, we in our most ordinary and unphilosophical conversation presuppose concepts which fairly bristle with philosophical problems—matter, mind, cause, substance, number. It is an important task of philosophy to analyse these concepts and see what they really mean and how far their application in the common-sense fashion can be justified. The part of critical philosophy which consists in investigating the nature and ·criterion of truth and the manner in which we can know is called *Epistemology* (theory of knowledge). It deals with such questions as—How are we to define truth? What is the distinction between knowledge and belief? Can we ever know anything with certainty? What are the relative functions of reasoning, intuition, and sense-experience?

The present book will be concerned with these two branches of philosophy as constituting its most fundamental and characteristically philosophical part. Allied to philosophy in the sense in which it is handled in this book, but distinct from it and having a certain independence of their own, are the following branches of study.

ALLIED BRANCHES OF STUDY

(1) Difficult to separate from epistemology but still regarded commonly as a distinct discipline is *Logic*. This is a study of the different kinds of propositions 'and the relations between them which justify inference. Some parts of it have very considerable affinities to mathematics, others might equally well be classed as belonging to epistemology.

(2) *Ethics* or *Moral Philosophy* deals with values and with the conception of 'ought'. It asks such questions as—What is the chief good? What is the definition of good? Is the rightness of an act dependent solely on its consequences? Are our judgments about what we ought to do objective or subjective? What is the function of punishment? What is the ultimate reason why we ought not to tell lies?

(3) *Political Philosophy* is the application of philosophy (mainly ethics) to questions relating to individuals as organized in a state.

It considers such questions as—Has the individual rights against the state? Is the state anything over and above the individuals in it? Is democracy the best form of government?

(4) *Aesthetics* is the application of philosophy to the consideration of art and the beautiful. It asks such questions as—Is beauty objective or subjective? What is the function of art? To what sides of our nature do the various kinds of beauty appeal?

(5) The more general term—*Value Theory*—is sometimes used to cover the study of value as such, though this might be put under the heading of ethics or moral philosophy. Certainly we may think of value as a general conception particular species and applications of which are handled by (2), (3) and (4).

ATTEMPT TO EXCLUDE METAPHYSICS OPEN TO OBJECTION THAT WE CANNOT HAVE EVEN CRITICAL PHILOSOPHY WITHOUT METAPHYSICS

Various attempts, some of which will be discussed later, have been made to exclude metaphysics as wholly unjustifiable and to confine philosophy to critical philosophy and the five allied branches of study just mentioned in so far as these can be regarded as an account and critical study of concepts of science and practical life. This view has sometimes been expressed by saying that philosophy consists or rather should consist in the analysis of common-sense propositions. This, if meant as an exclusive account, is clearly going too far. For (1) even if there can be no legitimate positive metaphysics, there will certainly be a branch of study the business of which it is to refute the fallacious arguments that have been at least supposed to lead to metaphysical conclusions, and this branch will obviously be part of philosophy. (2) Unless common-sense propositions are wholly false, to analyse them will be to give a general account of that portion of the real with which they are concerned, i.e. to provide at any rate part of the general account of the real which metaphysics seeks to give. Thus, if minds exist at all—and obviously they exist in some sense—the analysis of common-sense propositions about ourselves, in so far as these common-sense propositions are true—and it is quite incredible that all our common-sense propositions about human beings can be wholly false—will be giving us a metaphysics of mind. It may not be a far-reaching and elaborate metaphysics, but at any rate it will involve some genuine metaphysical propositions. Even if we say that all we know is merely appearance, appearance implies a reality which appears and a mind to which it appears, and these cannot themselves be again just appearance, so that we are still asserting some metaphysics. Even behaviourism is a metaphysics. Of course this is not the same as to say that metaphysics in the sense of an elaborate system giving us a great deal of information about the whole structure of reality and the things we most want to know is or ever will be possible. This can only be settled *ambulando* in trying to establish and criticize the metaphysical propositions in question. But, however ardent metaphysicians we may be, we cannot do without critical philosophy, or at least if we try to dispense with it we may be certain that we shall produce very bad metaphysics. For even in metaphysics we must start with the concepts of common sense and the sciences, having no others on which to build, and therefore if our foundations are to be in order we must carefully analyse and examine these. So we cannot quite separate critical philosophy from metaphysics, though of course a philosopher may emphasize one of these elements in his thought much more than the other.

PHILOSOPHY AND THE SPECIAL SCIENCES

Philosophy differs from the special sciences as regards (1) its greater generality, (2) its method. It investigates concepts which are presupposed by many different sciences at once besides questions which fall altogether outside the purview of the sciences. Concepts requiring this philosophical investigation are shared by the sciences with common sense, but there are some special problems raised or intensified by discoveries in a particular science which call for philosophical treatment because they are beyond the capacity of this science to discuss adequately, e.g. 'relativity'. Some thinkers, e.g. Herbert Spencer, have viewed philosophy as essentially a synthesis of the results of the sciences, but this view is not now generally taken by philosophers. No doubt, if philosophical results can be obtained by synthesizing and generalizing from the discoveries of the sciences, this should be done; but whether it can be done or not can only be settled by trying it, and philosophy has not succeeded in progressing very far or very profitably in this direction. The great philosophies of the past have consisted partly of an investigation of the fundamental concepts of thought, partly of attempts to establish alleged facts of a different order from those dealt with by science by methods which are likewise quite different from those of science. They have usually been influenced more than is commonly apparent on the surface by the contemporary state of science, but it would certainly be very misleading to describe any of them as in the main a synthesis of the results of the sciences, and even anti-metaphysical philosophers like Hume have been concerned in their philosophy rather with the presuppositions than with the results of the sciences.

Nor must we be too ready to assume that, because a certain scientific result or assumption is valid in its own sphere, it can be proclaimed without reservation as a truth of philosophy. Thus, e.g., it does not follow by any means that because, as recent physics seems to have shown, the time of physics is inseparable from space, therefore we can lay it down as a philosophical principle that time presupposes space. For this may be only true of the time of physics, and true of it just because the time of physics is time measured in space. It need not therefore be true of the time of our experience, from which the time of physics is an abstraction or construction. Science may progress by means of methodological fictions and by using terms in an odd sense which philosophy has to correct. The term 'philosophy of science' is usually applied to the branch of logic which deals in a specialized way with the methods of the different sciences.

THE METHOD OF PHILOSOPHY AND OF THE SCIENCES CONTRASTED

As regards its methods philosophy differs fundamentally from the special sciences. Except where mathematics is applied, the sciences proceed by empirical generalization, but there is little scope for this method in philosophy. On the other hand, the attempt to assimilate philosophy to mathematics, though more often made, has not been successful (except in certain branches of logic which have more affinity in their subject-matter to mathematics than to the rest of philosophy). In particular it seems humanly impossible for philosophers to attain the certainty and clear-cut definiteness of mathematics. This difference between the two branches of study may be ascribed to various causes. Firstly, it has not proved possible to fix the meaning of terms in the same unambiguous way in philosophy as in mathematics, so that their meaning is liable imperceptibly to change in the course of an argument and it is very difficult to be sure that different philosophers are using the same word in the same sense. Secondly, it is only in the sphere of mathematics that we find simple concepts forming the basis of a vast number of complex and yet rigorously certain inferences. Thirdly, pure mathematics is hypothetical, i.e. it cannot tell us what is the case in the actual world, for example, how many things there are in a given place, but only what will be the case *if* so-and-so is true, e.g. that there will be 12 chairs in a room if there are 5+7 chairs. But philosophy aims at being categorical, i.e. telling us what really is the case; it is therefore not adequate in philosophy, as it often is in mathematics, to make deductions merely from postulates or definitions.

So it is impossible to find an adequate analogy to the methods of philosophy in any other science. Nor is it possible to define precisely what the method of philosophy is except at the expense of grotesquely limiting the subject. Philosophy has not just one method but a variety of different methods according to its subject-matter, and no useful purpose is served by defining them in advance of their application. To do so is indeed very dangerous. It has often led in the past to wrongly narrowing the scope of philosophy by excluding everything that is not amenable to the particular method chosen as characteristic of philosophy. Philosophy requires a great variety of methods, for it must draw into its service and subject to its interpretation all kinds of human experience. Yet it is far from being merely empirical, for it is its task, as far as possible, to make a coherent picture of these experiences and to infer from them whatever can be inferred of the reality other than human experience. On the side of theory of knowledge, it must criticize all modes of human thought constructively, but any mode of thought which in our ordinary nonphilosophical reflections at their best appears to us as self-vindicating must be given a place in the picture and not rejected because it differs from others. The criteria for the philosopher will be on the whole coherence together with comprehensiveness; he must aim at giving a systematic consistent picture of human experience and of the world in which as much is explained as can from the nature of the case admit of explanation, but he must not purchase coherence at the expense of rejecting what in its own right is real knowledge or justified belief. It is a serious objection to a philosophy if it maintains what we cannot possibly believe in ordinary life. Thus it would be an objection to a philosophy if it logically led, as some do, to the conclusion that there is no physical world, or that all our scientific, or all our ethical, beliefs are really quite unjustified.

PHILOSOPHY AND PSYCHOLOGY

There is one science which has a very special bearing on philosophy, namely, psychology. Particular psychological theories are in practice much more likely to affect a philosophical argument or theory for good or evil than are particular theories in a physical science. The relation holds in the reverse direction too; except in the parts which border on physiology, psychology is in more danger of being affected adversely by mistakes in philosophy than is a particular branch of physical science. This is probably because, while the physical sciences have reached an established position long ago and so had plenty of time to clarify their basic concepts for their own purposes, psychology has only emerged as a special science recently. Till a generation ago it was usually taught by philosophers and was hardly considered as one of the natural sciences. Consequently it has not yet had time to complete the process of clarification of its fundamental concepts which is needed to make them, if not philosophically unassailable, at any rate sufficiently clear and serviceable in practice for the science in question. The contemporary state of physics suggests that, when a science reaches a more advanced stage, it may again tend to be involved in difficulties with philosophical problems, in which case the period of independence would lie not at the beginning nor at the more advanced stage of a science's career but in the long intermediate phase between the two. Certainly philosophy may be of some help in the pending reconstruction of physics.

SCEPTICISM

Philosophers have been concerned a good deal with a strange creature, the absolute sceptic, but there is of course in fact no such person. If there were, it would be impossible to refute him. He could not refute you, or indeed assert anything, even his scepticism, without contradicting himself, for to assert that there is no knowledge and that no belief can be justified is itself to assert a belief. But you could not prove him wrong, for all proof must assume something. It must assume some premise or other, and also the laws of logic. If the law of contradiction is not true, you can never refute anybody by showing that he has contradicted himself. A philosopher cannot therefore start *ex nihilo* and prove everything: he must make some assumptions. In particular he must assume the truth of the fundamental laws of logic, otherwise he could not use any arguments at all or indeed make any significant statement. Of these laws the chief are the law of contradiction and the law of excluded middle. As applied to propositions the former asserts that a proposition cannot be both true and false, the latter that it must be either true or false. As applied to things the former asserts that something cannot be and not be or have a quality and not have it, the latter that it must either be or not be and either have a particular quality or not have it. They do not sound exciting principles, but on them all knowledge and thought depend. If to assert something did not exclude its contradictory, no meaning could be attached to any assertion and none could ever be disproved because both the assertion and the disproof might be correct. It is true that there are cases where it may be misleading

22

both to ascribe a quality to something and not to ascribe it. There are many people whom it would be incorrect to call either bald or not bald, but this is because of the absence of an exact definition of 'bald', and because 'bald' and 'not bald' have therefore come in practice to signify extremes between which there is an intermediate class of cases where we should use neither of these terms but say 'partly bald' or 'more or less bald'.

It is therefore not a case of a person neither having a definite quality nor not having it. A person must either have or not have any particular degree of baldness, but when we say 'bald' or 'not bald' it is not clear what degrees these are intended to cover. The objections sometimes made to the law of excluded middle seem to me to rest on misunderstandings of this type. Similarly, the law of contradiction is quite compatible with a man being good in one respect and bad in another or being good in the same respect at one time and bad at another.

Philosophy must also accept the evidence of immediate experience, but this will not take us so far as might be expected. We do not normally have immediate experience of any minds but our own, and the evidence of immediate experience cannot possibly tell us that the physical objects we seem to experience exist independently of us. But more of this later. We shall soon find that more assumptions than have yet been stated must be made if we are to admit that we know what in ordinary life we cannot help thinking we do know. We must not however conclude that, because we cannot justify a common-sense belief by argument, that the common-sense belief is necessarily wrong. It may be that at the common-sense level we have a genuine knowledge or justified belief which can stand in its own right and does not require philosophical justification. It will then be incumbent on the philosopher, not to prove the truth of the belief, which may be impossible, but to give the best account he can of it and to examine exactly what it involves. If we use the phrase 'instinctive belief' for what we take to be evidently true prior to philosophical criticism and what continues to appear evidently true in our ordinary life after and despite of philosophical criticism, we may say with Bertrand Russell—certainly not a person who is likely to be accused of being over-credulous—that there can be no reason for rejecting an instinctive belief except that it clashes with other instinctive beliefs, and that one of the chief aims of philosophy is to produce a coherent system based on our instinctive beliefs amending them as little as is possible compatibly with consistency. And, since a theory of knowledge can only be based on a study of the actual things we know and the way we know them, we can say that, if a particular philosophical theory leads to the conclusion that we cannot know certain things which we obviously do know or that certain beliefs are not justified which obviously are justified, this is an objection to the philosophical theory in question rather than to the knowledge or beliefs which it assails. On the other hand it would be foolish to suppose that all common-sense beliefs must be true just as they stand. It may well be the function of philosophy to amend them, but not to throw them away or to alter them so drastically that they become unrecognizable.

PHILOSOPHY AND PRACTICAL WISDOM

Philosophy has been connected with practical as well as theoretical wisdom, as in the phrase 'taking things philosophically'. In fact success in theoretical philosophy is very far from giving a guarantee that one will be philosophical in this practical sense or act and feel in the right way in a practical situation. It was a favourite doctrine of Socrates that, if we know what is good, we shall do it, but this is only true if we include in the meaning of the term 'know' the realization with adequate emotional vividness of what we theoretically know. I might well know or believe that to do something I wanted to do would give somebody else, A, much more pain than it gave me pleasure and was therefore very wrong, and yet I might do it because I did not feel nearly the same degree of emotional repugnance at the idea of A suffering pain as I did at the idea of myself missing what I coveted. Since it would be quite impossible for any human being to feel the sufferings of everyone else as much as his own, the possibility of being tempted to neglect one's duty is always present and requires to conquer it not merely knowledge but the exercise of will. Nor are we so constituted that it is always easy to go against a strong desire even for the sake of our own happiness, let alone our own moral good. Philosophy is no guarantee of right conduct or of the right adjustment of our emotions to our philosophical beliefs. And even on the cognitive side philosophy cannot tell us by itself what we ought to do. For this we require, besides philosophical principles, empirical knowledge of relevant facts and ability to predict the likely consequences, and also insight into the particular situation so that we can apply our principles properly.

I am not of course saying that philosophy is no help to right living, but only that it cannot by itself make us live rightly or even decide what is right living. That it can at least throw out valuable hints I have already insisted. I should have much more to say about the connection of philosophy with right living if I were including in this book a discussion of Ethics, the philosophical discipline which deals with the good and with right action; but we must distinguish theoretical philosophy as an account of what is from philosophical ethics as an account of what is good and what we ought to do.

I do not by using this illustration wish to imply that I am a hedonist, or a person who holds that pleasure and pain are the only factors relevant to the rightness of an action. I am not.

The extent to which either metaphysics or critical philosophy can help us in deciding what we ought to do is very limited. It may lead to conclusions which will make it easier for us to bear misfortune cheerfully, but this depends on the philosophy, and it is unfortunately not a matter of universal agreement among philosophers that an optimistic view of the world is justifiable philosophically. But we must follow truth wherever it leads, since the mind, once awakened, cannot rest in what it has no justification for thinking may not be a falsehood. At the same time we must study with respect and not dismiss unheard the claims of those who think they have attained inspiring and comforting truths about Reality by means that cannot be brought under the ordinary categories of common sense. We must not take for granted that the claims to a genuine cognition in religious and mystical experience of a different aspect of reality are necessarily to be dismissed as unjustified just because they do not fit in with a materialism suggested but by no means proved or now even really supported by modern science.

Chapter Two

THE 'A PRIORI' AND THE EMPIRICAL

MEANING OF THE DISTINCTION, 'A PRIORI' CHARACTER OF MATHEMATICS

IN the theory of knowledge, the first point that confronts us is the sharp distinction between two kinds of knowledge which have been called respectively *a priori* and empirical. Most of our knowledge we obtain by observation of the external world (sense-perception) and of ourselves (introspection). This is called empirical knowledge. But some knowledge we can obtain by simply thinking. That kind of knowledge is called *a priori*. Its chief exemplifications are to be found in logic and mathematics. In order to see that $5+7=12$ we do not need to take five things and seven things, put them together, and then count the total number. We can know what the total number will be simply by thinking.

Another important difference between *a priori* and empirical knowledge is that in the case of the former we do not see merely that something, S, is in fact P, but that it must be P and why it is P. I can discover that a flower is yellow (or at least produces sensations of yellow) by looking at it, but I cannot thereby see why it is yellow or that it must be yellow. For anything I can tell it might equally well have been a red flower. But with a truth such as that $5+7=12$ I do not see merely that it is a fact but that it must be a fact. It would be quite absurd to suppose that $5+7$ might have been equal to 11 and just happened to be equal to 12, and I can see that the nature of 5 and 7 constitutes a fully adequate and intelligible reason why their sum should be 12 and not some other number. It is indeed conceivable that some of the things which make the two groups of 5 and 7 might, when they were put together, fuse like drops of water, or even vanish, so that there were no longer 12 things; but what is inconceivable is that there could *at the same time* be $5+7$ things of a certain kind at once in a certain place and yet less than 12 things of that kind in that place. Before some of the things fused or vanished they would be $5+7$ in number and also 12 in number, and after the fusion or disappearance they would be neither $5+7$ nor 12. When I say in this connection that something is inconceivable, I do not mean merely or primarily that we cannot conceive it—this is not a case of a mere psychological inability like the inability to understand higher mathematics. It is a positive insight: we definitely see it to be impossible that certain things could happen. This we do not see in the case of empirical propositions which are false: they are not true but might for anything we know have been true. It is even conceivable, so far as we can see, that the fundamental laws of motion might have been quite different from what they are, but we can see that there could not have been a world which contradicted the laws of arithmetic. This is expressed by saying that empirical propositions are *contingent*, but true *a priori* propositions *necessary*. What we see to be necessary is not indeed that arithmetic should apply to the universe. It is conceivable that the universe might have been constituted entirely of a homogeneous fluid, and then, since there would have been no distinction between different things, it is difficult to see how arithmetic could have applied to it. What we do see is that arithmetic must be true of whatever can be numbered at all.

We must not be misled here by the fact that in order to come to understand arithmetic we originally required examples. Once we have learnt the beginnings of arithmetic in the kindergarten with the help of examples, we do not need examples any more to grasp it, and we can see the truth of many arithmetical propositions, e.g. that $3112+2467=5579$, of which we have never had examples. We have probably never taken 3112 things and 2467 things, put them together and counted the resulting set, but we still know that this is what the result of the counting would be. If it were empirical knowledge, we could not know it without counting. The examples are needed, not to prove anything, but only in order to enable us to come to understand in the first instance what is meant by number.

The 'A Priori' and the Empirical

In geometry we indeed stand more in need of examples than in arithmetic, though I think this is only a psychological matter. In arithmetic we only need examples at the most elementary stage, but in geometry most people need a drawn figure, or at least an image of one in their minds, to see the validity of most proofs. But we must distinguish between an illustration and the basis of a proof. If the particular figure were not merely an illustration but the basis of the theorem, the latter would have to be proved by measuring it, but a measurement with a ruler or protractor never figures in Euclid's proofs. That the proof is not really based on the figure drawn is shown by the fact that we can still follow a proof concerning the properties of right-angled triangles even if the figure used to illustrate it is so badly drawn that it is obviously not a right-angled triangle at all. Again, if geometry were empirical, it would be a very hazardous speculation from the single example before us on the blackboard to conclude that all triangles had a property. It might be an individual idiosyncrasy of some triangles and not others. These considerations should be conclusive of themselves, but we might add that recent developments in geometry have had the effect of much loosening the connection between geometrical proofs and the empirical figure. It is possible to work out non-Euclidean geometries where we cannot depend on figures.

THE 'A PRIORI' IN LOGIC

Another important field for *a priori* knowledge is logic. The laws of logic must be known *a priori* or not at all. They certainly are not a matter for empirical observation, and the function of logical argument is just to give us conclusions which we have not discovered by observation. The argument would be superfluous if we had observed them already. We are able to make inferences because there is sometimes a logical connection between one or more propositions (the premise or premises) and another proposition, the conclusion, such that the latter must be true if the former is. Then, if we know the former, we can assert the latter on the strength of it, thus anticipating any experience. To take an example, there is a story that Mr. X., a man of high reputation and great social standing, had been asked to preside at a big social function. He was late in coming, and so a Roman Catholic priest was asked to make a speech to pass the time till his arrival. The priest told various anecdotes, including one which recorded his embarrassment when as confessor he had to deal with his first penitent and the latter confessed to a particularly atrocious murder. Shortly afterwards Mr. X. arrived, and in his own speech he said: 'I see Father —— is here. Now, though he may not recognize me, he is an old friend of mine, in fact I was his first penitent.' It is plain that such an episode would enable one to infer that Mr. X. had committed a murder without having observed the crime. The form of inference involved: The first penitent was a murderer, Mr. X. was the first penitent, therefore Mr. X. was a murderer—is of the famous kind to which logicians have given the name of *syllogism*. The importance of syllogisms has often been exaggerated, but they are as important as any kind of inference, and we cannot deny that in many cases a syllogism has given people information of which they were not in any ordinary sense aware before they used the syllogism and which they did not acquire by observation. Inference is only possible because there are special connections between the propositions involved such that one necessarily follows from others. It is a chief function of logic to study these connections, of which that expressed in the syllogism is by no means the only one.

(A *syllogism* consists of three propositions, two forming the *premises* and the other the *conclusion*. Each proposition can be expressed by a subject and predicate connected by the verb to be, the *copula*, and if we call everything which stands as either subject or predicate a *term*, there must be three and only three terms in the syllogism. The one common to the two premises is called the *middle term*, and it is on this common element that the inference depends. The other two, having been connected by means of it, occur without it in the conclusion. Thus in the usual example of the syllogism—All men are mortal, Socrates is a man, ∴ Socrates is mortal—man is the middle term connecting Socrates with mortality so that we could, even if he had not already died, know that he was mortal.)

The 'A Priori' and the Empirical

OTHER CASES OF THE 'A PRIORI'

A priori knowledge, while most prominent in mathematics and logic, is not limited to these subjects. For instance, we can see *a priori* that the same surface cannot have two different colours all over at the same time, or that a thought cannot have a shape. Philosophers have been divided into *rationalists* and *empiricists* according to whether they stressed the *a priori* or the empirical element more. The possibility of metaphysics depends on *a priori* knowledge, for our experience is quite inadequate to enable us to make on merely empirical grounds any sweeping generalizations of the kind the metaphysician desires. The term *a priori* covers both self-evident propositions, i.e. those which are seen to be true in their own right and those which are derived by inference from propositions themselves self-evident.

THE LINGUISTIC THEORY OF THE 'A PRIORI' AND THE DENIAL THAT 'A PRIORI' PROPOSITIONS OR INFERENCES CAN GIVE NEW KNOWLEDGE

At the present time even empiricist philosophers recognize the impossibility of explaining away *a priori* propositions as merely empirical generalizations, but they are inclined to the view that *a priori* propositions and *a priori* reasoning are merely concerned with language, and so cannot tell us anything new about the real world. Thus it is said that, when we make an inference, the conclusion is just part of the premises expressed in different language.[1] If so, inference would be of use merely for clarifying our language and would involve no real advance in knowledge. Some inferences are of this type, e.g. A is a father, therefore A is male. But are they all? That would be hard indeed to square with the *prima facie* novelty of many conclusions. Take, for instance, the proposition that the square on the hypotenuse of a right-angled triangle is equal to the sum of the squares on the other two sides. Such a proposition can be inferred from the axioms and postulates

[1] This theory is not applied to *inductive* inference

of Euclid, but it certainly does not seem to be included in their meaning.[1] Otherwise we should know it as soon as we understood the axioms and postulates. The example I gave of the murder discovered by a logical argument seems to be another case of a fact not known at all beforehand by the reasoner which is discovered by his reasoning. Extreme empiricist philosophers contend that this appearance of novelty is really illusory, and that in some sense we knew the conclusion all along; but they have never succeeded in making clear in what sense we did so. It is not enough to say that the conclusion is implicit in the premises. 'Implicit' means 'implied by', and of course a conclusion is implied by its premises, if the inference is correct at all.[2] But this admission leaves quite open the question whether or not a proposition can follow from a different one which does not contain it as part of itself; and since we obviously can by deductive inference come to know things which we did not know before in any ordinary sense of 'know', we must treat the empiricist's claim as unjustified till he has produced a clearly defined sense of 'implicit in' or 'contained in' which leaves room for that novelty in inference which we all cannot help really admitting. In any ordinary sense of 'know' the conclusion is not in the cases I have mentioned known prior to the inference, and since the premises are and indeed must be known before we know the conclusion, it is therefore in no ordinary sense of 'part' part of the premises.

It is indeed sometimes said that the premises include the conclusion in a confused form, but it is obvious that the beginner in geometry cannot be said to be aware of Pythagoras's theorem even in a confused form though he may know all the premises from which it can be deduced. Nor does awareness of the propositions that A was B's first penitent and that B's first penitent was a murderer include even confusedly the awareness that A was a

[1] It is no objection to this illustration that Euclidean geometry has not been proved true of the physical world, for the proposition in question undoubtedly follows from the premises of Euclid and therefore should on the theory we are discussing be included as part of them. What is denied by modern scientists is not that the conclusion follows from the premises, but that the premises and what follows from them are true of the world.

[2] Similarly, the phrase 'is contained in' is sometimes used just to mean 'follows from' or 'is implied by' and need not connote that the conclusion is actually part of the premises, as would be the case on the literal meaning of 'contained'.

murderer as long as the premises are not combined. When they are combined therefore something new appears that was not present to consciousness before in any way; there is a new discovery. We can also show by definite logical argument that the interpretation we are discussing does not enable one to avoid the admission of novelty in inference. For, what is it to know something in a confused form? It is surely to know some general attributes present in a whole but not others. To be aware of p even confusedly must involve discriminating some general attributes in p, and those are given in the premises, which are admittedly understood in some degree. If we do not discriminate any attributes, the confusion is too great for argument to be possible at all. Now it is admitted that, when we reach the conclusion, we do discriminate attributes which we did not discriminate before, even if they are alleged to have been contained in the confused whole which was present to our minds before we started inferring. It is further admitted that the conclusion follows necessarily from the premises. Therefore the general attributes which we discriminated at the time when we knew only the premises and not the conclusion must be linked with the attributes we discriminate afterwards in such a way that the latter follow necessarily from the former. So we still have to admit that sheer *a priori* inference can enable us to discover new attributes. In some cases it may take a good while to draw the inference, in other cases it may be practically instantaneous as soon as the premises are known and combined, but whether it takes a long or a short time to draw the inference cannot be relevant to the principle.

Nevertheless, the view that inference cannot yield new conclusions dies hard, and so it will not be superfluous to bring further arguments. (1) 'This has shape' admittedly follows logically from 'this has size' and vice versa. If the view I am criticizing were true, 'this has size' would, therefore, have to include in its meaning 'this has shape', and 'this has shape' would also have to include in its meaning 'this has size'. But this would only be possible if the two sentences meant exactly the same thing, which they obviously do not. (2) Take an argument such as—Montreal is to the north of New York, New York is to the north of Washington, therefore Montreal is to the north of Washington. If the view I am discussing is true, the conclusion is part of the premises. But it is not part of either premise by itself, otherwise both premises would not be needed. So the only way in which it could be part of both together would be if it were divisible into two propositions one of which was part of the first and the other part of the second. I defy anybody to divide it in this way. (3) The proposition 'Socrates was a philosopher' certainly entails the proposition 'if Socrates had measles some philosophers have had measles', but it cannot be that the second proposition is included in the first. For the first proposition certainly does not include the notion of measles.

What is really the same view is often expressed by saying that all *a priori* propositions are 'analytic'. A distinction has commonly been drawn between *analytic* propositions, in which the predicate is in the notion of the subject already formed before the proposition is asserted, so that the proposition gives no new information, and *synthetic* propositions in which the predicate is not so contained and which are thus capable of giving new information.[1] Analytic propositions are essentially verbal, being all true by definition, e.g. all fathers are male. As an example of a synthetic proposition we could take any proposition established by experience such as 'I am cold' or 'It is snowing', but empiricists often assert that there are no synthetic *a priori* propositions. That this view cannot be justified may be shown at once. The proposition that there are no synthetic *a priori* propositions, since it cannot be established by empirical observations, would be, if justified, itself a synthetic *a priori* proposition, and we cannot affirm it as a synthetic *a priori* proposition that there are no synthetic *a priori* propositions. We may therefore dismiss off-hand any arguments for the theory. Such arguments, whatever they were, would have to involve synthetic *a priori* propositions. Further, the view must be false if it is ever true that the conclusion of an inference is not part of its premises. For, if the proposition—S is Q—ever follows validly from —S is P, the proposition—all that is SP is SQ must be true *a priori*. But, unless the concept Q is part of the concept SP, the proposition

[1] This definition would have to be amended slightly to suit modern logicians who (I think, rightly) deny that all propositions are of the subject-predicate form, but this would not alter the principle though imparting a complication of detail with which we need not deal here.

—all that is SP is SQ—cannot be analytic. Therefore our arguments against the view that in all valid inferences the conclusion is part of the premises expressed in different language are also arguments against the view that all *a priori* propositions are analytic.

The analytic view seems plausible when we are concerned with the simplest propositions of logic and arithmetic, but we must not assume that a proposition is analytic because it is obvious. Though it may be very difficult to determine precisely where analytic propositions end and synthetic propositions begin, we cannot use this as a ground for denying the latter. It is very difficult to say precisely where blue ends and green begins, since the different shades run into each other imperceptibly, but we cannot therefore argue that all blue is really green. Taking arithmetic, even if there is a good deal of plausibility in saying that $2 + 2$ is included in the meaning of '4', there is none in saying $95 - 91$ or $\frac{216}{2} - \frac{287+25}{3}$ are so included. Yet, if the analytic view were true, all the infinite numerical combinations which could be seen *a priori* to be equal to 4 would have to be included in the meaning of '4'.

Some empiricists, without committing themselves to the view that all *a priori* propositions are analytic, still say these are a matter of arbitrary choice or verbal convention. They are influenced here by a modern development in the view of geometry. It used to be held that the axioms of Euclid expressed a direct insight into the nature of physical space, but this is denied by modern scientists, and the view is taken that they are arbitrary postulates which geometricians make because they are interested in what would follow *if* they were true. Whether they are true or not is then a matter of empirical fact to be decided by science. But, even if this suggests that the premises of our *a priori* arguments may be arbitrary postulates, this does not make the subsequent steps arbitrary. From the postulates of Euclid it follows that the three angles of a triangle are equal to two right angles. If the original postulates are arbitrary, it is not certain that the conclusion is true of the real world; but it is still not an arbitrary matter that it follows from the postulates. The postulates may well be false, but there can be no doubt that *if* they were true the conclusions must be so, and it is in this hypothetical working out of the consequences of postulates which may not be true that pure geometry consists. The *a priori* necessity of pure geometry is not therefore in the least invalidated by modern developments. What is *a priori* is that the conclusions follow from the axioms and postulates, and this is not at all affected by the (empirical) discovery that not all the axioms and postulates exactly apply to the physical world. (Applied Euclidean geometry is possible in practice because it is an empirical fact that they approximately apply. The divergencies only show themselves when we consider unusually great velocities or distances.)

If not only the postulates but the successive stages in the inference were themselves arbitrary, we might just as well infer from the same premise that the angles of a triangle were equal to a million right angles or to none at all. All point in inference would be lost. Dictators may do a great deal, but they cannot alter the laws of logic and mathematics; these laws would not change even if by a system of intensive totalitarian education every human being were persuaded to fall in with a world dictator's whim in the matter and believe they were different from what they are. Nor can they change with alterations in language, though they may be expressed differently. That the truth of *a priori* propositions does not just depend on the nature of language can be easily seen when we consider that, even if we do not know any Fijian or Hottentot, we can know that also in these languages and not only in the languages we know the propositions $5+7=12$ must be true. It is of course true that by altering the meaning of the words we could make the proposition we expressed by '$5+7=12$' false, e.g. if I used '12' in a new sense to mean what other people mean by '11', but then it would be a different proposition. I could play the same trick with empirical propositions and say truly, e.g., that 'fire does not burn' or 'there is an elephant in this room' if I used 'burn' to mean 'drown' or 'elephant' to mean 'table'. This does not in the least impair the obviousness of the contrary propositions established by experience. Finally, as we argued above that the proposition that there can be no synthetic *a priori* propositions would itself, if justified, have to be a synthetic *a priori* proposition, so we may argue that the proposition that all *a priori* propositions are a matter of arbitrary linguistic convention would, if true, have to be itself a matter of arbitrary linguistic convention. It therefore could not be vindicated by any argument and would be merely a matter of a new usage of words arbitrarily established by the persons who assert it, since it certainly does not express the usual meaning of '*a priori* propositions'. So we must reject any attempt to explain away the *a priori* as a genuine source of new knowledge. If the attempt had succeeded, we should have had to admit that philosophy in anything like its old sense was impossible, for philosophy clearly cannot be based merely on observation.

The views we have been criticizing contain the following elements of truth. (1) *A priori* propositions can be seen to be true and the conclusions of an inference seem to follow from their premises without any further observation, provided we understand the meaning of the words used. But to say that q follows from p once we understand the meaning of the words is not to say that q is part of the meaning of the words used to express p. 'Follow from' and 'be part of' are not synonyms. (2) If q follows from p you cannot assert p and deny q without contradicting yourself, but this is only to say that in that case the denial of q implies the denial of p. It is not to say that q is part of what you assert when you assert p, unless we already assume that what is implied is always part of what implies it, i.e. beg the question at issue. (3) An *a priori* proposition cannot be fully understood without being seen to be true. It may be impossible to understand something fully without understanding something else not included in it at all, so it may still be synthetic.

People have been inclined to deny synthetic *a priori* propositions because they could not see how one characteristic could necessarily involve another, but that this could not happen would be itself a synthetic *a priori* metaphysical proposition. People have also thought that it was necessary to give some sort of explanation of *a priori* knowledge, and could not see how this could be done except in terms of language. To this I should reply that there is no reason to suppose that *a priori* knowledge requires some special explanation any more than does our ability to attain knowledge empirically by observation. Why not take it as an ultimate fact? Human beings certainly cannot explain everything, whether there is ultimately an explanation for it or not.

The 'A Priori' and the Empirical

LANGUAGE AND THOUGHT

At the same time it is very right to stress the importance of language in connection with philosophical thought, even if this stress has lately been carried much too far. Language is not merely a means of communicating with others, but is necessary even for our own thinking. The function of words in this connection is to provide some sensuous imagery for the mind, so to speak, to take hold of. I cannot see any logical impossibility in thinking without the use of any sort of imagery, but as a matter of empirical fact it is very doubtful whether human beings are capable of such a feat, at least where the thoughts are at all definite. Actual mental pictures of the object may serve our purpose when we are dealing with a concrete physical thing, but obviously they will not go very far in philosophy. Words have the advantage that, while sensual in character, being sounds or black marks, they need not be like the objects for which they stand and therefore can be used to represent effectively concepts which are not themselves at all sensual. In abstract thinking words usually constitute the only imagery employed, but this does not mean that thinking is just talking to oneself. Clearly, if we are to use words effectively, we must be aware not only of words but of the meaning of the words. This awareness of meaning may be difficult or impossible to analyse adequately, but obviously it must be present since otherwise there would be no distinction for us between an abstract argument which we understood and a mere set of nonsense-syllables.

In view of its indispensable necessity for any but the most concrete thought it is easy to see that a consideration of language is likely to be very important for philosophy. The meaning of words, as used in common speech, is apt to vary in all sorts of ways of which it is easy to lose sight, with the result that fallacious arguments dependent on an ambiguity in the terms occur. I may have proved that S is P in one sense of 'P' but then confuse two different senses of P and draw a conclusion that in fact only follows if S is P in another sense of P. Or two disputants may be at loggerheads mainly because they are using words in different senses and therefore do not understand each other. It is therefore a good general rule that, when we are confronted with a philosophical question, we should first ask what is the meaning of the terms involved. If the meaning is not clear, we must then take the various alternative meanings that they might have and consider what follows from each of these meanings in turn. When we have done this, the question may turn out much easier to answer than before, and at least many sources of confusion will have been removed.

Language may also lead to philosophical mistakes because its verbal form gives misleading suggestions as to the structure of reality or because two sentences which really do not assert the same kind of thing at all are taken to do so because they have the same grammatical structure. Again we may fall into error through supposing that a word which owes its meaning to its context has a meaning in itself apart from the rest of the sentence and so stands for some definite entity or other. We do not tend to suppose this in regard to words like 'but' or 'and', but we certainly tend to suppose it in regard to nouns or adjectives. We shall encounter examples of these mistakes in the course of the book, but I shall just give one now because it illustrates both the last fallacies and because it is one which it is specially desirable to understand at this early stage in the argument. We have a word 'proposition', much used by philosophers, which stands for what we know, assert, believe, doubt, disbelieve, etc., and we say that we, for example, believe a certain proposition. We are then naturally apt to suppose that propositions are separate entities of a special sort because these are separate words for them. Also such a sentence as 'I believe a proposition' has the same grammatical form as 'I inhabit a house', 'I break a plate', etc. and therefore suggests that a proposition is something quite distinct from the believing, to which we do something when we believe it. But, if so, it is extraordinarily difficult to see what sort of thing it can be. The solution seems to be found in the fact that 'proposition' just does not stand for any real entity by itself, though 'believing a proposition' does so. Yet, provided we do not forget this, it is very useful and indeed necessary to talk about 'propositions'. When we do so we are by way of abstraction talking about that which certain different mental states of believing, doubting, supposing, etc., have in common.

The 'A Priori' and the Empirical

Again, we must remember that it is not the sole function of language to communicate information. It has also the functions of expressing emotions, commanding, conveying persuasion ('emotive functions' in general, as they are called). Sentences which assert the same thing objectively may have a quite different emotive tinge. I think this distinction has sometimes been run to death by recent philosophers, but it is no doubt a useful one.

THE DEFINITION OF MEANING IN TERMS OF VERIFIABILITY AND THE REJECTION OF METAPHYSICS

Another course adopted by many empiricists has been to identify meaning with the property of being verifiable (or falsifiable) by sense-experience, and to conclude that no metaphysics is possible because metaphysics would have to transcend sense-experience. Such a view dismisses metaphysical statements not as false or unsupported by evidence, but as meaningless. The following are the main objections to the verification theory. (1) There are other kinds of experience besides sense-experience the evidence of which has also a good claim to be heard, e.g. the experience of seeing logically necessary connections, ethical experience which tells us of values, religious experience. (2) I cannot have sense-experience of the past or of other minds, nor can sense-experience by itself directly establish any scientific laws. Therefore the strict verificationists will have either to interpret statements about such things in a very extraordinary way or declare these statements—and so almost every statement we can make—meaningless. They have sometimes themselves gone so far as to put forward the view that statements about the past were really only statements about the possible future evidence which would verify them and that statements about minds other than their own were really only statements about their own sense-data, but this is surely a *reductio ad absurdum* of the theory in question. (3) The verification principle is not itself verifiable by sense-experience. We cannot tell by sense-experience that there is nothing in the meaning of a statement which could not be verified by sense-experience any more than we

39

could tell by sight that there are no invisible microbes in this room. Therefore the principle is on its own showing meaningless. In order to meet such objections it has been suggested that the verification principle should be amended so as to make a statement meaningless only if sense-experience is not at all relevant to its probability or improbability, but thus amended the principle would not exclude metaphysics. The amount of pain in the universe is obviously relevant to the probability of the metaphysical proposition that it was created by a good omnipotent God. In fact most metaphysicians have based their metaphysics partly on an interpretation of and inference from our sense-experience. They may have been wrong in doing so, but this depends on the merits or demerits of their particular arguments and cannot without begging the question be deduced from the general consideration that sense-experience is not relevant to metaphysical propositions.

Many verificationists would consequently now admit that their principle was not put forward as a true statement but as merely a matter of method, the point of which is simply that in order to understand a proposition it is very important to ask how, if at all, it could be verified by sense-experience. This need not imply that anything that could not be thus verified is not a proposition at all, and is therefore not open to the above objections. But a person who takes this line must be very careful to avoid slipping back into treating the verification principle in his own thoughts as a dogma. He will be doing this if he ever draws any inferences from it and on the strength of this asserts what he infers as true. For we are not entitled to accept anything as true because we have inferred it from a premise, unless we know the premise to be true or are at least justified in believing it. Provided this caution is observed we need not object to the verification method, though we may doubt whether it has anything like the importance that is commonly attributed to it. Its chief use probably lies in helping one to distinguish science, which deals with what is in some sense verifiable by sense-experience, from metaphysics; but it is difficult (though perhaps not impossible) to define a sense of 'verifiable' which will leave a place for all scientific propositions and yet exclude metaphysics. We have also already seen in the first chapter by an independent argument that we cannot have even critical philosophy without some metaphysics.[1] (Of course, if 'verification' is not limited at all by sense-experience but interpreted in such a way as to include every conceivable means of establishing or making probable a proposition, everyone may agree that unverifiable statements, if not meaningless, at any rate should not be made and need receive no attention. But then even the most metaphysical metaphysician does not claim that his metaphysics is in this sense unverifiable.)

In general, attempts to establish the impossibility of metaphysics founder on the difficulty that we cannot show that metaphysics is from the nature of the case impossible without already presupposing some metaphysical beliefs.[2] To show that the nature of reality is such that we cannot know anything of it, we must already make some presuppositions about reality and about the ultimate nature of the human mind. How much metaphysics we are to admit is another question. The persistent disagreement of metaphysicians and the frequent discoveries of fallacies in their arguments certainly do not give much encouragement to hope that we shall be able to arrive at a system of metaphysics which is at once elaborate and securely founded. I think, however, that the significance of the perennial disagreement in question may easily be exaggerated. It may well be that, when two metaphysicians are disputing, what often happens is this. One philosopher asserts the truth of p and another the truth of q, p and q being apparently quite incompatible. Now presumably the facts are likely to be such that some of the criteria required if we are to assert p are present and also some of the criteria required if we are to assert q, otherwise there would be no dispute. It is in consequence of this that there will be both a tendency to assert p and a tendency to assert q. In that case we cannot say without reservations that either is right, because all the criteria required to justify the assertion are not present, but it does not matter whether we say p or q provided we

[1] *Vide* above, pp. 17–8.

[2] The most noteworthy such attempt was made by the great German philosopher Kant (1724-1803). His arguments are too subtle and elaborate to discuss here, but I think he is open to the objection expressed in this sentence, important as his contribution in very many respects may be. It should be added that he did not really exclude all metaphysics but retained the beliefs in God, freedom and immortality in so far as justified by ethical arguments.

41

add the necessary reservations. Both sides may then be right provided we look on them not as giving arguments to prove p or q, but on 'the q-side' as stating the reservations which have to be made if we are to say p and on the 'p-side' as stating the reservations which have to be made if we are to say q. The rival philosophies will then supplement rather than contradict each other, and they can thus both be regarded as making a positive contribution to the truth. Thus philosophers have often disputed whether reality is one or many, but we obviously cannot say that it is either without qualification. The pluralist, however, may be regarded as giving the points of which we still have to take account if we after all decide to say that reality is one and the monist as giving those of which we still have to take account if we decide to call reality many. I do not think all philosophical controversies can be treated exclusively in this way: there are such things as definite fallacies and definite contradictions between philosophers, but what I have said applies, at least partially, to a good many of the disputes between them.

INNATE IDEAS

The question whether *a priori* knowledge is possible must not be confused with the question whether there are 'innate ideas', i.e. ideas born with one. The theory of 'innate ideas' was put forward to account for the occurrence of ideas which did not seem derivable from sense-experience. The British seventeenth-century philosopher, Locke, criticizes it on the ground that it is absurd to suppose that new-born babies have ideas of God or of the law of contradiction, but all the advocates of the theory of whom we know have expressly denied that they meant to assert this and have said that all that was innate was a faculty to form the ideas. Locke's criticism, however, has its value as a reminder that, if 'idea' and 'innate' are taken in their proper senses, the theory is false, and a warning that its advocates had not thought out sufficiently the sense in which they were using innate ideas. The theory usually opposed to that of innate ideas asserts that all our ideas were ultimately derived from sense-experience (including observation of ourselves). Obviously it must be admitted that I can have ideas of things which I have never experienced by my senses, e.g. centaurs, but it was contended that such ideas were always formed by combining in some way ideas thus derived, e.g. in this case the idea of a horse's body and that of a man's head, or at least by comparing such ideas or abstracting elements in them. But there must be at least one idea that is not so derived. Inference is impossible unless we have the idea of logically necessary connection between the premises from which we start in our inference and the conclusion we reach, and this idea is clearly quite different from any which could be given in sense-experience. Other ideas which have been, at least plausibly, supposed not to be derived from sense-experience are God, good, duty, the laws of logic, substance, cause, and the ideas of geometry such as that of a perfect circle or square. It is particularly difficult to suppose that moral ideas could be derived from sense-experience, but the place for discussion of them is a book on Ethics.

But, if we deny that all ideas are derivable from sense-experience, we still need not hold the doctrine of innate ideas. A third alternative is to say that the ideas are not made by our mind but derived, like empirical ideas, by apprehension of the real, only to add that there are other ways besides sense-experience of apprehending the real. E.g., we may make three alternative suppositions about the idea of cause:

(1) We may suppose that we are innately so constituted that we call up the idea out of our own resources and apply it when we are confronted with experiences, such as that of regular succession, which suggest it. (2) We may suppose that the idea of causation is simply that of regular sequence in time, in which case we could easily explain it by sense-experience, since regular sequence is a relation which can be discovered by the senses easily enough. (3) If we think (as I do)[1] that causation cannot be identified with regular sequence or anything else which could be apprehended by the senses, we may still avoid the innate theory by maintaining that it is a relation in the real which we immediately apprehend by some means other than sense-experience on certain occasions, e.g. when we cause something to happen by an act of will or when we

[1] *Vide* below, chap. VIII

encounter physical resistance. Having acquired the idea of cause in this way, we might then apply it in cases where we do not immediately experience the relation. This would easily explain how we can be in error sometimes about the presence of what we are immediately aware of on other occasions. Similarly, if we accept the idea of substance as not an object of sense-experience, we might explain it either by supposing it innate or by maintaining that each person had an intuition of himself as substance and then applied the idea thus gained to other minds and material things. It would not be necessary to hold that we had this immediate apprehension each time the idea of substance or cause was applied, provided we had it occasionally. Again, if we can ever by thinking see two characteristics to be logically connected, this is sufficient to account for the idea of logically necessary connection without supposing it innate.

We need not suppose either that the fundamental ideas of logic and ethics are innate or that they are derivable from sense-experience or ordinary introspection. The fundamental characteristics or relations of ethics are apprehended in valuing or appreciating the value of something which really has them, and those of logic in thinking logically (i.e. apprehending the validity of inferences and the formal nature of propositions, etc.), and this does not mean that they are or are only characteristics of the experiences of valuing and of thinking logically. They are characteristics of what we value or of that about which we think logically.

LIMITS OF RATIONALISM

At the other extreme from empiricism we find an attempt to deny that there is any such thing as the merely empirically given. This is based on the psychological discovery, true no doubt as far as it goes, that what we perceive is always coloured by interpretation and cannot be derived simply from the sensations given by our sense-organs. E.g. ice positively 'looks cold', though coldness is not a quality given by sight; we perceive a cupboard as something which has an inside, though we do not see the inside. Sensations are supplemented by images and inextricably blended with beliefs and expectations. When we perceive anything we do not just apprehend it as it is to the senses now but as a member of a class of things and are subtly influenced by our experience of previous members. It thus becomes very hard to sort out from our total experience anything that is just given without any contribution by the mind. But that there is a given element present surely cannot be doubted, however difficult it may be to fix precisely where it ends and begins? For clearly whatever interpretation there is depends on something being given to interpret. No judgments are purely empirical, if by a purely empirical judgment is meant a judgment which involves no ordering or organization by the mind; but this does not make our ordinary judgments of perception *a priori* either in the sense of being logically necessary or in the sense of not being based on the given at all. Further, even in so far as the interpretation goes beyond what is given, it is dependent on what was given in past experiences. We see ice as cold because we have previously felt it as cold, we apprehend a cupboard as having an inside because we have seen the inside of cupboards in the past. All that is non-empirical here is the principle of method the mind has in organizing and interpreting the given, e.g. we do not know empirically that future cupboards will be like cupboards previously examined but we assume they will be so. The precise logical character of assumptions of this type is the main philosophical problem raised by scientific method and induction.

The rationalist thinkers of the seventeenth and eighteenth centuries tried to reduce sense-experience to a kind of confused thinking, but philosophers to-day would be almost universally agreed that this is impossible. Thought as the source of the *a priori* and sense-experience (including introspection of oneself) are quite different capacities and have quite separate, though both essential, functions in knowledge.

There is one limitation which we must impose on *a priori* knowledge at least as we know it. It always has the character of being primarily hypothetical. What we see *a priori* is a necessary connection between two facts or suppositions, which we express by the use of the word 'if' in what is called a 'hypothetical' as opposed to a 'categorical' proposition. (A categorical proposition asserts something unconditionally; a hypothetical proposition asserts only what will happen if a certain condition is fulfilled.) '2+2=4' means that, if there are 2+2 things, there must be 4 things. It does not tell us that there are 4 things in a particular place or indeed anywhere at all: that is an empirical proposition. We can indeed know negative categorical propositions *a priori*,[1] e.g. that there are no round squares or that there are no cases of 4 which are not cases of 2+2, but to know affirmative categorical propositions purely *a priori* is beyond our capacity. The only case in which it has been asserted that we can do this, in the 'ontological proof'[2] of God, I regard, with the great majority of modern philosophers, as a mere fallacy. This does not mean that we cannot use *a priori* propositions to enable us to obtain information about what actually exists. What it means is that we cannot obtain the information by the *a priori* propositions alone. We require in addition at least one empirical premise. When we know *a priori* that, if p is true, q follows, and we also know p empirically, we can infer q, but not otherwise. Thus, if we know the empirical premises that there were five people in a certain room an hour ago, that seven have entered since and none left (and we make the usually reasonable assumption that none have died in the meantime or miraculously vanished), we can then use an *a priori* proposition to infer that there are now twelve people there. If we have obtained by empirical means the measurements of two sides of a triangle and the angle between them, we can use an *a priori* proposition of trigonometry to infer the length of the third. Even the most abstract metaphysical arguments have some empirical premise, though it may be a very general and obvious one such as that something, at least myself, exists, or that there is experience of change in time.

INDUCTION

The chief use of *a priori* knowledge is to enable us to make inferences. Whenever we can make an inference from p to q, we

---

[1] I still call *a priori* propositions primarily hypothetical because the *a priori* negative categorical proposition that there are no cases of SP arises only from the insight that, if something is S, it cannot be P.

[2] *Vide* below, pp. 221-2

must know, or at least be justified in believing, the hypothetical 'if p, then q'. For q to follow necessarily from p that hypothetical proposition must be *a priori*; necessary connection is not a matter of empirical observation. An important distinction is, however, drawn between deduction and induction. Both are inferences, but they differ in that deduction proceeds from the more to the less general, induction from the less to the more general. Induction in all its more characteristic forms is a matter of empirical generalization, i.e. we argue that, because something has proved true in a number of observed cases, it will be likely to prove true in similar cases that have not yet been observed. The conclusion is not (except in very special cases) certain, but it may be highly probable, and all our rational predictions about the future depend on an inference of this kind. Induction has presented very serious problems to logicians and philosophers generally. The inference in induction is certainly not a merely empirical matter: we use it to enable us to forecast the future, but we have not observed the future empirically. The whole use of induction is indeed to enable us to infer what we have never observed. Therefore some *a priori* principle about the world is required if induction is to be justified. The principle must be of such a nature as to justify us in supposing that what has happened in observed cases is likely to recur in unobserved; but logicians have certainly not hit upon a principle which is both self-evident and adequate to justify inductive inference. The one which has been most commonly put forward as supplying what is needed is the principle that every change has a cause, but it would be much disputed nowadays whether this was either necessary or sufficient to justify induction. The meaning of 'cause' itself is also very much a subject on which there are varying views. So the justification of induction is one of the worst problems of logic. The fact that we must use induction if we are to have any science at all is a proof that science cannot be merely empirical (even where it does not use mathematics), but we cannot say that the conclusion of an inductive inference follows from its premises with the same necessity as does the conclusion of a deductive one.

Most of the propositions we call empirical are not justified by mere observation but by that together with induction. This applies to all conclusions of science, for these are never statements of single observed facts but generalizations about what usually happens or inferences from such generalizations. It applies also to all our ordinary judgments about physical objects, for we always read in more than is actually observed and the only justification for what we read in must be found in induction (i.e. we assume that objects will have besides the characteristics we actually observe at the time those characteristics which we observed in the past in similar objects, e.g. that the ice we see is cold though we are not feeling the cold). This does not mean that, whenever we observe, we are consciously making inferences. But we can speak of 'implicit inferences', meaning that without making conscious inferences we hold beliefs on the strength of experiences which could be used as premises to justify the beliefs by explicit inferences.

INTUITION

A necessary, though not always recognized, presupposition of inference is intuition. To argue validly—A ∴ B ∴ C—we must see a connection between A and B and a connection between B and C. But how do we know that that connection itself holds? We may be able to interpolate further terms, D and E, and say A, ∴ D, ∴ B, ∴ E, ∴ C; but we obviously cannot go on in this way *ad infinitum*. Sooner or later we must come to a point where we just see immediately that there is a connection, but cannot *prove* this to be so. When we see immediately something to be true otherwise than by observing it empirically, we are said to have an *intuition*. No doubt apparent intuitions are often to be explained as really implicit or suppressed inferences, but the argument I have just given shows that this cannot be so with all cases of intuition. Even when we have made explicit all the omitted steps, the logical point remains that for it to be possible to infer any one proposition from any other we must see the connection between them, and this connection cannot always be proved by interpolating fresh propositions, yet it must be known somehow. The connection may be said to be derived from the fundamental laws of logic, but the laws themselves are known intuitively. Further, before we can see their validity in the abstract, we must have seen their validity in particular cases. All of us have used syllogisms long before we knew anything about the rules of syllogistic inference. That was because we could see that a conclusion followed from its premises without knowing the general principle on account of which it followed, as we can move our arms effectively in definite pur- posive ways without knowing the laws of physiology which govern our motions or the laws of physics which make the selected motions the most effective ones for our practical purpose. The same applies whether the connection is such as to make the conclusion follow with certainty given the premises, or whether it is, as in most inductive arguments, such that the premises make the conclusion only probable. But, while logicians have easily agreed on the general principles governing deduction and we can see these to be completely self-evident, neither is the case as re- gards the general principles governing induction. Yet though neither the plain man nor even the logician is clear as to the fundamental laws behind the process, we can see in particular cases of induction that the truth of the premises makes the truth of the conclusion probable, as we can see that the truth of the premises makes the truth of the conclusion certain in particular cases of deduction. 'Intuition' as a source of knowledge or justified belief is often brushed aside with contempt, but the argument I have given at any rate shows that, if there are to be any valid inferences, there must be some intuitions.

Many philosophers have preferred to limit the term 'intuition' to cases of certain knowledge, but there are many cases where something presents itself to one intuitively as deserving a certain degree of credence but falling short of certainty or where an intuition has some value but is confused and inextricably blended with erroneous assumptions or inferences. These cases are par- ticularly plentiful in philosophy. It seems to me therefore prefer- able to use the term intuition to cover cases also where certainty is lacking. Anyone who dislikes this usage may substitute the term 'ostensible intuition'. For, whether all 'intuitions' are said to be certain or not, we must at least admit that what is taken to be a certain intuition is not always really one. It is largely a matter of terminology whether we then say that it is not an intuition or say that it is an intuition but not certain. But it is clear that there are all sorts of degrees of subjective certainty and uncertainty in apparent intuitions. Similarly, the *a priori* in general must not be equated with the certain. Empirical propositions may be certain, as are many established by immediate experience; and there are many cases of apparent *a priori* insight where we cannot be quite certain whether what we seem to see to be *a priori* true is really so. But any uncertainty there is in the *a priori* lies in the defects of the mind that reasons. We can only be uncertain in such matters because we are or may be confused. In some cases as in mathematics the confusion can be removed quite easily, in others as in philosophy it can persist for generations.

The main argument of those who attack the notion of intuition is that apparent intuitions are liable to conflict with each other and there is then no means of deciding which is right. But this is a mistake: we can in fact test them in various ways. We can consider whether they are capable of any clear and internally consistent statement. We can ask whether they fit into a coherent system with the rest of our well-established beliefs. We can also ask whether intuitions of the same kind have been confirmed in the past. We can ask whether an intuition stands or falls by itself or is a presupposition of a whole number of other beliefs which we cannot help holding, as some (though confused) intuition of the occurrence of causation or the uniformity of nature seems a necessary presupposition of all inductive beliefs. We can consider the plausibility of giving an alternative explanation of the intuitive belief. The result may then be negative or positive. It may be that our apparent intuition will evaporate when we think of the explanation, and then the latter is probably a correct one at least as to why *we* held the belief. Or it may be that the intuition will persist unshaken, in which case the explanation is probably at least inadequate. We can again consider whether the intuition repeats itself when considered in different contexts and different moods or with different examples.

So when two people have conflicting intuitions we need not suppose that there is just an irreducible difference of intuitive faculty between them and that there is nothing more to be done about it. Arguments may well be available which without strictly proving either side to be wrong put a disputant into a position in which he can see better for himself whether he is right or wrong or at least partially confirm or cast doubt on the truth of his view. In general, the clearer we have made ourselves about a subject by inferential thought, by analysing the different factors involved and by clearing up our terminology, the more likely are we to have correct intuitions on the matter if such are available at all. Again, intellectual confusions may be revealed which were responsible for the truth of the belief in question. Thus a person who really sees that A is B may confuse B with C and will then think he sees intuitively that A is C. Some such conflicts may be caused simply or mainly by ambiguities of terminology or the attaching of different meanings to some word. And of course we need not deny that differences of intuition may sometimes be due on one side or even on both to 'wishful thinking' or to the kind of cause which it is the business of the psycho-analyst (or of a patient and tactful friend) to remove. These remarks are specially applicable to ethical disputes. We cannot of course settle all disputes in these ways, but neither can we in practice settle all disputes in science. The most we can say is that they are soluble in principle, though we may not have the ability to hit on the right way of solving a particular dispute. Similarly, there is no reason to believe that conflicts between rival intuitions would not all be capable of a solution if these methods were applied aright and with good will on both sides, though in fact we cannot so apply them.

DISTINCTION BETWEEN KNOWLEDGE AND BELIEF

This is perhaps the best place to say a word about the distinction between knowledge and belief, which has played an important part in philosophical discussion. It is commonly and truly said that knowledge is certain and cannot be false, while belief may well be uncertain or mistaken. And some philosophers have assumed in consequence that we had a special faculty, that of knowing as opposed to believing, which was from the nature of the case infallible. This does not, however, necessarily follow. It may be that knowledge is only always certain and true for the same kind of reason as we have for saying that 'treason never prospers'. We can say it never prospers, because if it prospers it is no longer called treason. Similarly, it may be that we can only say that knowledge is always true because we should decline to call it knowledge if it turned out to be false. If I was absolutely certain of something and then later on I came to the conclusion that it is false or even only doubtful, I do not now say that I knew it but was mistaken. I say that I never really knew it at all. The explanation of this may be simply that 'I knew A' is a compound proposition including various elements: (1) I was subjectively certain about A, (2) A is true, (3) I was objectively justified in being certain about A, and it can only be legitimately asserted that I knew A if all three conditions were fulfilled. In that case to say that what I know or knew is true will be an analytic proposition. We shall not be using the word 'know' rightly if we admit that knowledge can be false. Knowledge will therefore be infallible for a quite different reason from any for which we might call, e.g., some very well-informed person an infallible guide about certain matters. We cannot first tell that something is knowledge and then conclude that we may therefore rely on it completely. On the contrary, we are only entitled to call it knowledge (in the strict sense) if we have first seen that we may rely on it completely. On the other side it is urged, and there is much plausibility in the argument, that if some things were not known as certain nothing could be even probable, and it is difficult to see how we could know anything with complete certainty if there were not a particular state of mind which we have towards certain things that could be regarded as from its nature infallible. But it does not seem possible to draw up an agreed list of the things we know with absolute certainty, and it is by no means clear that there are not cases of error which are psychologically indistinguishable from cases of knowledge.

Chapter Three

TRUTH

DEFINITIONS OF TRUTH

PHILOSOPHERS have been—like Pontius Pilate, though out of more respectable motives—much concerned with the question what truth is, and it is obviously of great importance for our whole philosophical outlook what we take as the criterion or criteria of truth. Considering first the question of definition, we find three main theories in the field.

(1) THE CORRESPONDENCE THEORY[1]

This maintains that truth consists in or depends on a relation between a belief or piece of knowledge and a fact in the real world. This is the common-sense theory in so far as common sense can be said to have a theory at all. We ordinarily think that, when we hold a belief, say, about the physical world, the belief is made true or false not by other beliefs but by something in the physical world to which it refers. My belief that this room contains a table is true because it corresponds to the facts about the room; the belief that there is an elephant in the room is false because it does not correspond to the facts about the room. I have taken examples from the physical world, but the same thing applies to beliefs about minds or experiences. My belief that I had toothache yesterday is only made true by the fact that I had toothache.

This theory seems only too obviously true, but there are three perversions of it against which we must be on our guard.

(*a*) I have used the terms, 'belief' or 'judgement' for what is true or false. Now this may be understood as referring either to

---
[1] Sometimes called 'accordance'.

our mental state of believing or to what is believed. But our state of believing is plainly not true; a psychological state cannot be sensibly called true or false. The theory therefore applies, if at all, only to 'belief' or 'judgement' in the sense of what is believed or 'judged'. ('Judgement' is used by philosophers as a term to cover both knowledge and belief.) The technical term in philosophy for what we judge or believe is 'proposition', and, strictly speaking, it is only propositions which can be true. We speak indeed of 'statements' as true, but they are not true in their own right but only because they stand for propositions which are true. Now, since in a discussion of this sort it is easy and indeed necessary to hypostatize propositions, we are apt to slip into thinking of them as entities which have a being of their own quite independent of being thought by anybody, and some philosophers have taken this view literally. But propositions, taken thus, would be such a queer kind of entities that it is better to avoid the view if we can possibly do so, and I do not see that it is necessary to regard them as anything more than elements in the states of mind of people who do what is called 'think of' or 'contemplate' the propositions. At any rate the correspondence theory is not necessarily committed to taking them as anything more than this. In that case there would still be *facts* if there were no minds, but nothing would then be *true* except in the hypothetical sense in which to say that S is P is true means that, if a mind were to judge S is P, that mind would be judging truly. But, granted that there are minds who do judge, the truth of their judgements may still be dependent on something which is not a mind, though there would not be judgements without a mind. There would be no answers to examination questions if there were no candidates, but it does not follow from this that whether a given answer is right or not depends on the candidate.

(*b*) The word correspondence suggests that, when we make a true judgement, we have a sort of picture of the real in our mind and that our judgement is true because this picture is like the reality it represents. But our judgements are not *like* the physical things to which they refer. The images we use in judging may indeed in certain respects copy or resemble physical things, but we can make a judgement without using any imagery except words, and words are not in the least similar to the things which they represent. We must not understand 'correspondence' as meaning copying or even resemblance.

(*c*) The theory must not be worded in such a way as to imply that we are never aware of the real but only of our judgements or propositions. If that were the case, we could never know that they did correspond. You cannot tell by inspecting a photograph whether it is a good likeness of a person you have never seen.

The correspondence theory as stated often seemed to fall under one or more of these perverted forms, and this aroused in philosophers the desire to find another theory which would avoid the notion of correspondence altogether.

(2) THE COHERENCE THEORY

Thus the coherence theory was developed in the nineteenth century under the influence of Hegel and the associated school of idealists. According to this theory truth is not constituted by the relation between a judgement and something else, a fact or reality, but by the relations between judgements themselves. This avoided the difficulty as to how we could know that judgements corresponded to something which was not itself a judgement. It was held that to say a judgement was true meant that it fitted into a coherent system with other judgements. Since coherence admits of degrees, it follows from this theory that a judgement can be more or less true. No judgement is absolutely true because we never attain a completely coherent system, but some judgements are truer than others because they approach nearer to this ideal.

The above is an objection to the coherence theory, because it is hard to believe such a conclusion. It would seem that a judgement is, strictly speaking, always either true or false and cannot be more or less true, and it is surely obvious that '2 + 2 = 4' and 'Washington is the capital of the United States' are absolutely true. It might be replied that the advocates of the coherence theory were not using 'truth' in the ordinary sense of the term, but we are looking for a definition of the word in the ordinary sense, not in some

Truth

exotic sense. 'Truth' in the ordinary sense is such a fundamental notion that it is a prime task of the philosopher to search for a definition of it in that sense, if one is indeed available. Further, I do not know how coherence itself could be defined without already presupposing truth. To say A coheres with B is either to say that A is consistent with B or that A necessarily follows from B, or something more complex definable in terms of consistency or of 'necessarily following from'. But these notions themselves already presuppose the notion of truth. To say A is consistent with B is to say that A and B may both be true; to say that A follows necessarily from B is to say that, if B is true, A must be true. So it seems that anyone who defines truth in terms of coherence is defining truth in terms of itself, thus committing a vicious circle. Finally, it is surely obvious that judgements are true not because of their relation to other judgements, but because of their relation to something objective which is not itself a judgement. This brings us back to the correspondence theory of truth.

(3) THE PRAGMATIST THEORY

Truth has been defined by 'pragmatists' as standing for beliefs which 'work'. Certainly true beliefs in general work better than false, but it does not follow that this is what is meant by truth. The pragmatist defends such a view on the ground that we cannot attain absolute truth and therefore must be content with what works. He points out that the object throughout evolution and in at least vastly the greatest part of human life has been not theoretical truth but practical success, and he insists that theory ought to be subordinated to what really counts. No doubt he will agree with everybody else that true beliefs must be consistent with each other and with experience, but he will say that this is only because, if they are not so consistent, they will not work.

The pragmatist definition of truth is open to the following objections. (a) It is quite conceivable that a belief might work well and yet not be true or work badly and yet be true. There are very many drunkards who would be greatly benefited if they believed that next time they took alcohol it would kill them, but this does

56

not make the belief true. (*b*) While true beliefs *usually* work, this is usually only because they are first true. It pays to believe that there is a motor car coming when this is true because if I do not believe it I may be run over, but it only pays because there really is a motor car, i.e. because the belief is first true. (*c*) What works for one man may not work for another, and what works for him at one time may not work for him at another. Does it follow that it has ceased to be true when it ceases to work, or that it is true for one man and not for another? The view that reality is a system in which everything is completely determined has worked for some men and the view that there was undetermined individual freedom for others, but both views cannot be true. God cannot both exist and not exist even if some men are helped by belief in his existence and others hindered. And he cannot have all the characteristics which have worked for all believers in all religions, for these are not all compatible. If a proposition is true at all, it surely must be true for everybody, and not just true for some men for whom it works and false for others for whom it does not work? Some pragmatists have welcomed such a subjective view of truth as is here suggested, but it is surely one that we cannot really accept. To take only one instance, if men evolved from animals at all, it will always be true that they did so, and will not become false in a particular generation when the effects of believing it happen to be bad and true again in another. (*d*) The pragmatist definition of truth is open to an objection already brought against the definition in terms of coherence, namely, that the truth of a belief depends on its relation to something objective not just on its functioning as a belief.

RETURN TO THE CORRESPONDENCE THEORY. THE VIEW THAT TRUTH IS INDEFINABLE

But the correspondence theory while, I think, true of at any rate most truths, does not give us much information unless we can succeed in defining correspondence, and unfortunately nobody has been able yet to give a satisfactory definition. This does not indeed destroy the theory, for it may well be that correspondence is indefinable. But, if this view is taken we shall have to admit that the theory has very little to tell us, for it will then have done little more than substitute an undefined technical term 'correspond' for the ordinary term 'is true'. Its only service seems to be that it has called attention to something which is obviously a fact but has been overlooked by certain theories, namely, the dependence of truth on a relation to something not itself a judgement at all. It would surely have been better frankly to admit that truth was indefinable and then say what could further be said about it, namely, that it was a relation between propositions and facts, without claiming to have given a definition and veiled the difficulty by the use of a technical term. Further, it may be objected that the correspondence theory only applies to certain kinds of true propositions and not to other kinds. It is hard to apply it to propositions about the future, because there is nothing for these propositions to correspond to, as the future does not yet exist. It is also hard to see how it can be applied to those hypothetical propositions where neither the protasis nor the apodosis expresses a fact, e.g. if Germany had won the war Britain would have been ruined, or if I had six wives I should have $4+2$ wives. There is no fact in the existent world to which such propositions correspond, and yet they are true propositions. The examples I have given may sound unimportant, but many such hypothetical propositions are of the greatest practical importance, since our motive for refraining from doing most things that we deliberately refrain from doing is the belief that, if we did them, such and such consequences would ensue. This is a belief in a hypothetical proposition such that, since we are not going to do them, neither the protasis nor (we hope) the apodosis is or ever will be true.

To say that truth is indefinable is not to say that we cannot know anything about it. It is only to say that we cannot analyse it in terms of anything else, and this is by no means an unplausible statement. It seems that we must admit some indefinables if there are to be definitions at all, since we cannot define A in terms of B and C, B and C in terms of D and E, and so an *ad infinitum*. But, if there are indefinables, truth seems as likely to be one as is any concept. It is such a fundamental notion that it is not in the least surprising if it turns out that there is nothing more fundamental in terms of which to analyse it. Only it must be emphasized that, if we are to attach any meaning to an indefinable, as opposed to an undefined term, we must be able to point to an experience in which the characteristic can be seen immediately to be present. To take an example of an indefinable that has commonly been used by philosophers, the colour yellow, we cannot analyse yellow in terms of anything else, otherwise we could explain sufficiently what it was like to a person who had never seen it;[1] but if we are not colour-blind, we can know perfectly well what yellow is like by seeing it, and this is the only way of knowing it. Can we point to an experience that tells us what truth is like in an analogous way so that, though we cannot define it, we can understand what is meant by the term? Surely we can. For we sometimes know something with immediate certainty to be true, if only of our present experience. And in doing that we surely see what truth is. If we did not, we certainly could not see any particular proposition to be true any more than we could see the colour of a yellow thing without seeing its yellowness. Having acquired the notion of truth in such experiences, we can apply it to propositions the truth of which is very much in doubt or is a matter of probable inference. But even if truth is indefinable, philosophers may still dispute about its relations, its criteria and exactly what it qualifies.

CRITERIA OF TRUTH

We shall now turn to the question of the criterion or criteria of truth. This question has not always been carefully separated from the question of the definition of truth, but I think it ought to be. The question, what truth is, is in itself different from the question how we are to find out whether a proposition is true. If we know that truth is to be defined as *A*, it may be thought that this at once gives us also the criterion of truth, because we could then always look for the characteristic *A* in order to decide whether a proposition was true. But it might well be the case that A was some-

---

[1] The scientific 'definition' of yellow in terms of wave-lengths is not an analysis of what the colour is, but of certain physical phenomena which accompany it. People knew what yellow was long before they knew anything about the wave theory of light.

thing which we could not thus directly discover but must determine by indirect means. For instance, only at the best in a minority of cases could we claim to see by direct inspection whether a proposition corresponded to the real, since to do so we should have to have an immediate awareness of the latter, whereas most of the propositions which we believe are established by inference and not thus immediately seen to be true. Yet this admission would not necessarily contradict the view that correspondence constituted the definition of truth. So we had better handle separately the question of the criterion and the question of the definition of truth. The only way of determining the criterion or criteria is to investigate the different kinds of well-authenticated knowledge and belief we have and see what the criteria are that convince us of their truth. There is no means of proving *a priori* what the criteria should be apart from such an investigation of what we find we must actually believe in ordinary cases.

We might well speak of 'correspondence' as the criterion of truth in cases of straightforward sense-experience or introspection. We can then observe the fact in question immediately and see whether our judgement corresponds. But, as we shall discover later, it is difficult to hold that we ever directly sense external physical objects, and in any case most of our judgements about them certainly go beyond anything we experience immediately.

What is to be the criterion of these? It may be contended that the best single word to describe it is 'coherence'. Certainly something that we may describe as a coherence test is needed to decide between rival scientific theories or even to distinguish illusion from genuine perception. Many of our sense-perceptions are unhesitatingly rejected just because they do not fit into a coherent system. That is the case with dreams. Why do we not believe our dreams when awake? Because they do not cohere with the perceptions of waking life. A dreamt that he was hanged last night, but that does not agree (cohere) with the fact that he is still alive. I sometimes dream that I am in a place hundreds or thousands of of miles away from where I am when I wake, though no known means of locomotion can have transported me from there. The lack of coherence with waking life would be still more obvious if somebody else were in the room at the time I dreamt and could observe my presence. Again, if we always believed in the sense-perceptions even of waking life, we should have to suppose that the same physical thing had all manner of different shapes, since the shape varies with the position of the observer, and rather than do this we reject very many of our perceptions as illusory. In water an oar appears bent, but to assume that it is really bent would not agree (cohere) well with the fact that we can use it to row effectively. All this can be cited to show the very important part which coherence plays in our actual thinking as a test of truth. It may be said to be the sole criterion by which we distinguish illusions and correct perceptions.

A great deal of stress has rightly been laid on the supreme importance for science of observation, but it may be doubted whether there is a single accepted proposition of science which could be established by observation alone, and I do not think this is altered when we add to observation deductive logic and mathematics. An obstinate person could always adopt the course of the opponents of Galileo when the latter claimed to have discovered the satellites of Jupiter. When they denied the existence of these bodies, Galileo challenged them to look through the newly invented telescope and see them for themselves. They replied that they knew already there were no such satellites and would not look through the telescope because, if they did, the devil might make them see them although they were not there. This is ridiculous enough, but it must be admitted both that the view is logically possible and that a similar course is adopted by all of us in regard to the objects of dreams and other appearances condemned as illusory (except that we do not attribute the deception to the devil but to our sense-organs). These objects do not conform to our intellectual standards of coherence, and so we just say they were not really there, though we have seen them perfectly well. (Of course we do not mean they are not real at all. We give them reality as a sort of mental images, but not as physical things.) Even without resorting to such heroic expedients as Galileo's opponents, most physical theories that have been held at any time could avoid outright refutation if a sufficient number of arbitrary *ad hoc* assumptions were made. Take the Ptolemaic theory, for instance. If we relied on observation primarily, the right reply to Copernicus's suggestion would be that put by Bernard Shaw in the mouth of a medieval soldier: 'The utter fool! Why could not he use his eyes?' It may be retorted that the ptolemaic theory, although in accordance with experiences such as that of seeing the sun rise, was logically incompatible with observations of a more recondite order, so that these latter refuted it. But this is not the case: it would be possible to maintain the ptolemaic system compatibly with the evidence of the senses provided we made sufficient arbitrary *ad hoc* assumptions unconnected by any principle. This was what was done in face of the first criticisms of Copernicans, but eventually as the number of such assumptions became greater the ptolemaic theory became less and less plausible until it was quite dead, although never strictly refuted, and this is what happens with most discarded theories of science.

Advocates of the coherence theory are well aware that complete coherence must be regarded as an unattainable ideal, but views may still be judged according to their greater or less distance from it. The nearest approach to it is to be found in mathematics. Here the different propositions are so connected that each follows necessarily from others and that you could not deny any one without contradicting a vast number of others. If we assumed that $2+2$ was equal to 5 we could, I think, without making any further mistake draw conclusions which contradicted every arithmetical truth there is about any number. Other sciences cannot attain to this degree of coherence, but in any science we assume that of two theories, equally compatible with observed facts, the one which brings us nearer to this ideal is the more likely to be true. To be successful a theory must not be inconsistent with empirical facts, but coherence must not be interpreted in terms of mere consistency. Two truths might be quite compatible and yet quite independent and logically unconnected, e.g. that Washington is the capital of the United States and that I have a pain in my big toe. A successful theory must not just enumerate logically compatible facts without connecting them or causally explaining them. It must, if possible, bring them under laws, and the only evidence for the laws may be said to be their coherence with experience. We bring together into a coherent system what previously appeared unconnected by deducing different facts from the same set of laws, e.g. the fall of apples in an orchard and the movements of the stars. We may have no insight into the causal laws governing nature, but nevertheless in deciding what these laws are we can be swayed only by two considerations. Either we must see the laws accepted to be those which can easiest be reconciled with our experience, i.e. cohere best with it. Or we must see that they increase the coherence of our experience by bringing different elements of it together under the same law, instead of two separate unconnected laws. It is difficult to see what other criteria there could be for a scientific law, and these certainly can be brought under the heading of the principle of coherence. In our psychological interpretation of people's actions and testimony we similarly apply the coherence test, accepting the explanation which we say 'makes the best sense' of their actions. We presuppose it even in a detective story, for the correct theory as to the origin of the crime will be the one which accounts for the facts and fits them into a coherent system. The fundamental principles of logic themselves can be justified by this criterion on the ground that there could be no coherent system at all without these principles. But the argument does not in any way support the view that coherence by itself is the sole criterion, but rather *coherence with experience*. This would probably be admitted by most advocates of the coherence theory, but it may then be urged that 'coherence with experience' really means 'coherence with propositions based on experience', so that we have now admitted a second set of propositions not themselves based on coherence but on the mere fact that we can see them to correspond to our experience. The coherence criterion cannot without being thus supplemented by the correspondence criterion ever do justice to the empirical element in our knowledge. Only we must not think of the empirical data as known completely quite apart from the use of the coherence test and thus serving as an altogether independent starting-point already there in its entirety. In order really to know the empirical data, we must have already fitted them into some rough kind of system. We cannot know them, still less communicate our knowledge, without classifying them and bringing them under universal concepts, and this already presupposes a conceptual system in the light of which we make all our judge-

Truth

ments and which is tested by its ability to give a coherent interpretation of our empirical data. We must remember that with the exception of proper names almost·every word we use stands for a universal concept of one sort or other, and this means that it is part of a conceptual system which men have gradually built up in order to describe their experiences to each other and interpret them to themselves.

There are other gaps in a purely coherence theory of truth besides its inability to deal with empirical data. It is true that the coherence theory cannot get on without admitting immediate empirical cognitions not just based on coherence. But it is true also that it cannot get on without immediate cognitions of a different sort. The advocates of the coherence theory reject the view that any propositions are self-evident in their own right. They would say that the fundamental logical propositions, like the law of contradiction, which seem self-evident, are validated not by their self-evidence, but by the fact that they are presupposed if there is to be any knowledge or any coherent system at all. Of subordinate principles they would say that they must be accepted as true because, although these are not themselves necessary presuppositions of knowledge, they follow from general principles which are. But I find it hard to believe that we only know the law of contradiction because we see that without it we could have no knowledge or that we only know that numbers can be summed because we see that otherwise we could have no arithmetic or no consistent arithmetic. But, however that may be, there is in any case a definite proof that the coherence theory cannot dispense altogether with the notion of self-evidence or intuition. Suppose a belief is accepted or a proposition known because it coheres with the system. But how do we see that it coheres with the system? We might see it as the result of a process of mediate inference, but that could not go on *ad infinitum*. Sooner or later we should have to come to a proposition of which we could only say that it is evident that it coheres with the others or that we just see immediately that it coheres. We may thus apply to the coherence test the general argument which I used earlier to show that all inference must presuppose intuition.[1]

[1] *Vide* above, p. 48.

Again, I do not see how, if we were never immediately aware of the presence of goodness or badness, rightness or wrongness in any particular instance, we could ever establish any ethical proposition by the coherence test. Ethical propositions cannot be proved by argument from non-ethical, so some ethical propositions must be known immediately if we are to know any at all. Finally, I do not see how the coherence theory can give a satisfactory account of memory judgements. These are clearly not inferences, they are not established, though they may be confirmed, by coherence; they are as much given as the data of sense-perception. They represent still another kind, and a very important and all-pervasive kind of immediate cognitions.

It seems to me therefore that 'coherence with experience' is not a formula adequate to cover the whole of knowledge and justified belief. There are other immediate cognitions besides those of objects of our present introspection and sense-experience. But a parallel formula might be found to cover all cases. We might say that the criterion is 'coherence with direct cognitions in general'. By an 'immediate cognition' or 'direct awareness' I mean a 'cognition otherwise than by inference', thus covering alike sense-perception, introspection, memory, intuition of the logically self-evident and of immediately apprehended ethical propositions. To say that correspondence was the sole criterion would be to try to bring all criteria under the heading of this direct awareness, but the correspondence theory has to admit that we are able to make inferences beyond our immediate experience or memory. Similarly, the coherence theory has to admit that coherence by itself is not the sole criterion, but at least coherence with experience, and, I should say, 'coherence with immediate cognitions in general'. When this has been admitted, either theory has left a place for the other, and the difference between them has become one of relative emphasis.

It is clear in any case that we cannot do with just one criterion of truth. Neither sense-experience nor coherence can fulfil this role for all truths, if only because there are both *a priori* and empirical propositions. Intuition we have to introduce as a third criterion, if only because all inference presupposes intuitions by which we see that a stage in the inference follows from the preceding one. Since intuitions are usually concerned with facts of a kind that could not be confirmed or refuted by sense-experience or memory, coherence provides a specially valuable test for them; but coherence is also absolutely essential for building up our ordinary conception of the physical world and of human minds. Nor can we dispense with memory as a fourth means of attaining knowledge and justified belief. Memory is not sense-perception or present introspection, nor is it inference, and it can rightly claim to be its own adequate guarantee in a vast multitude of cases. Memory, introspection and perception of the immediate object of sense may perhaps be all appropriately brought under the correspondence formula as cases where we just see immediately that the propositions believed or known correspond to the facts, but it seems less appropriate to apply this formula to knowledge by inference.

The discussion has brought out the fact that there are two elements in knowledge and true belief to both of which it is essential to give an adequate place in our philosophy, (1) active construction and systematizing by the mind, (2) an objectively given basis independent of the first element and the foundation of its work. Extreme empiricism neglects the former element, most forms of the coherence and pragmatist theories the latter.

Are we to add to the other criteria the pragmatic test of which so much is said nowadays? Now no doubt a belief in a true proposition will usually (though not always) work well and a belief in a false proposition badly, and therefore practical success may commonly serve as a criterion which will at least make it likely that the proposition in question is true. But I cannot regard this criterion as an ultimate one. How are we to know that a belief works badly? Because the consequences which should follow if the belief were true do not in fact occur? But this is a direct theoretical refutation which every theory recognizes. The point which shows the belief false is not its practical bearing, i.e. that it injures somebody, but the fact that it conflicts with experience. A false belief might be refuted by a conflict with experience of a kind which was highly agreeable to the believer, as when he has a pleasant surprise. And it may be urged that we know by perception and inference a great many propositions without seeing how

66

they work at all. To this it may be retorted that, since we do not assume all our perceptions to be correct and do not see the canons of at least inductive arguments to be logically self-evident, we must in judging what we perceive and making inductive inferences at any rate presuppose certain general principles which can only be justified by their working. The question is not whether a particular proposition works, but whether it is a consistent deduction from the application of principles of inference which have worked in dealing with experience and are justified by their working. But we may reply that this is a vicious circle. What the pragmatist is trying to justify is the belief in induction, i.e. the argument from what we have observed to the unobserved, and the argument offered to justify it is that the belief has worked in the past. But this is no argument that it will work in the future unless he already assumes the principles of induction which he is trying to justify. And, since he has not yet shown that they will work, these principles must be assumed independently of any test by their working. We may of course interpret 'working' as 'systematizing empirical facts', but then we shall be falling back on the coherence test. The question is: Can the mere fact that some belief produces good consequences, apart from any further argument which shows that the belief in question would not be likely to produce good consequences if it were not true, itself supply a criterion of truth? I am not clear why it should. If we were perfectly adjusted to the real, true beliefs would perhaps always work better than false, but then nobody can claim that we are perfectly adjusted.

Chapter Four

MATTER

THERE is nothing more obvious, at least to the non-philosopher, than the existence of physical things, yet there are few topics about which more philosophical difficulties have been raised, and we are at any rate no nearer to a generally accepted proof of the existence of the most ordinary physical objects than we are to such a proof of God's existence. Before studying the question we all think ourselves to be immediately aware of physical objects, and if asked how we knew they existed would think it sufficient to say: We see them. Most philosophers would, however, hold the view that we are not immediately aware of them at all, and there are certainly weighty arguments supporting such a conclusion. For (1) empirical evidence strongly supports the view that what we perceive depends for its qualities at least partly on our sense-organs. It is not only that we cannot e.g. see without eyes but that, if our optic nerve is affected in certain ways, we shall see what is not there. In order to see stars it is not necessary to look at the heavens on a dark night, it is sufficient to receive a blow on the head. If we get drunk, things look double; if we have jaundice, everything looks yellow; if we merely change our position, the things perceived alter drastically in shape and size. All this strongly supports the view that the objects we immediately perceive, though their nature may be causally determined partly by external physical things, depend for their existence on our perceiving them.

(2) What we perceive immediately we presumably perceive as it is, but physical objects we commonly do not perceive as they are. This seems proved by the fact of illusion. Further, two different people looking at the same thing at the same time from different positions in space may see it differently, e.g., as having

different shapes. But the same thing cannot really have two different shapes at the same time. Therefore they are not really seeing the same thing. Such arguments have led to the formation of what is commonly known as the *representative theory of perception*. According to this view what we *immediately* perceive is not the physical object we say we perceive, but a sort of image produced in our mind by the latter acting on us through our sense-organs. This image has been sometimes called a representation, sometimes an idea, sometimes a sense-datum, and sometimes a sensum. The view is very paradoxical, but it is hard to meet the arguments in its favour.

If indeed we mean by sense-data only those elements in experience which can be ascribed simply to sensation, it may be doubted whether we are ever aware of pure sense-data. What we are immediately conscious of is probably always or almost always mingled with memory and interpretation and not just the result of objects acting on our sense-organs at the time. The point of the representative theory is not that this immediate object is simply given by sensation alone, as the term sense-datum might imply, but that it is not to be identified with part of any physical object conceived realistically or to be regarded as existing independently of being perceived. Whether it is given by sensation alone is a question not about the nature of what we perceive but about its causation.

THEORIES OF PERCEPTION

If we do not hold the representative theory at least about some perceptions, there seem to be only three alternatives, each of them extremely difficult to credit. The first is to deny altogether the existence of physical things independent of human perception of them. In this case our theory will no longer be representative because there will be nothing behind human ideas or sensa for them to represent. This alternative we shall discuss later. The second is to assert that everything we ever perceive exists in the physical world just as we perceive it. But it seems hardly possible to reconcile the existence of all these incompatible things. It is self-contradictory that two different colours should be in the same space at the same time, but if everything that anybody ever perceives existed independently just as he perceives it, I do not see how all these different things and qualities could be fitted into physical space without two or more often overlapping in such a way that two different colours did occupy the same space. Further, the theory would not really achieve its object, because it would make at least one perception illusory, i.e. the perception of change I have when I see an object grow smaller or change in shape as I alter my position. On such a theory this perception would be illusory because the different shapes and sizes which I perceived as changing into each other would really be all there all the time. But if any illusions are admitted the main object of the theory is lost, which was to enable us to hold that we always perceived directly the physical objects we think we do before we reflect, and in order to save what is left of the theory, it seems hardly worth while accepting such paradoxes as the objective existence of all the objects and qualities ordinarily regarded as illusory.

The third alternative is to hold that we always perceive physical things directly but are mistaken in our perceptions of them. At first sight this seems the least paradoxical alternative, but in reality it is perhaps the most. For it leads us into holding that our immediate experience itself is radically mistaken, while the other views condemn as mistaken not the experience itself but beliefs suggested by it. To make this point clear let us take the case of a stick which is really straight but, being partly in water, appears bent. On the representative view there is something really bent, the representation or sensum; the evidence of my immediate experience on this point is not doubted. But on the other theory there is nothing really bent at all, only something straight which appears bent. I do not see what 'appears' can mean here except 'is mistakenly taken as bent'. Now we may well go on believing that the physical object itself is straight, but if there is one thing clear about the situation from our immediate experience it is that we really see something bent, from which it follows that something bent really exists if only as an image in our mind. If it did not exist, we could not see it. We must accept the evidence of immediate experience, for on this all other empirical evidence depends. The error of supposing that we were seeing something

Matter

bent when there was nothing bent to see, if an error at all, could not be explained as due to an over-hasty and superficial analysis of our experience. However carefully and long we look at the stick, we see that there is something bent. Further, we should have to suppose a like error in all or almost all cases of immediate experience. For in all or almost all cases an element of illusion is present, if only due to our varying position in space. Most philosophers would hold that we *never* can be mistaken as to qualities that we immediately experience, but whether this be so or not it is at any rate clear that we cannot admit such widespread error as all this without plunging into the abyss of an almost total scepticism. If we cannot trust our immediate experience, is there anything to which we can give credence at all?

It seems therefore almost necessary to adopt the representative theory as regards at least some cases of perception, but need we adopt it in all? Such a partly representative view as is here suggested may be regarded as the view of common sense. The general pre-philosophical attitude seems to be that we perceive the ordinary objects of physical life directly, but that things like rainbows, mirror images, or the pink rats seen by a man suffering from delirium tremens are only appearances. But few philosophers have compromised in this way. The chief objection to the compromise is that it is very difficult to find any perception at all where no element of illusion comes in, if only because our position in space must influence what we see and the structure of the part of our body we use in touch must influence what we feel. We may also recall how different objects look according as to whether they are viewed with a microscope or by the naked eye.

PHENOMENALISM OR IDEALISM *v.* REALISM

But if we adopt a wholly representative theory, the question may be asked how we are to justify the belief in external independent physical objects at all. If you ask me why I believe there is a table in this room, the natural answer is: Because I see it; but if I did not, strictly speaking, see the table but only a representation of it, what then? Unless it is admitted that I sometimes at least perceive physical objects directly, I cannot compare my representations with the reality in order to determine whether they are good likenesses of it or not, and it is certainly at least conceivable that my representations might be all illusory and produced by quite different causes from those physical objects to which common sense attributes them.

We reach here one of those great dividing-lines between philosophers which splits them into different schools. Some answer these difficulties by maintaining that we can only intelligibly, or at least justifiably, talk of matter or 'physical objects' if we interpret our statements simply in terms of experiences and the laws governing experiences. On this view to talk about a table is simply to talk about the experiences human beings have when they see, touch, or use what we call a table, or at least if we do mean anything more than that when talking about tables we are making assertions which cannot be justified or defended. These philosophers are called *phenomenalists*, or if they combine their view with a metaphysics which makes mind fundamental to reality, *idealists*. In this chapter we shall discuss the negative phenomenalist position rather than the more positive metaphysical idealist views often linked with it.[1] The philosophers opposed both to phenomenalism and idealism are commonly called *realists*. According to the realist physical objects are quite independent of experience and possess at least some of the qualities which the plain man and the scientist ascribe to them in a sense in which this statement could not be reduced to a statement about human experience or sense-data. Thus the realist would maintain that a coin literally has the same property of circularity that I see or some similar property[2] even when nobody is looking at it; the phenomenalist that we can only say it has it if we mean by this that sensations of circularity would be produced in people who went through the experiences which we ordinarily describe as 'seeing and handling the coin' or that our experiences go on as if the coin were circular in the realist sense. He may either say that physical objects do not exist apart from experience at all or that, if they do, we cannot say

---

[1] For these *vide* below, pp. 138–41.

[2] The realist need not commit himself to saying that physical space is *just like* the space we perceive, at least if he holds a representative theory of perception.

anything about what they are like as thus existing, only about their effects on us.

The view that physical objects cannot be conceived as existing independently of being perceived was first put forward by Berkeley in 1710. At first sight such a view may seem too absurd to be worth discussing, as indeed it did to almost all Berkeley's contemporaries. But familiarity with it very often removes this feeling. We must in any case distinguish between a view which seems absurd only because it is in violent conflict with our ordinary beliefs and a view which is absurd in the sense of being self-contradictory and therefore logically impossible. Berkeley's view is not absurd in the latter sense, and it might seem absurd in the former sense and yet be true. At any rate a discussion of the view is essential for many problems of philosophy. Various attempts have been made to soften the paradox by those who held it to be true. (1) They insist that a good sense can still be given to all the statements about physical things ordinarily made by the plain man and the scientist if we interpret them in terms of human experience. Since the phenomenalist does not deny the occurrence of any experiences ordinarily recognized as occurring, he can point out that in his view our experience will go on just the same as if independent physical things existed; and he will say that he does not contradict any verifiable statements of science, since scientific statements can only be verified by reference to human experiences. We can still even in his view make just the same predictions about the sensa we shall experience as we can in the ordinary view; all we cannot do is to say what physical things are like in themselves apart from their effects on us. (2) Berkeley and other idealists, while using the phenomenalist arguments, have none the less maintained that physical objects were independent of human beings, though dependent on mind, because they held them to be dependent on a super-human mind.

Berkeley's principal arguments against realism and indeed all those that have subsequently been brought by philosophers may be classified as follows:

Matter

(1) ARGUMENTS FROM THE THEORY OF KNOWLEDGE

It is contended that physical objects, if they are known by us, must be related to mind, and that we therefore cannot tell what they would be like apart from mind, since we cannot know them without *ipso facto* relating them to mind. Some thinkers going a step further have said not merely that we cannot know what anything existing independently of mind would be like but that we can positively know that nothing could thus exist whatever it was like. They have argued that the conception of something existing independently of mind is a self-contradictory one, because even to suppose or conceive such a thing would be to bring it into relation to mind and therefore contradict the proposition that it was independent of mind. If so, we can assert definitely that physical objects in the realist sense could not exist with the same justification as we can deny the existence of anything self-contradictory such as round squares or things which were at once blue and red all over. These arguments have commonly been reinforced by pointing to the large amount of constructive activity done by the mind in framing concepts even when dealing with quite simple matters of fact.

To this realists have replied that, so far from the nature of knowledge implying that its object is 'relative to' in the sense of dependent on mind, it implies that the nature of the object must be independent of the knowing of it, since otherwise knowing would distort what we supposed we knew and would therefore always falsify itself. They distinguished between 'internal relations' which made a difference to the terms related and 'external relations' which did not, and insisted that the relation of knowing was external at least at one end, i.e. if it did make a difference to the knower, it made no difference to the object known. The constructive activity by the mind which their opponents had emphazied they were prepared to admit, but only as a preparation for knowing and not as identical with knowing, and they insisted that what the mind constructs or alters in the process consists not of the object known but of mental concepts distinct from it used as tools with a view to knowing it.

74

Matter

In this controversy I am on the realist side. All the idealist arguments that I know from the theory of knowledge seem to me to involve some definite fallacy. Thus Berkeley argues that I conceive physical objects and what I conceive is 'in the mind'; but this phrase is plainly ambiguous. To say that something 'is in my mind' may indeed mean that it is an idea of mine, but it may also mean merely that I am thinking of it, which is quite compatible with its existing outside my mind. If I say that the quarrel between the western Powers and the Russians is very much 'in my mind', this is certainly compatible with recognizing the objective existence of this quarrel outside me. I am not implying that it is only a quarrel in my mind. Again it has been argued that object is relative to subject and therefore implies a subject (mind), but it does not follow from this that an object cannot exist independently of a subject, any more than it follows that, because 'pupil' implies 'teacher', the men who are my pupils could not exist without a teacher. The correct answer is that, as these men could not *be pupils* without a teacher, so physical things could not *be objects* without a subject, but the physical things might still exist without a subject as the men might exist without a teacher.

It is a good test of most of the arguments from the theory of knowledge to ask whether, if valid at all, they would apply only to physical things or to all objects of knowledge. If the latter is the case, they would lead to the conclusion that not only physical objects but other human minds and the laws of logic depended on my knowing them, and that surely can be regarded as a *reductio ad absurdum*. Thus when Berkeley argued that physical objects are conceived, and therefore existed in the mind, he might equally well have argued: I conceive other human beings, what is conceived is in the mind, therefore other human beings are only ideas in my mind. He was not prepared to accept the latter conclusion, but if so was he justified in accepting the parallel conclusion about physical objects?

It has been pointed out that the phenomenalist or idealist case gains a spurious plausibility from a certain ambiguity in various expressions. Sensation, perception, conception, knowledge may all be used in two senses, one to mean a mental state of sensing, etc., the other to mean what is sensed, etc. Now in the former case

Matter

the words obviously stand for what cannot exist except in a mind, but it does not follow that they do so in the latter. Thus when the phenomenalist or idealist argues that the notion of physical object consists of 'sensations', it may be that he is confusing 'sensations' in the sense of 'feelings' and 'sensations' in the sense of 'qualities sensed'. The former cannot exist independently of mind, but the latter might well do so. In order to avoid the risk of this confusion it is best to use 'sensation' only in the former meaning, and to employ 'sensum' or 'sense-datum' to signify what we sense as opposed to the act or state of sensing it.

(2) ARGUMENTS FROM THE SPECIFIC CHARACTERISTICS OF PHYSICAL OBJECTS

Berkeley also argued—and again his arguments have been repeated by most subsequent idealists—that when we examine the different characteristics ordinarily ascribed to physical things, we find they all involve a reference to experience and are unthinkable without this. Thus he contends that taste, warmth, sounds, colours are 'sensations', and so on all along the scale. Now I have just referred to a confusion between two meanings of 'sensation' which is probably responsible for some people's acceptance of phenomenalism, and this confusion is relevant to the present as well as to the previous argument. Colours, etc., clearly are sensations if we mean by that 'something sensed'; but it does not follow that they are 'sensations' if we mean by that 'feelings', and therefore that they only exist in a mind. But that is not conclusive. If we recognize this and similar distinctions, there can be no verbal contradiction in asserting realism; but the phenomenalist or idealist might still maintain that on careful inspection it was clear that, although we could distinguish sensed qualities like colour from sensations in the sense of feelings, we could not separate them. We can distinguish but cannot separate the properties of convex and concave in a curve or the property of being 4 and that of being 96 − 92, and similarly the idealist might say that we can distinguish but cannot separate any one of the qualities in question, e.g.

76

Matter

colour from the property of being experienced. (By saying that one property is inseparable from another I mean not merely that it does not in fact exist apart from the other, but that it could not possibly do so.) Whether the qualities ordinarily ascribed to physical things are thus inseparable from experience or not is a question that can only be settled by considering each case on its merits and trying to see if we really can conceive the quality as ever existing without being experienced by anyone. The result may be different in the case of some qualities from what it is in the case of others. One quality given in sensation we indeed all agree in regarding as inseparable from consciousness and so as incapable of belonging to unconscious physical objects. That is pain. But it does not follow that all other qualities given in sensation are in the same position. Common sense certainly makes a distinction between them, and talks of physical objects as having temperature, colour, size, but not as having pain. Proceeding down the scale let us now take taste. Most people, I think, would hesitate to say that this quality ever belonged to unexperienced objects. We do indeed speak of sugar as sweet when it is not being tasted, but by this we seem to mean only that it would produce the feeling described as a sweet taste if we put it in our mouths. We do not mean that the actual sweet taste is itself present in the sugar though nobody is tasting it. I should myself not be prepared to say that it is inconceivable that the taste should be thus present, though I have no evidence that it in fact is, but most people would probably disagree with me even as to its conceivability. But when we come to warmth and sound there would be a greater inclination to say that the qualities in question could exist independently of being experienced, and still more so when we come to colour. Yet it is still plausible to say that the nature of a colour is inseparable from how it looks, and that therefore the colour could not exist without being experienced. But a similar statement seems less plausible in the case of shape, size and velocity.

For this reason and also for others which will become clear shortly, many realists make a distinction between *primary* qualities which they conceive as existing in physical objects independently of being perceived and *secondary* qualities which they do not. The former comprise such qualities as shape, size, velocity, duration,

Matter

texture; the latter such qualities as colour, sound, taste, smell.¹
Now it has been found that science can explain our experience
adequately for its purposes without ascribing secondary qualities²
to physical objects, but not without ascribing primary. Colour
vision itself can be explained scientifically without supposing that
physical objects really have colour, but not without referring to
the size, structure, etc., of the light waves and the things which
reflect them. Faced with this distinction idealists have brought
three arguments in order to show that the realist account of primary is no more tenable than that of secondary qualities. (*a*) It is
pointed out that we are just as subject to illusions in regard to
primary as in regard to secondary qualities. This argument will be
dealt with later. (*b*) It is argued that primary qualities cannot be
conceived as existing without secondary and that therefore the
two are in the same position. This I think is invalid. It is true that
it would be self-contradictory to suppose that there could be an
object having only primary qualities. What has shape and size
must have some other quality or qualities besides. For to talk
about the shape of a physical object (or of a sense-datum for that
matter) is only to talk about its boundaries, and there must be
something within the boundaries. To talk about its size is to talk
about the extent it occupies, but there must be some quality or
qualities to occupy the extent. To have motion or velocity you
must have some qualities which change their position. All the
primary qualities are really relations, and relations imply terms
which stand in the relations. Therefore the philosophers like
Descartes, and probably Locke, who thought that physical objects
had no qualities but the primary ones must be wrong. It does not
follow, however, that the other qualities they have need be identical with any of the secondary qualities we perceive. It might be
that the qualities other than the recognized primary ones which

¹ Temperature occupies an intermediate position. As felt warmth or cold it was
regarded as a secondary quality, as the motion of particles supposed to explain this
feeling as primary.
² I am using 'secondary qualities' in the sense in which Berkeley and subsequent
philosophers, not in the sense in which Locke used the term. Locke used it to mean
not the actual seen colour but the power in a physical object to excite the sensation
of the colour. In that sense secondary qualities do belong to physical objects if
primary do.

Matter

physical objects possessed were quite unknowable to us, though they appeared as colour, hardness, warmth, etc. Consequently, the realist is committing no logical absurdity if he ascribes primary qualities to physical objects but refuses to ascribe secondary.

(*c*) Some idealists[1] have had recourse to an argument from relations in order to show that primary qualities really imply mind. They certainly involve relations, and it is argued that relations imply mind. If A and B are related, they are at once separate and together in a mysterious way, and it is contended that this combination of separateness and togetherness is only intelligible if we think of A and B as existing for a mind which at once distinguishes them and yet holds them together in the same unity of consciousness. But most philosophers do not now find it evident that relations imply mind, and I cannot produce a further argument on the subject.

(*d*) Many philosophers would claim to see directly that it was just as evident that primary as that secondary qualities implied mind. But we are here again driven back to something which we cannot settle by argument but either see or do not see to be true. However, we certainly must not regard the idealist contention with contempt in view of the great number of philosophers who have found it evident that physical objects could not exist unexperienced while holding in other respects the most varying views.

I am not discussing here one argument which plays a large part in Berkeley, the argument that material substance as something over and above its qualities is a quite unintelligible and absurd concept. This is an objection to Locke's particular view of matter rather than to all forms of realism. A realist need not hold this theory of substance. He may hold like Whitehead that physical objects are just events or series of events.

(3) NEGATIVE ARGUMENT

The most popular and plausible argument against realism is a negative one based on the difficulty of justifying realism. We have already seen that, if we hold realism, it is difficult for us to avoid

[1] E.g. T. H. Green, *Prolegomena to Ethics.*, bk. I, ch. I, esp. § 26-9

a representative theory of perception, and that if we hold a representative theory it is difficult, since we never see physical objects directly, for us to justify realism. Most realists have tried to meet the difficulty by an argument to the effect that physical objects were necessary to explain our experience causally. But we cannot understand by a physical object just an unknown X which causes our experience; if we are to understand such objects as common sense and science understands them, we must be able to ascribe to them more or less definite qualities. Now how can we tell what are the qualities of a cause from the qualities of its effects? It is commonly agreed that we can do so only because we have in the past experienced similar causes producing similar effects, e.g. though I have been asleep at night and not seen it rain, I can infer that the puddles in the road were caused by rain because I have on other occasions seen rain cause puddles. But if the representative theory is true, we have never directly experienced physical objects, and therefore we cannot know in this way what they are like. Nor are we entitled to say that the cause is necessarily like the effect. A draught is not even supposed to be like a cold in the head or the tearing of my flesh by a knife like the pain it causes. This argument is supported by pointing to the numerous cases of admitted illusion which suggest that we can never say what the real shape, size or colour of any physical object is, even if we admit that they have some shape, size and colour. So it may plausibly be contended that, if we do introduce the conception of external physical objects, we can produce no good reason for saying anything whatever about them. If so, the conception becomes that of an unknown X, and it may be questioned whether it can be of any help towards the explanation of our experience to postulate an unknowable X.

CAUSAL ARGUMENT FOR THE EXISTENCE OF PHYSICAL OBJECTS

The phenomenalist arguments have had a very wide vogue both among the more rationalistically and the more empirically inclined philosophers. The former have regarded them as constituting a preface to a metaphysics which claimed to show that reality was fundamentally mental or spiritual; the latter on the other hand have been inclined to be phenomenalist because any other view seemed to go beyond what was justified by experience. And phenomenalism has recently become popular even among scientists, or rather those scientists who also aspire to reflect philotophically on what they are doing. Scientists have recently taken very much to talking in terms of actual or possible observers. A notable example of this is provided by the theory of relativity where the fact that observers travelling at different rates might not apprehend the same events as simultaneous is taken as an adequate ground for the denial of an absolute objective simultaneity altogether. We must not, however, go too far in stressing the phenomenalist implications of relativity, for the theory after all defines simultaneity in terms of objective spatio-temporal relations of some kind.

Let us now consider what the realist can say in his defence. In the first place he can produce a more formidable version of the causal argument for physical objects than our previous discussion suggests. Suppose he argues in this way. It is universally recognized that, if we can make a great number of detailed predictions from a particular scientific hypothesis, and the predictions come off, this is a strong argument that the hypothesis or something like it is true. The reason for this seems to be that it would be an extraordinary and inexplicable coincidence if predictions based on the theory all came off by mere chance. Suppose I had a theory as to the causes of the weather and on the basis of it predicted that it would rain to-morrow. This would arouse little attention because in any case it was very likely to rain. Even if it was mere guess-work, the prediction that it would rain to-morrow would have something like a thirty to fifty per cent chance of being fulfilled in the part of the world where I wrote this book, and therefore my success in predicting would be no considerable argument for the truth of my theory but could easily be regarded as a mere coincidence. But suppose I predicted correctly whether it would rain or not for every day in the next year. In that case experts would have to sit up and take note of my theory. It might still not be exactly true, but at any rate something very like it would have to be true in order to account for my extraordinary success in making predictions. It would remain logically possible that my success was due to mere chance, but nobody would believe this. It would be altogether too improbable a coincidence. The improbability may be illustrated in mathematical form. Suppose it rains on the average one day in two at the place for which I make my predictions. In that case the chances of my prediction being right on any particular day if it were mere guesswork would be $\frac{1}{2}$, on two particular days $\frac{1}{2^2}$, on three $\frac{1}{2^3}$ etc. By the time it had got to twenty-one days it would be already about one in a million, and as for my prediction being right by chance on every one of the 365 days, the probability of that would be $\frac{1}{2^{365}}$ the denominator being a number large enough far to exceed that of the electrons in the solar system. Now a vast number of predictions are always being made on the basis of the hypothesis that physical objects exist and have certain definite characteristics like some of those which we under favourable conditions perceive when we observe them. These predictions are constantly coming off. Far more than 365 are made by me every day and most of them are fulfilled. It is true that some of the predictions are not fulfilled, but this can only diminish slightly an improbability which is so astronomical that it can suffer enormous diminution and yet remain amply sufficient to justify the belief that the success of the predictions cannot be attributed to chance. We must remember that, where a prediction is not fulfilled, this can always be explained as due to a mistake about the particular characteristics of certain physical objects and does not suggest that no independent physical objects exist at all.

So there seems to be ample evidence to support the belief in physical objects in the realist sense. For how can the success of the predictions be explained unless the beliefs as to physical objects on which they are based are approximately true? They need not be exactly true, but the truth must be at least sufficiently like them to account for the predictions reached by inference from them turning out true so often and it would seem to follow that the causes of our perceptions must at least be very like what we ordinarily think them to be. To put the argument in a slightly different way, human experience has been going on for centuries or rather millennia as if physical objects existed, and surely that makes the belief in these objects a highly probable one. From the assumption that, in the absence of any special cause for thinking the contrary, the primary qualities seen by us in a clear light from the optimum distance for clear observation really belong to physical objects independently of being perceived, men have in the course of human history made billions on billions of predictions which have been fulfilled. Does not this make it extremely probable that this hypothesis or something sufficiently like it to be legitimately called realism is true? (The realist need not hold that physical qualities are exactly like, only in general similar to, some of those we perceive.)

But unfortunately the argument has two serious limitations. In the first place, it does not refute a view like that of Berkeley, who denied the existence of matter in the sense of a set of unperceived bodies in space and attributed our perceptions to the direct action of God on our minds. If God thought it well to produce ideas or sense-data in us which followed just the order we should expect if they had been produced by independent physical objects of the type ordinarily postulated by the realist without there being any such objects, he could no doubt do so, and it would be senseless to talk of a coincidence. The fact that our experience went on as if there were independent physical objects would be adequately explained by God's intention that it should go on like this. However, such a view would not be so different from realism as might be supposed. For God must know what he is doing when he gives us the sort of experiences we should have if there were independent physical objects, and he would therefore need to have ideas of physical objects himself, as Berkeley indeed suggests. Such ideas, being quite independent of human beings, and being the causes, indirect if not direct, of their perceptions might well be regarded as themselves a kind of physical objects in the realist sense of the word, and Berkeley, sometimes at least, so regards them. However, Berkeley's view cannot be proved or shown to be probably true; and against the ordinary phenomenalist who does not postulate a God to account for the order of our perceptions the argument I have given is in my opinion a very cogent one. It seems to me to show that we must suppose the existence of something over and above human beings and their sensa and, further, that we cannot be completely agnostic as to what these external things are. The argument from successful predictions does provide evidence as to their characteristics. It also shows how we can distinguish between illusions and genuine perceptions. We condemn those perceptions as illusory which do not fit into our causal system. An oar may appear bent in water but it rows as if it were straight; mirror images and rainbows do not act causally like 'real' physical objects. This, I think, is the most important criterion on the whole, but in most cases of illusion there is either disagreement between different observers or between the senses of sight and touch, in which case we give the preference to that one of the visual appearances which does not contradict the appearance to touch. It is a significant fact that, provided we take the ordinary realist view of physical objects, we can causally explain even the illusions.

But, unfortunately, even apart from the reservation in favour of Berkeley, the argument from successful predictions does not provide conclusive evidence for as much as we might think. This brings us to its second limitation. This may be expressed by saying that it cannot be used as an argument for ascribing secondary, only primary qualities to physical objects. Science finds it perfectly possible to make all the predictions it does make without assuming that physical objects have any qualities except the primary ones, shape, size, motion, velocity, etc. It can even give a satisfactory causal explanation of our sensations of colour without assuming that physical objects are really coloured, or of sound without supposing that sounds exist objectively in the physical world. It assumes indeed the objective physical existence of light-waves and sound-waves, but it does not ascribe to these waves any but primary qualities. So we cannot argue that secondary qualities are present in the physical world on the ground of our success in predicting, since the predictions are not based on the assumption that physical objects have the secondary but only on the assumption that they have the primary qualities. The distinction between primary and secondary qualities has often been attacked, but there is a strong philosophical basis for it in this fact that the ones are needed to explain our experience and to make predictions and the others not.

It is further argued that we have really no ground for saying that even the primary qualities of physical objects are like what we perceive them as being, for all that is absolutely needed to account for the success of our predictions is that their 'structure' should be the same as it appears to be. This requires explanation with the help of an imaginary illustration. Suppose I were abnormally constituted so that I saw grass as green but leaves as always blue. In that case it would be easy to detect the difference because I should deny that grass and leaves were ever the same colour and say leaves were like the sky on a fine day. But suppose I differed in my perception of colour from other men in such a way that I saw the colour I call blue whenever other people saw the colour I call green and saw the colour I call green whenever other people saw the colour I call blue. Then I could, it would seem, never discover the difference, yet it would be a very real one. This situation could be expressed by saying that the content of my experience was different from theirs in these respects, but the 'structure' of my experience the same. Similarly, the sort of relations I perceived under the heads of shape and size might conceivably be different from those perceived by others without our ever detecting it, provided our perceptions, though different, corresponded in this regular way. And, similarly, physical objects might really have different qualities and relations from those we perceive and yet our predictions come off, provided the qualities and relations, though different, were arranged in the same kind of way. Call the relations of physical things as we perceive them $r_1 r_2 \ldots$ and as they really are $v_1 v_2. \ldots$ Then we could still make successful predictions if whatever appeared to us to be related by r_1 was really related by v_1, and whatever appeared to us to be related by r_2 was really related by v_2, etc. That is what is meant by saying their structure is the same.

The above considerations suggest a compromise between realists and phenomenalists on the following lines. The former might admit that we cannot have any ground for saying that physical objects are qualitatively like what we perceive; and the latter would find it hard to avoid admitting that our perceptions have causes, that these causes are external to ourselves, and that our success in making predictions strongly supports the view that there is a resemblance in structure between things as they are and things as they appear to us. We might thus conclude that the material world as such is unknowable by us, but add that we have probable arguments which justify certain beliefs about its structure. Perhaps this argument carries the antithesis between content and structure a little too far, but it would be generally accepted nowadays that we cannot know anything from science about what a particle of matter is in itself but only about its relation to other particles of matter.

But another line of argument is possible. If, as seems to be the case, the representative theory of perception is true, we can only perceive physical objects by the mediation of sense, and we can only infer their existence or properties by using some sort of causal argument from these sensa. Now, since particular causal laws can only be established by experience, it is difficult to see how we can pass by a causal argument to something quite different in kind from anything we have ever experienced. Further, if sensa are to represent physical objects adequately, the latter must contain in themselves elements which are like the sensa. (Berkeley supported his idealism by asking what can be like an idea but an idea, and 'idea' is his equivalent of the modern 'sensum' or 'sense-datum'.) We can only apprehend physical objects in so far as we apprehend sensa which we in our ordinary experience of perception regard as parts of them, since at the common-sense level we do not hold the representative theory; we can only describe them in terms of characteristics of sensa; we can only determine their positions or characteristics either by taking 'on faith' our sensa as giving characteristics belonging to them, or by a causal argument from our sensa. All this suggests the conclusion that physical objects are best regarded as groups of entities qualitatively the same in kind as our sensa but existing independently of being perceived. It would indeed be ridiculous to identify a physical thing with a single sensum, but it might well consist of a group of entities of the same kind as sensa, only existing unsensed (the term 'sensibilia' has sometimes been used for such entities). In that case it would really have something like the colour, shape, hardness or softness which we under the most favourable conditions perceive in it. And we could still conceive of it as existing unperceived by anybody, unless we accept the arguments of the idealists. The arguments from illusion against the physical reality of secondary qualities do not show that physical objects cannot have colour, but only that we cannot decide conclusively what the colour is. Realists have usually assumed that physical objects are quite different in kind from our sensa, even when they held that nothing but our sensa was immediately perceived. But this is an assumption they are certainly not justified in making. We have immediate experience only of two kinds of thing, sensa and minds, and if so how can we be justified in asserting the existence of a third thing generically different from either? The causes of our perceptions may be generically different from either sensa or minds, but we certainly have no means of discovering that they are thus different.

ARGUMENTS FROM COMMON SENSE. ANALYSIS OF PROPOSITIONS ABOUT PHYSICAL OBJECTS

The next argument for realism is commonly called the argument from common sense and is no doubt the most influential. We cannot really believe, except for a short time in a philosophical discussion, that physical objects do not exist, and it seems unreasonable of philosophers to defend conclusions that nobody outside a mental hospital would seriously hold in ordinary life. We may not be able to prove the existence of physical things, but in the last resort we must accept some beliefs that we cannot prove. We cannot abandon our instinctive beliefs altogether if we are to have anything left on which to philosophize. The philosopher may well accept slight amendments to them, but if he has to amend them too drastically it is a serious objection to his own philosophy. Even Lord Russell has admitted that the only ground there can be for rejecting one 'instinctive belief' is that it clashes with others, and certainly no one would accuse him of being an unduly credulous person, too ready to accept instinctive beliefs. Nor can we point to any other instinctive common-sense belief with which the belief in physical objects clashes. We cannot prove the belief false, the worst we can say is that we cannot prove it true.

Matter

To this argument many modern philosophers would reply by drawing a distinction between knowing a proposition and knowing its analysis. They would say that we know quite certainly that physical objects exist and they would refuse to make this a philosophical question at all. But although we know the truth of countless propositions about physical objects, they say, we do not know how they are to be analysed and the philosophical problem is to find their analysis. By 'giving the analysis' they say they mean determining exactly what the common-sense statement asserts, not criticizing or amending this assertion or giving some additional philosophical information not already contained in it. It is an inquiry into what people really mean when they make the ordinary statements of life. Of course it must be admitted that a person can in some sense know what he means without being able to give the philosophical analysis of it, but it would be denied that he could know in the full sense what he meant without doing this. By using this distinction philosophers are enabled to accept the argument from common sense, at least seemingly, and yet also to accept phenomenalism. For they can say that, although our ordinary propositions about physical objects are true, they have to be analysed as merely statements about the experiences or sensa human beings have under given conditions. In that case we need no longer feel that phenomenalism contradicts common sense, for common sense is then itself not talking realism at all but phenomenalism. It is then true that there is a table in front of me; but this only means that I have visual sensa of a certain describable kind and would have tactual sensa of a certain other kind if I went through the experience described as touching the table, and that other experiences would follow certain causal laws, e.g. the experience of seeing books put on the table would be followed by the experience of seeing them remain there and not the experience of seeing them fall, etc. The phenomenalists would usually admit that we cannot hope to give a complete list of the simpler propositions about actual and possible sensa which constitute the analysis of any proposition about a physical object, for this would be to give a complete list of all the conceivable criteria which might make us likely to think the proposition true and all the empirical effects which we might regard as following from its truth; and this admission is certainly not without its difficulties for them. But they would insist that at any rate we can see that the analysis has to be in terms of a class consisting of an indefinite number of such propositions and must not introduce any propositions which do not refer to human sensa in this way. The phenomenalist analysis has the merit of including all that matters to our experience, for it does not *ex hypothesi* matter to us empirically what things are like when nobody is experiencing them. And it does not like realism go beyond human experience, a point which appeals to the empiricist temper of the age. Consequently, even physical science nowadays shows phenomenalist tendencies.

The view I have just sketched must be carefully distinguished from the one I suggested above which analysed physical objects in terms of sensa in the sense of holding that they were groups of entities like sensa, only existing unsensed. On that view physical objects are conceived as actually there all the time whether experienced or not; but on the view which I am now discussing, to say that they are still there when not actually being perceived is only to assert hypothetical propositions about the sensa we should have under certain conditions and not to attribute qualities to anything actually existing. For example, to say that my table was still in this room at midnight when there was nobody there is only to say that, if a normal observer had looked then in a normal light, he would have seen a brown oblong surface, that if he had had the experience of putting his hands on the place where he saw it he would have felt something smooth and hard, that if he had had the experience of putting books on the place he would not have had the experience of seeing them fall to the ground, etc.

Now this seems to me a fatal objection to the theory as an analysis of common-sense propositions. It may perhaps be impossible to justify more than this philosophically, but it is surely plain that, when we speak of my table as being in the room at a time when there was nobody there to observe it, we are meaning to ascribe to it the same kind of existence as we are when we talk about the table now that there is somebody here perceiving it. When I talk about physical things which nobody perceives, I am surely talking about what actually exists, not merely about what would exist if something had happened which has not happened.

Matter

Geologists and astronomers give an account of what the earth was like long before there were any living beings on it: surely they are saying that the earth actually was in a molten state in those days, and not merely talking about the experiences which human beings would have had if there had per impossible been any there to observe it. There is great interest in an historical account of the way in which things actually developed; but what interest could there be in asking what *would* have happened millions of years ago if something else had happened which could not possibly have happened? When I say that the perceived motion of the hands of my watch is caused by the machinery inside, I am surely attributing to the machinery an actual existence all the time, and not merely meaning, when I make statements about it, that we should have perceived something *if* we had looked, which we did not. The machinery is thought to have caused the perceived movements, and a cause must surely be something which actually exists, or existed at the time it acted as cause. The mere hypothetical fact that I should have perceived something *if* I had looked could not possibly be a cause. An event cannot be caused by what has not actually happened but only would have happened if something else had happened which has not. These arguments may not be conclusive as showing that physical objects in the realist sense exist, but at least they show that our ordinary assertions about them must be analysed not phenomenalistically but realistically, i.e. not merely as saying what has happened or would happen to our sensa or experience but as saying what actually exists whether perceived or not. We might indeed accept the phenomenalist analysis as regards some common-sense propositions about physical objects. It is more plausible to say that, when we speak of sugar as sweet, we are merely saying that if we put it in our mouth we should get a sweet taste, and similarly about most other people, than that we are saying that the sugar has the sweet taste as an actual quality all the time whether anybody is tasting it or not. It is perhaps more plausible to say that, when we speak of a coat in a closed cupboard as green, we mean merely that a normal observer would perceive it as green if he looked in a normal light than to say we mean it actually has the colour green now, though it is not being perceived by anybody and is in the dark. But if we accepted this analysis in regard to all the qualities of the sugar or the coat, there would be nothing left to cause the sensations of colour or taste.

An important element of truth in the phenomenalist analysis is that we must not admit into physical science propositions about physical objects which could not be verified by any experience, but it does not follow that in order to exist in the full sense physical objects need actually be experienced. But the point that has most influenced its supporters is that they thought it enabled them to say that we *knew* physical objects to exist. At the common-sense level we certainly say this, yet if the realist analysis is correct we have seen that it may be doubted whether we really do so. But I think the advantage of the phenomenalist analysis here is largely illusory. It may be argued indeed that if, when we talk about physical things, we are only talking about our sensa, we are talking about things which we know exist. But propositions about physical objects cannot possibly be analysed merely in terms of our own present sensa. If they were, I should have to say that the crocodile in my bed about which I dreamt really existed. If we take the phenomenalist view, we must analyse them in terms of the sensa of normal human observers in general and our own possible future sensa under different conditions; and we cannot perceive those directly any more than physical objects. To say what other human beings perceive is a matter of inference as much as it is to say what physical objects are like on the realist view. It is true that cases of 'telepathy' occur, but those are far too rare to form the basis of our interpretation of the belief in physical objects and are certainly not the ground of the vast majority of assertions about the physical world. In the absence of telepathy the position in regard to our knowledge of other people's perceptions is not very different from the position in regard to our knowledge of the physical world as conceived by the realist. We have seen above[1] that, provided the perceptions of other human beings correspond uniformly to ours in their variations, we have no scientific means of deciding whether they actually do or do not perceive the same qualities as we do, so that as with physical objects on the realist view so with the perceptions of other human beings we can make

[1] p. 85.

very probable inferences as to 'structure' but not as to 'content'.

If we reject, as I should do, the phenomenalist analysis of common-sense propositions about physical objects in the sense in which an 'analysis' is claimed to stand for the strict equivalent of the proposition analysed, we are then entitled to use the argument from common sense for what it is worth on behalf of realism. Till this question had been discussed, we were not entitled to do so, because till then we could not say whether common sense asserted realism. Now it does seem to me that the argument from common sense has a great deal of weight. I do not of course suppose that on a purely philosophical issue the opinions of common sense ought to be preferred to those of the philosopher. That would be to ascribe a special authority over philosophy to the opinions of those who had not studied philosophy. But the question whether physical objects exist and what they are like is not a philosophical issue. We do not need the philosopher to tell us that we have bodies, that the earth exists, and that iron is heavier than feathers. And, if a philosopher asserts that according to his philosophy these statements must be false, it is a condemnation of his philosophy rather than of the statements which he criticizes. Any philosophical arguments he can use are surely less certain than is the truth of the statements just mentioned by me. Therefore, if these statements have to be analysed in a realist and not a phenomentalist way, this is a strong argument for the philosophical truth of realism.

DIRECT COGNITION OF PHYSICAL OBJECTS

It is not as if the philosopher could reasonably claim to show the common-sense propositions about physical objects to be false. The most he can show is that they cannot be proved true or even probable. But it might be asked: Do they need a philosophical proof? Are not they evident in their own right? The absence of a proof does not prove that they are not known without a proof. We cannot prove everything. It may be thought that I have already ruled out this suggestion by admitting that we do not perceive physical objects directly, but it is possible that what we do not perceive directly we might still know directly. This occurs in the somewhat analogous case of memory. I do not perceive by my senses what I had for breakfast this morning, yet I remember it. When I remember it I know directly what I ate; what I know is not the result of an argument but something that is seen as true in its own right. If anybody challenges the correctness of my memory I may give arguments, but then I shall no longer be appealing to memory. In memory I know something to be a fact without argument. Or at least, if I do not *know* it, I have a justified belief about it. Often memory amounts only to justifiable belief and not to certain knowledge, but in a very important sense it is direct in either case. For memory, whether fallible or infallible, is not an inference any more than is perception as such. On the other hand, it is clearly indirect if we mean by this that what we remember is not a direct object of our senses. It does not even *seem* direct in this sense, while perception seems direct but probably is not really so. I do not directly sense my past breakfast; I only know it through something that arises in my present state, whether an actual memory-image of the breakfast (which need not occur) or some other modification of my present consciousness; yet what I know in memory is the past and not only the present modification in question. Now memory is not completely analogous to perception, but if we can be directly aware in memory of something that we do not directly sense, this shows at any rate that it is not absurd to suppose that I might know an empirical fact directly without perceiving it directly. If we use the word 'cognize' to cover the case where I do not know with certainty but have a justified belief based on contemplation of its object, we may put our contention by saying that the intuitive conviction we all have of the existence of physical objects is based on a direct cognition. There are many cases of memory where not certainty but justified belief is attained without inference, as well as the cases where something is really known in memory, so that we need not dismiss the possibility of a direct cognition in cases where it does not give what is in the strict sense knowledge. Our direct cognitions may be mixed up badly with assumptions and errors and yet contain a core, not always easy to pick out, which is cognized correctly. Our cognitions of physical things may be genuine, though often at least and perhaps always partly confused and mistaken, apprehensions of reality. We certainly are convinced when perceiving things in the ordinary way that we do apprehend real objective facts, and this cannot be refuted, though at the common-sense level we do not avoid the confusion between claiming that we sense them directly and claiming that we cognize them directly. The claim that we have this direct cognition of physical objects cannot be seen to be self-contradictory even if we do not perceive them directly, and it could only be rejected on the ground of a theory of knowledge to the effect that such a kind of cognition is impossible. But a theory of knowledge can only be based on the kinds of well-accredited cognition we are found to possess. We cannot tell *a priori* that one particular kind of cognition which we claim to have is not a possible one, we have not enough *a priori* knowledge of our faculties to say that, and therefore we must base our theory of knowledge on a generalization and systematization of the particular kinds of successful cognition. Now cognition of physical objects is obviously a kind of successful and well-accredited knowledge. Therefore, rather than reject it because it does not conform to our theory of knowledge, we must base our theory of knowledge partly on it. We must not deny it because it is unlike other kinds of cognition. Since the objects of cognition are very different, ranging from sensa and material things to laws of pure mathematics and ethical values, we may expect cognitions themselves to be very different from each other in kind.

Besides appealing to our intuitive conviction we may use two other arguments to support the view that we have a genuine and direct cognition of physical objects. (1) We are certainly directly aware of ourselves, but it may be argued that consciousness of ourselves necessarily involves consciousness of a not-self as a background with which the self is to be contrasted, and since the former awareness is direct the latter must be also. But, since we are not directly aware of other minds, the only existing things other than ourselves of which we could be directly aware are physical objects.

(2) We certainly suppose at the common-sense level that we are directly aware of physical objects in perception, and it is on the basis of this supposed direct awareness that we make the pre-

dictions which I have mentioned and which are so remarkably
fulfilled. We attribute qualities to physical objects in the first
instance because we see and feel them to be there. So, if the argument from predictions is an argument for physical objects in the
realist sense, it is also an argument for our intuitive convictions of
their existence being genuine cognitions. Tested by their results
the convictions work to such an extent that it would be an extraordinary coincidence if they were not genuine cognitions of the
objects about which the predictions are made. The reliability of
an alleged capacity is to be tested by its results, and here the
results are very good.

If we have a direct cognition of physical objects, the position
in regard to colour is altered. For colour seems as much an immediate object of awareness as shape, therefore on this score we
have no ground for denying to secondary qualities the physical
reality which we attribute to primary, though we cannot in the
case of secondary qualities supplement this conviction by the
argument from predictions or any sort of causal argument. It is
a common mistake that science has refuted the view that physical
objects are coloured; all it has really done is to show that our
experience can be causally explained without assuming that they
are coloured and to add to the difficulties of giving a plausible
account of what colours they have if they are coloured. Most
'secondary qualities' other than colour are not regarded even by
common sense as qualities of the physical objects which produce
the perceptions of them. At a common-sense level we seem to
think of sounds and smells as somewhere in the air between us
and the object which emits them but not like colours as qualities
actually pervading the surface of the object, while we do not
ordinarily regard tastes as belonging to objects at all except when
actually tasted.

PHYSICAL SUBSTANCE

We have so far been talking of physical objects simply in terms
of their qualities, but we ordinarily think of them as substances,
and as such we regard them as something more than mere groups
of qualities or even series of events. Yet when we are asked what

this something more is we cannot answer. We suppose that beyond the qualities there is something which has the qualities (or in which they 'inhere', to use the technical term). But what is this something over and above the qualities and relations of physical objects? We cannot say. It becomes a mere unknowable X, and our failure to know it has been deplored as an instance of the weakness of our faculties and of the mystery which shrouds the real world. But is it unknowable because of the weakness of our faculties, and not rather because we have defined it in such a way that it could not be known, even by Omniscience itself? For anything that could be known about it would have to be stated in terms of qualities and relations. When we have taken these away, what is left over in our concept of a physical object is a completely vacuous notion and therefore no notion at all, and this may well make us sceptical of the substance theory in this form. It does not follow that the conception of substance ought to be altogether rejected. If it is clear that there is no sense in talking about what a substance is apart from its qualities and relations, it is also clear that qualities and relations, if they are to have any place in the existent world, must be qualities and relations of something. Perhaps the answer to our problem is that we ought not to ask questions such as: What would qualities be like without substance? What are substances apart from their qualities? What are terms apart from their relations or relations apart from their terms? Perhaps what we should say is merely that the concepts of substance and quality are inseparable and correlative, neither being prior to the other, but both being necessary parts of our idea of matter. And we might treat the antithesis between a relation and its terms in the same fashion. At the least a substance is not just any collection of qualities but a collection of qualities arranged in a particular way very difficult to define. But it does not follow that there is something else in the substance when you have taken away the qualities.

The question of substance is one where language has probably had a misleading effect. We use one word, a noun, to represent a thing and other words, adjectives, to represent its qualities, and this suggests that, since different words are used, the element in the thing represented by the noun is different from any and all the elements represented by adjectives. But we need not accept this suggestion as metaphysically true or pragmatically valuable.

The concept of substance is also used to give us a sense of stability and unity in change. We think of attributes as changing while the thing which has them remains the same, but we are confronted with the difficulty that we cannot possibly say what the permanent element is, unless indeed we can fix on some permanent attribute or attributes, in which case it might be objected that we are still dealing with the attributes and not with the substance. It seems that what we need is a conception of substance not as something over and above the attributes but as the unity in which the changing attributes are contained. Again, it seems best to think of the two opposed concepts not as representing different parts of a thing but as correlative ways of looking at a thing, as ordering concepts that have their significance and utility only in connection with each other.

Whatever our conception of substance, I do not think we can find any metaphysical ground for saying when one substance ends and another begins in the physical world. We call the human body the same even though its matter has been almost entirely changed every seven years, because the form of the whole is preserved. If one tile from the roof of a house is replaced, it is still the same house. How many tiles and bricks would have to be replaced to make it a different house? Or how much exactly would its shape have to be altered to produce this effect? Are we to call a book one substance or a page or each organic particle in the page? Modern science till recently seemed to provide us with permanent unchanging substances absolutely distinct from each other in the shape of atoms, but the developments in science during the twentieth century have had the effect of denying the absolute indestructibility of the atom, and of raising very serious doubts whether its successor as the ultimate unit of matter, the electron, is anything more than a useful mental picture to symbolize certain mathematical relations. To conclude with a story for the benefit of those who are still inclined to deny the relativity of the conception of a single substance, it is said that a nobleman once got into financial straits and as a result his housekeeper, to save money, darned a pair of his black silk stockings with green wool.

Matter

This process went on till they were all green wool. Now at what point did they cease to be the same pair of stockings? It is obvious that the answer is a purely verbal matter. Exactly when we say that the one pair ended and the other began is a question of language, of no philosophical or scientific significance, like the question how few hairs a person must have on his head to entitle us to call him bald.

Chapter Five

MIND

PRIMARY CERTAINTY OF EXPERIENCE
REPLY TO BEHAVIOURISM

THE discussion of physical objects should have been sufficient to counteract the assertion that their existence is the chief and primary certainty. The primary certainty is experience, and this is not a physical object but something mental. When I think I perceive a physical object, it is conceivable that I might be dreaming, but I could not even dream that I existed without existing. And here by 'I' is meant my mind, not my body. It might conceivably be a mere dream or illusion even that I had a body, but it could not be an illusion or dream that I thought, at least in the wide sense of the term in which I am always thinking of something when I am awake at all. And similarly it could not be an illusion that I experienced. For to believe or even doubt that I am thinking or experiencing, I must already think and experience. This is the famous argument used by Descartes: I think, therefore I am (*cogito, ergo sum*). We may grant that the argument as he used it went rather too far. He talked as if it established a permanent self, while all it does establish is the present existence of a thought as experience. But with the appropriate limitations the argument is valuable as showing the primary certainty of experience against those who are disposed to talk as if matter alone were real.

Of course what we cannot practically help holding as certain is not limited to what can be theoretically proved such, but if we are to get back to the ultimate foundations of belief and knowledge we should ask what is logically certain. This falls into two classes, (1) Certain *a priori* propositions which could not be denied without logical absurdity, like the law of contradiction or the law

99

of excluded middle. (2) My own present existence as a thinking being. The certainty has, however, a different foundation in the two cases. We can see that the laws of logic could not conceivably be false, but it is quite conceivable that I should not have existed. My father might well have never met my mother. What is inconceivable is that I could deny or doubt my existence without existing, and therefore for me, but only for me, such a denial or doubt would be self-contradictory. But the *logically* certain need not be co-extensive with the certain. Besides what is logically certain there are a number of immediately known propositions which we can regard as absolutely certain although there would be no self-contradiction in our denying them. In this class I put more specific propositions based on introspection. I cannot see any self-contradiction in supposing that I might make mistakes in introspection, and there is therefore no *logical* absurdity in supposing that I might be mistaken now when I judge that I feel warm or that I have a visual presentation of a table. But I still cannot help being absolutely certain of the truth of these propositions and I do not think that I ought to be otherwise. I should not say this of all judgements of introspection, but I should certainly say it of some. Again I cannot help being absolutely certain of the truth of some (though by no means all) of my judgements of memory. As we have seen, it is however hardly possible to claim this absolute certainty for judgements about physical objects, and, as we shall see, there are similar difficulties in claiming it for judgements about minds other than one's own.

Descartes' assertion *Cogito, ergo sum,* is commonly regarded as the beginning of modern philosophy and in particular as initiating the subjective tendency which has been so characteristic of subsequent philosophical developments. Since his time philosophers have tended more than in earlier days before looking outwards first to look inwards in order to form a decision as to the human capacity for knowledge, and this tendency has often been carried much too far. But he was fundamentally right as to the starting-point, though not as to the way in which he used it. It has been objected that the *cogito* implies the existence of something thought as much as of a thinker, but there is nothing in the argument which proves that what is thought need be independent of the thinker. It might be just a mental image dependent on my imagining it for its existence.

Descartes' argument brings out the absurdity of 'behaviourism' as a philosophy. Some psychologists, who call themselves 'behaviourists', have tried to explain away the concept of mind or even mental events in psychology altogether and substitute for it the concept of behaviour studied as a physical process. Probably most of them merely mean that the observation of outward behaviour and not introspection provides the most useful way of acquiring data in psychology, but some would go further and put forward their behaviourism as a philosophy and not merely a methodology of psychology. In that case their position can easily be seen to be untenable. Such philosophical behaviourism may mean one of two things. (1) It may mean that there are no mental events at all. But in that case no one can possibly believe behaviourism to be true, for believing itself is a mental event. (2) It may mean that there are mental events but these are simply to be identified with physiological events. The kind of physiological events with which behaviourists identify thinking are usually movements of the vocal organs. People often, when they think, move these as they do when they talk, only less markedly, and behaviourists have advanced the view that this is what always happens when we think, and further that this is just what thinking is. Nineteenth-century materialists were on the other hand inclined to identify thinking, and mental events generally, with processes in the central nervous system or brain. In order to refute such views I shall suggest your trying an experiment. Heat a piece of iron red-hot, then put your hand on it, and note carefully what you feel. You will have no difficulty in observing that it is quite different from anything which a physiologist could observe, whether he considered your outward behaviour or your brain processes. The throb of pain experienced will not be in the least like either the act of withdrawing your hand or the movement of your vocal organs to say whatever you do say, nor would it be like anything described in textbooks of physiology as happening in the nervous system or brain. I do not say that it does not happen in the brain, but it is quite distinct from anything that other people could observe if they looked into your brain. The behaviourists pride themselves on being empiricists, but in maintaining their view they are going clean contrary to experience. We know by experience what feeling pain is like and we know by experience what the physiological reactions to it are, and the two are totally unlike. We know by experience what thinking is, and we know by experience what movements of our vocal organs are, and we see the two to be totally unlike. It is not a question of *a priori* speculative metaphysics whether mental and physiological events are to be distinguished. The difference is as plainly marked and as much an empirical matter as that between a sight and a sound. The physiological and the mental characteristics I have mentioned may conceivably belong to the same substance—I shall discuss that question in the next chapter—but at least they are different in qualities, indeed as different in kind as any two sets of qualities. The element of truth in behaviourism is that I can only acquire knowledge about other minds through their bodily behaviour, including under that what they say about themselves. But it is only because I interpret their behaviour in terms of my own immediate experience of my mental states, not my body, that it can give me information of a psychological kind at all.

We should not regard the conception of the mind as a metaphysical hypothesis concerning what lies behind experience, but rather as the conception of the different experiences of ourselves or some other person as related in a single whole. In this sense its existence cannot be denied. A distinction has been made, chiefly by theologians, between mind, soul and spirit, but this distinction has been avoided by most philosophers and 'mind' used to cover the whole of the man's inner nature and not merely his more intellectual side.

DIFFERENT ELEMENTS IN THE MIND

Now what do we find in our experience? Into what elements is it analysable? In the first place we discover a number of sensuous elements the qualities of which resemble rather those of physical objects as conceived by common sense, than those attributable to mind as such. I am referring to sensa and images. These may be

Mind

regarded as mind-dependent, but not as qualities of the mind. When I look at the sky on a clear day my mind is not blue, when I hear the din of a big railway station my mind is not loud. We must remember here the distinction already pointed out between 'sensation' as signifying 'sensing' and 'sensation' as signifying 'what is sensed'. The former but not the latter is an attribute of mind. But certainly, even if they are not attributes of mind, the investigation of the sensa and images we have under certain conditions, is a major part of the work of psychology. Further they, or at least images, are very closely linked with our processes of thought. It may be doubted whether we can ever think in the least definitely without using some sort of imagery. Words themselves are after all sensuous images of black marks on paper or of sounds.

Turning to the more specifically mental side of ourselves, we find that it has been subjected to a threefold classification, represented by the distinction between affective, cognitive, and conative. By the affective side of our nature is meant the feeling side, by the cognitive side the side concerned with knowing, believing, reasoning, perceiving, by the conative side that concerned with acting, willing, striving, desiring. We must not, however, think of it as if the three sides operated quite separately. On the contrary practically all mental processes involve all three at once. Except perhaps when we are half asleep there are probably no times in our life when we are only feeling beings, and certainly none when we are only cognitive or conative beings, since the feeling element at least must always be present. Thus having an emotion like anger or fear involves at once having more or less strong feelings, striving in a certain direction, e.g. to escape or get the better of our opponent (conative), and recognizing the situation as one of a certain character (cognitive). Cognition is essentially linked up with conation in the form of striving to attain some end by the cognition, if only the end of discovering truth for its own sake, and in the form of voluntarily turning the attention in certain directions. Attention in its turn is bound up with 'interest', and interest with feeling pleasure or its opposite in a pursuit.

On the other hand, while the three sides of mental activity mostly involve each other, a thinker may emphasize one in preference to the others, and this variation in relative emphasis is one of the chief sources of difference between philosophers. Those who emphasize the cognitive element most are apt to think of reality as primarily something satisfying the intellect, and so as a rational system in which there is a reason for everything or for most things of importance, and the different parts are all logically connected. Others make cognition subject to the conative side and insist that cognitions are always primarily means to a practical end. They exalt the importance of will at the expense of reason both in their estimate of man and in their view of reality in general. The most fundamentally real thing to them is given in the awareness of activity. Thirdly, the philosophers who derive knowledge exclusively or almost exclusively from sense-experience might be described as making the affective element predominant, since sensations are in my opinion best classified as feelings.[1] Hume's psychology would be a good example of one which tends to reduce everything to feelings. Similarly, in the realm of moral philosophy we can distinguish those who make the chief good a cognitive state, whether that of contemplation of the supreme being or simply that of having clear ideas in general; those like Kant who find the chief good in a state of the moral will; and those who find it in the feeling of happiness or pleasure. But it seems more likely that a right view will do justice to all three sides of our nature.

Some philosophers, while accepting images and sensa, have denied the existence of mental acts or processes like knowing, believing, willing, etc., on the ground that these are not accessible to introspection. The trouble is that we cannot introspectively detect such acts by themselves, but that seems to be because they are essentially bound up with some object. We cannot know without knowing something, believe without believing something, will without willing something, etc. If so it is not to be expected that we can introspect these activities by themselves, but we can still have an idea of what they are like because we can see the distinction between willing and not willing something, or that between believing and doubting the same thing. It does not matter if we cannot observe some attribute, A, by itself; we can still know

[1] Many psychologists, however, classify them as cognitions.

what it is like if we can observe the difference between AB and CB, and this is how we know what it is like, e.g. to believe. That we cannot give an adequate account of the self in terms of images and sensa alone may be shown by, for instance, taking the case of thought. One can go a certain distance in the interpretation of thought by means of images, but in very many cases the only discernible images are words. You may be able to think about physical things by forming images of them, but if you open a book on philosophy or economics at almost any page, you will not find a sentence the content of which is capable of being imaged. This being so, we are dependent on words for thinking about such topics. It seems to be a psychological necessity to have some sort of sensuous picture in our mind, but we cannot produce pictures that are like the objects about which we think, therefore we employ verbal images which can be used to represent some fact without needing to be like what they represent. A person who wishes to deny any mental events or processes over and above sensa and images will therefore have to maintain that thinking about philosophy is reducible simply to a combination of verbal images. Now he may be right indeed in maintaining that verbal images are a necessary condition of such thinking, but he cannot be right in maintaining that they are also a sufficient condition. For he will then not be able to make any distinction between a set of words about an abstract topic which we understand and a string of nonsense syllables. If we were dealing with physical objects we could often analyse the meaning in terms of non-verbal images, but this is not always the case even here. The meaning of most scientific theories could not be expressed adequately in terms of images of physical objects and even in cases where propositions about physical objects could be thus expressed we may understand them perfectly well without in fact using the imagery. Some people very rarely use any but verbal images. In any case, as I have said, in e.g. philosophy and economics (or even politics) the meaning of most statements cannot possibly be expressed in terms of sensuous imagery which is like the subject-matter of our thought. Yet we can understand some statements in philosophy and economics. Therefore understanding is something mental which cannot possibly be explained entirely in terms of images. It cannot be explained entirely in terms of verbal imagery, for we must make a distinction between using verbal imagery and understanding it; and, as we have seen, it cannot be explained in terms of non-verbal.

Attempts have also been made to analyse belief in terms of behaviour, thus excluding the need to posit any specific mental act or attitude of belief. On this view to believe that A is B is to act as if A were B. The view is, however, in my opinion, open to several very serious objections. Firstly, what can be meant by 'acting as if A were B'? Surely nothing but acting as if we believed A to be B, in which case belief is being defined in terms of itself. If A were B without our believing it to be so, it would not alter our actions though it might alter their effects. Secondly, I often have beliefs on which I never act. In such cases the theory can only be maintained by referring to hypothetical action. But I can tell whether I believe something without first having to decide how I should act under certain hypothetical circumstances which may never be realized at all. I know immediately in many cases that I believe something on which I am not at present acting, but it cannot be a matter of immediate knowledge how one would act if something were to happen which in fact has not happened. For instance I believe that Chimborazo is the highest mountain of the Andes, and I should therefore refrain from trying to climb it if I were in that neighbourhood because I should think it too formidable a task. But I surely cannot identify the belief with this hypothetical fact. That I should not try to climb Chimborazo is an inference and not anything immediately known at all, further it is an inference from my belief about the height of Chimborazo as premise. It already presupposes the latter belief, which therefore cannot be defined in terms of it. And the same with all propositions about future or possible actions based on a belief. We cannot avoid these criticisms by identifying the action with repeating to oneself or others the words which we say express the belief. For we might do that without having the belief. Thirdly, the theory does not allow for human folly and immorality. We often hold a belief quite genuinely and yet because of some strong desire which carries us against reason do not act as if it were true.

It seems equally impossible to analyse desiring, willing, liking,

Mind

etc., in terms of imagery. So we have two very different kinds of attributes given in our immediate experience: specifically mental attributes and the attributes of sensa and images. I should say that the latter kind could and the former could not be conceived as existing unexperienced, but the idealist would contradict the first part of this statement. However, no sensible person would deny the second part and say that, e.g. pleasure and pain could exist unexperienced.

When we start talking about the more specifically mental side it is disappointing how little philosophy and psychology can say about it. This is largely because we very soon arrive at characteristics which we can know by experience but cannot define further. Analysis presupposes unanalysable characteristics and we very soon reach these in the process. The unanalysable is of course not the unknowable, it is what we know well enough by experience but cannot explain in terms of anything else so that a person could understand what it was like if he had never had the experience.

DISPOSITIONAL PROPERTIES

The terms applied to the mind both in psychology and in ordinary non-scientific conversation are, however, by no means limited to actual characteristics. They commonly refer to dispositions or capacities. For example, if I talk about somebody's 'beliefs', I am certainly not committing myself to the view that he is at the time I speak actually thinking of what I say he believes. I am sure that I am right in saying that Pollitt believes the present government to be bad for Britain, but for anything I know Pollitt may be asleep at the moment or thinking about something quite different. Therefore, though I use the present tense, I am not speaking about the actual present state of mind of Pollitt. I am speaking about a disposition, by which is meant that I am saying something about not what he necessarily does now think but what he would think if his attention were turned to the subject. Most of the psychological terms we use stand for dispositions and not actual states of mind. When we speak of a person knowing, desiring, fearing, valuing something, we do not ordinarily mean that he is at the moment we speak in a state of actual desire, fear, etc., but that he has a disposition (tendency) to be so in regard to the object in question. (No doubt we must distinguish between long- and short-term dispositions, e.g. he is afraid of dogs and he is afraid that he will not be able to go out to-day.) But dispositional terms have to be defined in terms of actual states. In order to understand what 'believe' in the dispositional sense means we have to know from experience in ourselves what an actual state of coming to believe is like, to understand what 'fear' in the dispositional sense is we must know what it is like to feel an actual emotion of fear, etc. It follows that we cannot explain psychological events by referring to dispositions. To explain a man's bad temper by a disposition to get angry is only to say that he does easily get angry. The only utility in talking like this is that it distinguishes the man's general bent from circumstances for which we can assign more specific causes. For instance, it implies that a particular outburst of bad temper on the part of the man is not to be explained adequately by saying that he was tired out and therefore 'not himself' or that the occasion, though trivial, was for him associated with some more important desire the frustration of which in most normal men would give rise to some symptoms like bad temper. It is important to realize that when we talk about dispositions we are only saying what a man does or would do, thinks or would think, feels or would feel under certain circumstances. For it is all too easy to suppose that when we have referred a psychological event to a disposition we have given an explanation of it as we have when we refer a physical event to some physical machinery. The difference between the two cases is that we can form an idea of what the physical machinery is like even when it is not producing the event in question. Physical machinery can be observed when it is not working, but psychological cannot be. The only way in which we can think of a disposition is as a law determining or inclining us to have certain experiences and perform certain actions. There may be an actually existent basis for the law in the mind, but if so we cannot say what it is like. We can only form an idea of the mind in terms of introspectively observable events, and we cannot introspectively observe our dispositions but only their manifestations in experience. A disposition, as we know it, can only be expressed in terms of a hypothetical proposition, i.e. I shall do and feel so and so if . . . , and is not anything that actually exists in between its manifestations. It is to psychology what a law is to physical science, except that it does not allow of precise mathematical calculation and that a man's dispositions are laws peculiar to him, not common to everybody. Of course the acquiring of even a long-term disposition can sometimes be explained, e.g. by experiences in early childhood, but in order to explain it we have to fall back on more permanent and general dispositions, e.g. the 'instincts'. The ideal of psychology as a science would be to explain all dispositions peculiar to an individual by deduction from dispositions common to all men together with the peculiar environment or physiological heredity of the individual man. Whether we think this ideal could conceivably ever be attained will depend on our views on issues such as determinism and pre-existence, but no doubt a great deal may be done in this way.

'UNCONSCIOUS' DESIRES

Dispositions of course need not be conscious: I need not be aware of the laws which govern my experience and behaviour. But an additional kind of unconscious has figured very largely in the writings of modern psychologists. They have produced evidence to support the view that desires very commonly exist in a man without being introspectively observable, and it is not meant merely that they are present in the sense in which a desire to overcome the Labour Party is present in Churchill even when he is not thinking of the subject at all. In the case of Churchill he could no doubt detect the desire by introspection as soon as he thought of the subject, but the unconscious desires of the psycho-analyst are supposed not to be introspectively discoverable at any time, at least until the technique of psychotherapy has been applied. Thus it is said that A may hate B without ever being consciously aware of feelings of dislike towards B but rather of the reverse. It has been even said that desires are normally unconscious, and that the Unconscious includes a much greater part of our nature than what is conscious. Now it is easy to see how a disposition can be unconscious. A disposition is only a general tendency to act and feel in a certain way or a causal law affecting our actions and feelings, and there no doubt are many true generalizations about ourselves which we have never made and many causal laws affecting us which we have never discovered. But it is a different matter to claim that a desire in the non-dispositional sense, i.e. an actually existing desire, can be unconscious, and the claim may even seem self-contradictory at first sight. If I never experience a desire for A, surely, it may be said, I cannot desire A, any more than I can have a pain which is never felt. The answer may be found in a distinction between two senses of 'conscious' which I regard as of very great importance for avoiding confusions. By 'conscious desire' may be meant a 'felt desire'. In this sense a desire, unless the term is used only dispositionally, like any other element in our experience, must be conscious. Or the phrase may signify a 'desire which is introspectively noticed'. In this sense it is plain that all our experience need not be conscious. For even the most introspective person is not introspecting all the time, and when he does introspect he does not introspect every element in his experience. There is always the sense of something more beyond what we explicitly notice in our introspections. It may therefore without self-contradiction be supposed that we have desires which are felt as elements in our experience making their contribution to its whole tone but are not picked out and identified. It is certainly admitted that the unconscious desires make a difference to our total experience, for they make us feel uneasy, but the element in our experience to which the uneasiness is primarily due may not be sorted out. I may similarly feel physically uneasy in a vague way without sorting out the particular sensations which constitute my malaise. In this sense the unconscious would be part of an experience of which we were more or less vaguely conscious as a whole, but would not be distinguished from the other parts of this experience and so would not be an object of consciousness *per se*. There is no self-contradiction in saying that a desire is unconscious in this sense, or even in the rather stronger sense of 'unconscious' in which it signifies not merely what is not introspectively observed but what cannot be

Mind

so observed. All we can say is that it is very surprising that so important an element in experience as these desires should often be inaccessible to introspection, but this is a paradox and not a contradiction. I do not indeed think that all the cases of 'unconscious desires' detected by psychologists need be brought under this heading. In some cases the desire may have been introspectively observed at times by the person who has it, but he may have forgotten what he observed; in others what the man fails to be aware of may not be the presence of an element in his experience but the effects or causes of the latter. For instance, when a psychologist says of a man who gives away large sums of money and thinks very highly of himself on this account that he is really *unconsciously* motived by desire for applause, what he means, if he is sensible, is probably not that the man had no conscious desire for applause, but that he did not realize that this desire was a main cause of his actions. Or when a psychologist says that somebody's philanthropy is really a sublimation of the sex instinct, he may mean merely that his philanthropy was caused by events of a sexual character such as an unfortunate love-affair, not that he has unintrospected feelings of a sexual character towards the objects of his philanthropy. Indeed for the purposes of psychology as a natural science and for the purpose of effecting cures it may be that all the psychologist need assume is that men have unconscious desires in the sense of acting as if they had such desires, leaving it an open question whether they really had them without introspectively noticing them, whether they noticed them at times but failed to remember them, or whether they did not have them at all but were led by some unknown cause, e.g. an obscure physiological brain-state, unintentionally to simulate the effects of desires which they did not have. Of course great practical and theoretical importance must be attached to the fact that our introspections and memories can be drastically limited by what we wish not to know and that this may occur even against our conscious will, though I think the extent to which it happens has been very much exaggerated. We may however admit that the larger part of our mind is 'unconscious' if that means 'is not introspectively discriminated'. And we must remember that dispositions need not be conscious at all.

SELF-IDENTITY AND THE CONCEPTION OF
THE SELF AS A SUBSTANCE

But what is the mind or self? Most people would have the feeling very strongly, if challenged, that it was not merely a set of experiences connected by causal laws but at least a relatively permanent substance. This view is backed by the following arguments.

(1) Knowledge presupposes self-identity. For knowledge is always of a multiplicity, a, b and c, but to compare or connect a, b and c the *same* being that knows a must know b and c. If there is to be consciousness of a connected argument, the same self which recognizes the premises must recognize the conclusion, and this takes time. Therefore the self must preserve its identity in time. (2) A thought implies a thinker distinct from any thought. Thoughts are only events, but could a mere series of events know anything? (3) Memory tells me that the same 'I' who does so-and-so now did so-and-so in the past. But the past events are all over and not now in existence, therefore the self cannot be reduced to a series of events.

These are important arguments, but on the other hand it is very hard to form any idea of what a self existing as a 'substance' over and above its experiences could be. We are here confronted with similar difficulties to those which we encountered when we asked what a physical substance was over and above its qualities and relations.[1] Does the substance behind my experiences (or the Pure Ego, as it is sometimes called) change or not? If it changes, I am no longer myself; if it does not change, it is not what I understand by 'I', for I certainly always think of myself as capable of changing and, I hope, improving.

The case for a pure Ego is, however, stronger than the case for a physical substance in the sense of a substratum over and above its qualities. For, in the first place, we have the above-mentioned arguments for the pure Ego which obviously could not be applied to a merely physical substance. And, secondly, while we certainly cannot claim ever to perceive a physical substance as such in

[1] *Vide* above, p. 96.

distinction from its qualities, we may with some plausibility claim to be immediately aware of a pure Ego over and above its experiences. In memory I am immediately aware that something happened to me in the past, i.e. that the being to whom it happened was the same Ego as I now am, yet the experiences now and then are different. This is an important point. The notion of a pure Ego or any substance over and above its qualities could not be defined in terms of anything else, so how can I know at all what it is like, and if I have no idea of what it is like, how can I attach any meaning to statements about it? *Ex hypothesi* the pure Ego cannot be analysed in terms of its qualities and relations, for it is different from these. Its nature therefore must be incapable of analysis, but if so our knowledge of what it is must depend on a unique and irreducible experience, and we can only attach meaning to the term if we can point to such an experience. Now we certainly do seem to have some experience of the 'I' which we do not have of anything else, but it is extraordinarily difficult to be clear what we are immediately aware of when we have the experience. It may be claimed that we are thus aware of a substance over and above its experiences, but it may also be held that all we are immediately aware of is a unique and unanalysable relation between our experiences, and this seems easier to conceive. The conception of a pure Ego would be less difficult than it is if we could regard a disposition as some actual quality other than our experience which caused or tended to cause the experiences. We could then think of the Ego as distinct from its experiences and yet give it a content by ascribing to it the dispositional properties in question. But unfortunately we can form no idea of a dispositional property except a hypothetical one. The only actual qualities we can ascribe to a mind are experiences, yet we hesitate to identify the self with its experiences, especially as it is apparently not always having experiences. But if we think of it as something apart from its experiences, we are back at the notion of a substance over and above its qualities. The problem is therefore one of the hardest of philosophy: thinkers are groping after an intermediate alternative between that of an unchanging substance-Ego over and above its experiences and that of a self which is merely a string of experiences, but they have not succeeded in finding one capable of clear

Mind

statement. We must not, however, try to gloss over the difficulties on either side of the question. We cannot solve the problem satisfactorily by making the body the substance, for as we have seen, similar difficulties arise about substance in the physical world. As we have also seen, the case against making a physical object something over and above its characteristics is stronger than the similar case against the self-substance regarded as purely mental. So to make the body the substance of the self would still be to reduce it to a number of connected events. But the question of the relation between the mind and the body I am deferring to the next chapter, and so shall pass on now.

If we reject the pure Ego theory, we shall still have to face the question what the relation is which constitutes a self. My experiences are related in some way to those of many other human beings, but it is clear that, even if there is no substance-self over and above experiences, there still is at least some very special relation between experiences which holds when the experiences belong, as we say, to one self. In that case they will belong in the sense of being actually parts of the self. They will belong in a sense analogous rather to that in which a brick belongs to a house than to that in which the house belongs to its owner. Only the different parts of which I am thinking are successive in time rather than co-existent in space, although I do not mean to deny that there are co-existent elements in the self. (It has occasionally been disputed, but it must happen whenever we compare two objects, for our thoughts of them must occur simultaneously.) Now, if the pure Ego view is rejected, what relation can reasonably be said to make two experiences parts of one self? Mere causal connection or resemblance is not enough. Different minds may affect each other causally, and I now resemble myself as I was when I was a baby less than I resemble most grown men. Nor can we say that what 'belonging to the same self' means is 'being attached to the same body'. If that were the case, it would be verbally self-contradictory to assert survival of bodily death, and whether the latter is a fact or not, certainly its assertion is not self-contradictory like saying that I at once am and am not the same self. Further, I can remember many experiences in the past as mine without remembering anything definite about the state or appearance of my body and therefore without being aware of my body as the same body that I now have. Yet if 'belonging to the same self' meant 'being attached to the same body' I could not know that two experiences were related in the former way without knowing that they were related in the latter. Similar objections apply to the attempt to find self-identity in a similarity of organic sensations. Attempts have also been made to define self-identity in terms of memory, but I think these involve a vicious circle. To remember an experience is already to know that it was mine, and I cannot make an experience mine by knowing that it was mine. So if we adopt a view of the self according to which its identity is constituted not by a single substance over and above its experiences but by a relation between the experiences, it is probably best just to say that the relation is unique and indefinable. We must not, however, in any case think of the various experiences which make up the self as just existing one after the other and unaffected internally by the relation which unites them. The relation between different experiences of what we call the same self is in any case radically different from the relation between members of a mere aggregate like a heap of stones. It is so close that they could not conceivably be what they are without belonging to a whole of this particular kind, i.e. a self, while a stone might quite well not belong to a heap at all. Also in any case it is misleading to speak of the self as a series of events, since these events are only abstractions from a continuous process.

Considerable attention has been attracted by certain cases of abnormal psychology where it looked as if a self had actually split into two or more different selves, present in the same body and taking turns to dominate it. Whether this was really so is difficult to say, and there are certainly not enough even apparent cases of this to make sweeping generalizations, but such instances do suggest, though they are very far from proving, the possibility that self-identity is much more a matter of degree than we are usually prepared to admit. We are all familiar with sayings such as 'He was not himself last night' or 'He was quite like a different person', and when we reflect how different we can feel and be in different moods and different environments, we can easily conceive a series of intermediate cases between the normal man and the extreme cases of dual personality. There is the difference that in his varying moods the normal man still retains memory, but perhaps this too is no more than a difference of degree. It is a well-known psychological fact that, e.g. in a gloomy mood it is more difficult to think of cheerful things and vice versa, so presumably it will be more difficult also in such moods to remember them. Increase this difficulty indefinitely, and you have the case of the man who cannot remember one set of facts at all so that there is a complete breach in the personality. If the appearances of multiple personality be accepted at their face value, they rather make against the pure ego theory, but not conclusively so, for there is no way of proving that a pure ego may not split up, although it has been generally supposed that it could not do so, and in any case they are too rare to provide an adequate foundation for a theory.

Earlier philosophers have often tried to prove the immortality of the soul from the premise that it is a substance. They thought that substance as such must necessarily be permanent and that consequently a substance could only in the natural course be destroyed by being broken up into its parts, which were themselves substances. This fitted in well with the view that the atoms of which physical objects were made were themselves indestructible. What we usually call physical substances are really groups of substances and therefore can come to an end by separation of their parts. But the destruction of a simple substance would be a different story, and this was supposed *a priori* impossible (at least without a special miraculous act on the part of God). Now it was argued that the soul must be a simple substance because otherwise we could not account for the unity of thought. In order to have the thought 'wolves eat lambs' a single being must apprehend all three of its terms. If one being thought of wolves, another of eating, and a third of lambs, this would by no means constitute the thought that wolves eat lambs. Few philosophers would now use this as an argument for immortality. It does bring out an important point, the essential unity of thought; but to show that the mind functions as a unity, which is certainly true, is not to show that it is in itself a single 'substance'. Further, it would be generally doubted nowadays that we knew the *a priori* proposition that a

Mind

simple substance must be permanent, and as regards the physical world the conception has been largely dropped. There may be good ethical and religious arguments for survival of bodily death, and there may be empirical arguments derived from psychical research, but we cannot claim to know enough about the nature of the self for us to venture on a metaphysical demonstration of this. Neither can we have a metaphysical demonstration of its negative.

All this brings out the point that the modern tendency is to answer questions about the unity of the self not in terms of unity of substance but in terms of unity of function. It may be contended in its support that the arguments for the unity of the self are really arguments from the unity of our experience and therefore do not apply to a supposed substance apart from its experiences. The tendency was started mainly by Kant, who insisted that the argument from the unity of knowledge showed that the self functioned as a unity in knowing objects, but not that the self was a unity apart from its relation to its environment of known objects. The contents of our awareness at any one time are connected by a unique relation, the unity of consciousness, which does not relate to anything else. Our own experiences and mental states at different times are likewise related in a way in which no two selves ever are. What I do and how I feel are uniquely influenced by what has happened to me in the past in a direct way in which nothing else could influence me. If I have learnt something I tend to remember it, but I do not tend to remember something because somebody else has learnt it; I may be influenced by the good and evil fortune of others, but only if *I* first know of it; I am disappointed if *I* do not obtain what I desire, but not if anybody else fails to do so, unless through sympathy I have formed a desire of my own that he should fulfil his desire; I cannot literally feel another's pain, though I may feel a similar pain or a painful feeling of sympathy with his pain. In all these simple empirical ways and many others each self can be seen to be a unique unity without invoking trans-empirical metaphysics to support this conclusion. The self also no doubt contains a great deal of diversity, and the unity varies greatly in degree, but it is undoubtedly there as an empirical fact except in the very rare

117

cases of 'dual personality'. It is not incompatible with conflicts in the self, on the contrary the very conflicts presuppose it. There is a struggle between two desires of mine just because they both impel me, the same person. The sting of these conflicts just lies in the fact that the same person cannot do two incompatible things, e.g. eat his cake and have it. The fundamental separation of different selves is brought out most clearly in the difficulties of communication which prevent our knowing even whether another man sees the same colour that we see and in the impossibility of literally sharing the feelings of another, however strong may be our links with him in friendship and love. Everyone must, humanly speaking, fight his own battle alone. Matthew Arnold expressed an important truth when he said:

> *Yes: in the sea of life enisled,*
> *With echoing straits between us thrown,*
> *Dotting the shoreless watery wild,*
> *We mortal millions live alone.*[1]

Some philosophers have contended that the distinction between different human selves is not by any means so fundamental as it seems and have even argued that it is best to regard them just as different manifestations or modes of one and the same mind, meaning not merely that they were created by one mind, as is held by the ordinary theist, but that they just are one mind, strictly speaking. This does not seem to me to do justice to the empirical facts of individuality which I have cited. If there is a fundamental separation anywhere in the universe, it seems to me to lie between the different minds. The upholders of a contrary view cite the cases of co-operation and love and contend that what we really care about, or at least ought really to care about, is not our individual welfare as separate beings but the triumph of causes which transcend our personality. But it may be retorted that the value of co-operation and love lies just in the fact that they involve unity between *different* selves. The closest love presupposes difference; in the sense in which a man loves others and in the sense in which this love is of great value he cannot be said to love himself. It is the unity in difference, not mere unity, that

[1] *To Marguerite*, (Oxford Book of English Verse, p. 891.)

is of value here. And the same with co-operation in general: the point of co-operation lies in the fact that each man makes his specific different contribution to the good of the whole.

In a socialist age the value of individuality must not be ignored. It would not be good for all to be alike; we must all look at life through our own, somewhat different spectacles, and it is good that we should. On the other hand, we can only realize our individuality through intercourse with others. To realize even ourselves adequately we must be unselfish, and even the most selfish of us is willy nilly dependent for nine-tenths of what he knows and does on others and has his life incessantly moulded by his relations to them. To be ourselves we must concentrate our attention on things other than ourselves. But this must not be allowed to obscure the other, the individualistic side of the antithesis. Man is fundamentally a social being, and he is also fundamentally an individual being. To hit on the right course to do justice to both facts is perhaps the chief problem both of politics and of practical ethics.

However, mind is revealed not only in strictly individual experiences but in the great constructions by co-operative mind which have developed in the course of civilization. These may be regarded as objective manifestations of mind, super-individual not in the sense of having a separate being over and above the thoughts and experiences of the individuals in whom they are realized, but in the sense that they can be studied historically as a whole in which what is important is not the individuals who made the contribution but the development of the idea. Examples of these manifestations of mind are science, art, philosophy, law. We must realize that a study of these provides us with at least as good a clue to the nature of mind as does ordinary psychology.

KNOWLEDGE OF OTHER MINDS

A problem that has troubled philosophers a good deal, though certainly not the plain man, is how we can know of the existence of minds other than our own. The term *solipsism* (from *solus ipse*) has been used to stand for the view of a person who should believe in his own existence but not in that of any other mind. It may be doubted whether such a view has ever been seriously held, but logically it is hard to disprove it conclusively. As the *cogito, ergo sum* makes clear, I am immediately aware of my own mind, but I do not seem to be thus aware of the minds of others, even those I know best. There no doubt are cases of telepathy, but these need not be regarded and, I think, are best not regarded, as involving direct awareness of another's mind or experience. One mind may in telepathy, intentionally or unintentionally, cause another to have thoughts or experiences similar to its own without the second mind being immediately aware of the first, as on the representative theory of perception a physical object causes us to have certain sensa and thereby know the object without our perceiving it directly. In any case conscious telepathy is far too rare a phenomenon for it to be possible to base our knowledge of other human beings on it. I have this knowledge, and yet like the majority of people have had no conscious experience of telepathy and derive my information about the latter phenomenon solely from hearsay, i.e. from first assuming the existence of other minds and believing what they tell me. We are therefore confronted with difficulties similar to some of those which arose when we considered how to justify the belief in physical objects.

Various suggestions have been made to overcome these difficulties: (1) It has been suggested that we all of us really are sometimes immediately aware of other people's minds or experiences, although this immediate awareness is mixed up with a great many other beliefs not based on direct awareness and is therefore not recognized as such. But it would be odd if we were frequently immediately aware of something without even seeming to ourselves to be so. (2) An argument from analogy has very commonly been used to justify the belief. Other people's physical bodies are like our own, a mind is attached to our own body, therefore it is argued that a mind is probably attached to the other bodies of the same kind we see. Although there is some force in this argument, it certainly seems inadequate to bear the weight put on it and give anything in the remotest degree approaching the certainty we feel about the matter, particularly as the analogy for each of us is based on only a single instance, our own self. It would be hard to find any other case in which we regarded an argument from a single instance as a very strong argument from analogy. But two stronger arguments remain.

(3) We may argue that our experience constantly goes on as if purposes other than our own were at work and does this on such a scale that it would be fantastic to suppose that the purposes were not really present. Once we have admitted that it is extremely probable that there are purposes other than our own operating we have admitted that there are probably other minds, for purpose is inconceivable except in mind. To the suggestion that the purposes in question might be unconscious purposes of my own I might reply by asking what could be meant by saying they were purposes of my own. I am not introspectively aware of them, they are often incompatible with my conscious purposes, they are as a whole very much more pervasive and influential than my conscious purposes and can achieve many feats of genius that would be absolutely beyond any capacities shown in my conscious life, and they are related causally to bodies other than my own in a similar way to that in which my conscious purposes are related to my own. They are excluded from the characteristic unity which constitutes myself, for the various relations I have mentioned a few pages back as constituting such a unity are lacking, e.g. they make ingenious physical machines and have therefore presumably learnt how to make them but I *qua* conscious never knew how to make the machines. They are certainly excluded from the unity of consciousness which characterizes my conscious mental processes. I should, if I adopted this line of argument, have to draw a very sharp distinction between the conscious and the unconscious part of my mind and assign far more importance to the latter than to the former. But, once I had made all the necessary admissions, it may be doubted whether I should be saying anything more than that there are different minds in the ordinary sense but they are all one and the same mind in some metaphysical sense, a view which has been maintained by philosophers whom no one would regard as solipsists at all.

(4) We may use an argument similar to that which we used about physical objects. A great many of the predictions I make are based on my beliefs as to the mental states of others and these predictions are on the whole fulfilled in a remarkable fashion like

the predictions based on my beliefs about physical objects. So we have again a very strong argument in favour of the beliefs on which they are based being approximately true.

Even these two arguments would not, however, refute a theory about other human minds such as Berkeley put forward about physical things. Granted a single other, sufficiently powerful and intelligent, mind besides my own, like Berkeley's God or Descartes' demon, that other mind might give me all the sensa and experiences I have and yet make them such as if there were a great many other minds, though there was in fact only one. I know no logically adequate refutation of that view, though I have no doubt that it is false. But, if we are to be sceptical, we might go still further. I do not know how to refute by argument the view that I came into existence in the last minute and all my seeming memories are illusions.

We must carefully distinguish an account of the arguments in favour of the existence of other minds from an account of the processes by which we come to form our beliefs about them. I am not suggesting that I or anybody else originally came to believe in other minds through using the arguments I have mentioned. The existence of his mother is not for a baby a hypothesis to explain the success of his predictions. The belief in other minds is too natural and instinctive for it to be possible to account for it by argument at all. But, however the belief originated, there is the question how we are to justify it and this is the question under discussion.

Chapter Six

THE RELATION OF MATTER AND MIND

GRANTED mind and matter, there are still many problems about the relations between them, whether we are thinking of the human body and mind or of the relations between matter and mind in general. Taking the first problem first we find two main issues of controversy: (1) Do a man's body and mind interact? (2) Are his body and his mind the same or different substances?

INTERACTION OF BODY AND MIND

The affirmative answer to the first question may seem too obvious to call for discussion, but to be a philosopher one should be an adept at casting doubts on the apparently obvious, and the seeming interaction has been in fact very commonly questioned. However, if it is rejected, some other way must be found of explaining the empirical facts which show that there is at the least a very frequent correlation between certain bodily and certain mental events. The most popular way of doing so in modern times has been to assert that the bodily and the mental correspond to each other because they are different attributes of the same substance. So the first and second questions have a certain connection, and the main theories on the subject have commonly been classed as (1) interaction theories, which both assert causal interaction and assert that body and mind are different substances, (2) parallelist theories which deny interaction and explain the appearance of it by saying that the series of bodily and the series of mental events in a man correspond (run parallel) not because there is a causal connection between them but because they are different sides of the same thing. But it is perfectly possible to assert both that body and mind are the same substance and that there is causal interaction between bodily and mental states. It would also be possible to assert that body and mind are different substances and do not interact, only there would then be a great difficulty about explaining the appearance of interaction, unless we were prepared like some seventeenth- and eighteenth-century philosophers to attribute it to the intervention of God.

Before discussing this matter it is well to have certain points clear which must rank as quite established. (1) Bodily and mental processes are at any rate different qualitatively even if they should turn out to be only different aspects of the same substance. I have already insisted on this point in combating Behaviourism.[1] Throbs of pain are not at all like nervous impulses, thoughts not at all like the movements of the vocal organs or the vibrations in the brain which are all that could be observed by the physiologist. We can observe both bodily and mental qualities and we can see them as a matter of purely empirical observation to be quite different. Therefore, if we identify body and mind, all we can sensibly mean is not that bodily and mental qualities are the same but only that they are different qualities of the same substance.

(2) Bodily and mental events accompany each other according to regular laws, whether we explain this by causal interaction or in some other way. Dozens of these laws are known to us at the common-sense level, though with a certain lack of exactitude, e.g. the law that if a man burns himself he generally feels pain, and physiologists have some evidence of a much more widespread correlation than is apparent to the ordinary observer. The principle that there is a complete correlation between bodily and mental events so that a characteristically different change in the brain accompanies every different mental event, in which many physiologists have believed, outruns immensely anything that has been or, as far as we can see, ever could be scientifically established, but it would be unwise to found any positive theory on our inability at the present time to suggest even on what general principles the correlation could be worked out. If the correlation is an empirical fact, it is however important to realize that it is compatible with any of the main philosophical theories. The complete correlation,

[1] *Vide* above, pp. 101–2.

if it occurs, might be due to the interaction of two different substances, or to the mutual causal influence of two different sets of qualities in the same substance, or to the same substance appearing under parallel non-interacting aspects, or simply to the action of God if you like that type of explanation.

(3) However much has been said about the advance of brain physiology, it remains true that we can know a great deal more about the psychological than about the physiological antecedents of most mental events, and can make predictions about them much more effectively from the former than from the latter set of data. Since the brain is not normally observed and can hardly be observed when a man is conscious, prediction from brain-states is impossible except in a few cases when a whole big area of the brain has been destroyed or injured, and prediction of future mental events from past outward behaviour is usually only effected by the indirect process of going back to the mental states which we suppose accompanied or immediately preceded the outward behaviour and onward directly from them to the future mental events we predict. We do not argue directly from a man's past actions to his future actions, but suppose, e.g. that his honourable conduct in the past is the expression of honourable intentions and therefore expect it to continue.

The common-sense doctrine of interaction has been attacked mainly on two grounds. Firstly it is urged that the alleged causal connection is inconceivable because the terms between which it is supposed to hold are too unlike each other. The notion that the mind can affect the brain has been compared contemptuously to the notion that the coaches of a train could be held together by a friendly feeling between the driver in the front and the guard in the rear. This argument, however, loses much of its force when we realize that even in the case of two ordinary admittedly interacting physical things we are unable to see why they should be causally connected in the way they are. The explanation of this is disputed: some philosophers would say that it is just a fact that they are so connected, and not anything having a reason which a mind could see, others that there is an intelligible connection to explain their interaction, only we do not possess sufficient intelligence and knowledge to discover it. But the fact of our inability cannot be denied, whatever its explanation may be, therefore it no longer seems to constitute a special objection to interaction between body and mind, that we cannot see the connection. Further if, as is generally admitted by realists, we cannot know anything about the internal nature of matter, it is difficult to see how we can claim to decide what it can or cannot cause. Nor is it clear that we know *a priori* that cause and effect cannot be unlike.

The argument has sometimes been amended so as to take a somewhat different form. It is said that in any other case of causation the terms linked by it are also related in other ways within a system. Two interacting physical objects are both in space and so in the spatial system, and a mental event which directly affects another occurs in the same mind, but there is no such common system to which both body and mind can be said to belong and therefore they do not fulfil the precondition without which causation is impossible. There are again various things that may be said in reply. We do not know *a priori* that membership of such a system is a necessary presupposition of all causal connection, and even if it is we may reply that bodily and mental events are at any rate both in time and that mental events are in some way spatially localized. Or the contention may be contradicted in a more outright fashion by asserting that we are directly aware not of body and mind as separate things but of the two as constituting a special unique whole, and that this provides the union in a common system said to be required. I do not know whether such union in a system as is suggested is really a prerequisite of causation or not, but certainly we seem to start by being aware of body and mind together rather than of a separate body and a separate mind. The distinction between bodily and mental has to be learnt as we grow up and requires a considerable feat of abstraction, though this does not alter the fact which I have emphasized that we can by inspection see bodily and mental characteristics to be radically different.

But, secondly, the main motive for the denial of interaction has been the desire to preserve a complete water-tight mechanical system. The assumption that all physical causation is explicable in terms of the Newtonian laws of motion or something very similar has worked exceedingly well in science for centuries, and scientists have therefore naturally been very reluctant to admit any causation which did not accord with it. However the objection is less plausible nowadays, since the internal progress of physics itself has brought us up against the limits of this kind of causal explanation even in the inorganic world, though many physiologists and biologists still assume its universality in their own sphere. The specific form which this objection to interaction took was usually based on the principle of conservation of energy. According to this principle the total amount of energy (actual and potential) always remains constant in quantity in any physical change and can only be redistributed among different bodies, from which it follows that the mind cannot add new energy to bring about a movement of the body or the body divert energy from the physical world to bring about a change in the mind. But this only disproves interaction if we assume that all causation involves the transmission of energy from the cause to the effect, and this assumption cannot possibly be proved. It is not true even of the inorganic world, e.g. the movements of the string make no difference to the energy of a pendulum but alter the direction and velocity of its motion; and even if it were true of the inorganic world, that would be no good reason for supposing that it must be true of the interaction of body and mind if this takes place at all. Mental characteristics are very different from merely bodily characteristics, and so there is no reason to suppose that the mode of causation they exercise is not very different too.

It is not possible, I think, to produce conclusive arguments on the other side either, but I cannot help thinking that the *onus probandi* is altogether on the opponents of interaction. According to all the ordinary empirical criteria which we accept in other cases bodily processes are causally related to mental and vice versa, and therefore it seems only reasonable to accept this evidence unless there is a strong argument against it. Further, the parallelist, as we shall see, can only explain the correlation between physical and mental events, which is an empirical fact, by introducing metaphysical hypotheses of a far-reaching and not very plausible kind.

Of one alternative to interaction we can dispose in a more conclusive fashion. In the late nineteenth century 'materialists' put forward the doctrine of *epiphenomenalism*, according to which bodily events cause mental but mental cause neither bodily nor even other mental events. This view is open to the following objections: (*a*) Nobody can ever be justified in believing epiphenomenalism. For, if it is true, it entails the conclusion that the belief in it is due only to physiological changes in the brain of the believer and never to the awareness of any good arguments for it, since coming to be aware of an argument is a mental event.

(*b*) Unless his physical actions were affected by his deliberate intentions, it is quite incredible that a person could produce an elaborate work like *Hamlet* or Kant's *Critique of Pure Reason*. But if they are thus affected, physical processes are affected by mental. The argument must not be misunderstood. The epiphenomenalist does not assert that Shakespeare could have produced *Hamlet* if he had not gone through mental processes. Even on the epiphenomenalist theory that would not be the case, for the theory admits that mental processes accompany, and must according to the laws of nature accompany, the physical as their effects. The complex brain changes necessary for the production of Shakespeare's *Hamlet* could not have occurred without the corresponding changes in Shakespeare's consciousness even on that view. (Of course I am referring here to causal and not to logical necessity.) But the epiphenomenalist does deny that these mental processes can themselves have any effect on anything physical, and is thus debarred from supposing that his own mental processes, though existent, had any part in causing Shakespeare to write what he did write, an odd conclusion enough, and one which makes the intelligent and purposive character of the work quite inexplicable, in fact an incredible coincidence. For it is then not caused by any purpose or intelligence whatever, directly or indirectly, but merely by physical motions.

(*c*) That epiphenomalism is false is assumed in all practical life. In deciding what we are to do we must always make the assumption that our will and motives can affect our physical actions, and it is silly to adopt a philosophy the denial of which is implied by us every time we do anything voluntarily.

(*d*) Since the physiological events in question are admittedly accompanied by mental processes, it is arbitrary to say that they are the sole cause of any subsequent mental events and that the mental processes which accompany them have nothing to do with causing the latter to occur. Why pick out one element of the antecedent like that and attribute everything to it?

Objections (*a*), (*b*), and (*c*) also apply to some but not to all forms of parallelism. One remark must be added: there is a widely held view which equates causation with regular sequence or concomitance. If this view be true, interaction must certainly be accepted as a fact, for there is no doubt that there is a regular sequence or concomitance between many physical and many mental events, e.g. getting burnt and feeling pain, willing to move one's arm and moving one's arm. (No doubt there are exceptions to these regularities, but there are few regularities we can find anywhere absolutely without exceptions.) But I shall not use this argument, as I do not believe that causation can be reduced to regular sequence or concomitance.

ARE BODY AND MIND THE SAME SUBSTANCE?

Let us now turn to the second question, the question whether the body and the mind are the same or different substances. At first sight the view that the mind is best regarded as an attribute of the body is a highly plausible one. We have one substance here, the body, it may be argued, why posit an additional one? We have mental attributes certainly, and these are different from bodily attributes, but may they not still both belong to the same substance? And, if so, is there any need to posit an additional substance beyond the body itself? A reason which has probably been influential in leading people to reject a one-substance view is that mental attributes are not in space in the sense in which physical objects are. They seem to be localized vaguely, usually in the brain,[1] but they are not extended or spread out in space. If they were it would be good sense to say that my thought of God at this moment was 0·74 inches across, while we are quite clear that we cannot say things like that, not because we cannot in practice

---

[1] This may be only the result of our upbringing. The Greeks did not locate thought in the brain but in the midriff, so they can hardly have experienced it as so obviously localized in the former as it seems to modern man.

measure our thoughts spatially, but because in principle they are incapable of such measurement. Similarly it seems on principle impossible for a thought of mine to be 9·47 inches from a thought of yours, as it is intrinsically impossible for a thought to be yellow or a virtue rectangular. It must therefore be admitted that mental characteristics are in an important sense non-spatial, but it is not clear that we know *a priori* that a spatial object cannot have non-spatial attributes. The view has also been rejected on the ground that the unity of thought was incompatible with its being an attribute of the body, for the matter of the human body is divisible. But one may reply by means of the distinction already made between being a single substance and functioning as a unity. A number of different substances like the atoms composing a physical object might in producing certain effects function as a unity. For example, a billiard ball is composed of a vast number of physical particles, yet when it strikes another it acts as a unity. If we say that our body is the substance of which our mental characteristics are attributes, we shall have to remember that it is not really a single substance; but there is nothing to prevent a group of substances taken together from having attributes which never belong to its members singly at all. A house has attributes which do not belong to any of the individual bricks, etc. of which it is composed, and the same is still more obviously true of the human body in relation to its cells. It might well be still more the case in regard to mental attributes.

If one rejects interaction, the view in question has the advantage of explaining the regular concomitance of physiological and mental events. But the view is not incompatible with causal interaction between the physical and the mental side of the one substance. Different attributes of the same substance may certainly interact. Nor is the view 'materialistic' in the sense of necessarily implying that the material attributes are of primary importance. It was in fact somewhat misleading to describe this view as the view that the mind is the attribute of the body. For, if the latter has mental as well as material attributes, it is no more or rather less appropriate to speak of it as the body than as the mind-body or body-mind, unless we mean to imply that the material attributes are more important than the mental. We had better talk of the 'view that body and mind are the same substance' without speaking of one side rather than the other as the substance.

But when we ask what can be meant by saying that body and mind are the same substance, the difficulties thicken. It is not meant that bodily and mental attributes or events are literally the same, otherwise we fall into the absurdities of behaviourism. What is meant then? In order to answer this question we must consider the meaning of 'substance'. Now theories of substance fall into two kinds, those which define substance in terms of a relation between successive events constituting the substance and those which define it in terms of a substratum over and above its characteristics and the events happening to it. If we adopt the former, relational view of substance, it is incumbent on us to explain clearly what the relation is which makes body and mind one substance, and this has never been done. We must remember that it will be nonsense to say that body and mind are the same substance if the relation which makes of a mind one substance is different from the relation which makes of a body one substance, yet there is no relation which has been suggested as doing the former that is capable of doing the latter. Felt continuity of experience, for instance, which has sometimes been put forward as the relation in terms of which a self is to be defined is obviously a relation between mental events and not between physical. To say that what is meant by saying that two mental events belong to the same self is that they are attached to the same body will not help, for the whole problem is in what sense they are attached to the body.

If, on the other hand, we adopt the view of substance as a substratum over and above its attributes, we are confronted with the fact that in that case we can form no idea of the substance of at any rate our body. It is arguable that we are immediately aware in introspection of a pure Ego over and above its experiences, but if we adopt that view we must either renounce any one-substance theory or identify the substance of the body also with our Pure Ego, which would give the theory a quite different form. If, on the other hand, we deny the Pure Ego, we can form no intelligible notion at all what the one substance is. The substance of both body and mind would be completely unknowable to us, and it does not seem a subject capable of profitable discussion whether there are one or two unknowables.

The only intelligible form of the one substance theory left seems to be that according to which the mind is the reality and the body (or brain) the appearance. This view has fairly often been held, though we do not hear much of it nowadays. It is at least capable of giving an understandable account of the relation between body and mind, but it has the disadvantage of being untenable without far-reaching metaphysical assumptions which there is little or no ground for making. For we could hardly hold that human bodies alone of material objects were the appearances of something psychological; we should have to extend the theory, and make the whole of the physical world the appearance of something mental or quasi-mental, thus adopting 'panpsychism', or the view that everything, even inorganic matter, is really alive. The more popular view which makes the body rather than the mind the substance has never been made intelligible, plausible though it may seem till we have investigated the notion of substance.

A possible view is that the question whether two events or attributes belong to the same substance is one the answer to which depends on several criteria and which therefore could not be answered with a firm Yes or No unless all the criteria were present or absent, but is a matter of degree and convenience, further that there is no substantial unity or relation constituting self-identity over and above these criteria. In that case whether we ought to speak of the mind and the body as one substance or two would become in a sense a verbal question. If we thought of the great qualitative difference between bodily and mental events, of the differences between the causal laws which govern the one and those which govern the other, of the fact that bodily states can be observed by anyone and mental states only by a single individual, of our ability to predict facts about a man's state of mind with great probability from our psychological knowledge of him when we cannot predict them from his brain-states, we should speak of the body and mind as different substances. On the other hand, if we dwelt on the dependence of mind on body for its experiences, actions, and even thoughts, and wished to treat them together in science, as physiological psychologists do, we should speak of them as the same substance. We could no longer say that one of these views was right and the other wrong, only that one terminology was more convenient than the other. But in that case the question whether we called the body and the mind the same or two different substances would have no metaphysical significance, but merely be an issue between two ways of describing the same empirical facts. We could not for instance possibly conclude that the mind could not survive bodily death merely because for certain purposes it was useful to treat it as an attribute of the body.

SURVIVAL

An upshot of the discussion is that it is not possible to give a philosophical disproof of survival. The apparent dependence of mind on body is a prima facie argument against it, but if there are religious, ethical or empirical reasons for accepting survival, the facts can easily be interpreted in accordance with it. It may still be that the mind really only uses the body as an instrument and can find other instruments or even do without such instruments altogether when the body dies. If we take such a view, we must indeed not overlook the very close connection between mind and body, but we must neither overlook the fact that we can see no *necessary* connection, we cannot see that mental processes are impossible without bodily. On the contrary it was just our inability to see any connection between them that provided one of the arguments often brought against interaction. We do not see in the least why the mind need have a body at all, and if we are unable to see this we must not claim to see that it could not do without one after death, although if we accept survival we may reasonably think it more likely that the soul takes on some other sort of body than that it at once undergoes such a drastic transformation in its mode of life as would be involved in ceasing to have any body whatever. On the other hand, if we speak of the body as merely the instrument of the soul, empirical facts drive us to make two admissions which rather tone down the force of our statement. (1) The instrument may drastically affect its user. Illness and injuries to the brain affect intellect and character. In such cases the brain has a resemblance to an old-fashioned cannon which was very liable to blow up and wound the man who employed it. But this does not necessarily make the brain part of or one with its user nor exclude the possibility of the latter surviving it and recovering from these effects after bodily death. (2) The brain is, at least under present conditions, an instrument necessary not only for expressing our thoughts in action and speech to others, but even for private thinking. It does not necessarily follow that it will always be so, any more than it follows that, because windows are necessary for me to see the sky now, I shall be unable to see the sky when I go out of doors because there are no windows. The philosophical theory of the relation between body and mind should be neutral on the question of survival. Against their close causal connection should be set their great qualitative dissimilarity.

It is not part of the scope of this book to discuss the alleged empirical evidence for survival produced by 'psychical research', but we have certainly no *a priori* grounds for rejecting it with contempt, and the evidence is at least such that, if anybody is inclined to believe in survival on ethical or religious grounds, he need no longer admit that empirical facts support the contrary view more than his own and need not hesitate on that account. For the prima facie suggestions of mortality are now countered by evidence which, if it does not conclusively prove, at least finds its easiest and most natural explanation in survival of bodily death. I refer to the communications, afterwards verified, of truths which were known to the dead man in his lifetime but to no other living person and of which the medium could not possibly have acquired knowledge in any normal way, to the extraordinary display by mediums of all the mannerisms and characteristic behaviour of the dead man down to his handwriting, and to the 'cross-communications' in which two messages given by different mediums unknown to each other's conscious mind are found to be unintelligible when taken by themselves but perfectly intelligible and specially associated with the dead man when combined. I did not say that these proved survival, since they might conceivably be explained by telepathy and pre-cognition, but I think it is certainly fair to say that survival at any rate provides the easiest and most natural explanation, though not necessarily the right one.

The Relation of Matter and Mind

At any rate the evidence is such as greatly to lessen the antecedent improbability of survival, which otherwise might deter many from accepting it on ethical or religious grounds.

THE MIND CONCEIVED AS THE 'FORM' OF THE BODY

An intermediate position between the one and the two substance theories was adopted by Aristotle, and was largely taken over by St. Thomas Aquinas and incorporated in the official Roman Catholic theology. According to this the mind is not an independent substance but the 'form' of the body. Here it is necessary to say a word about the Aristotelian antithesis between form and matter, which must not be just identified with the physical matter of the scientist. Everything in the world of men consists of these two elements. Matter is in itself indeterminate and valueless. It is in its own nature quite unintelligible, so that we cannot know anything about it as such but only about the forms combined with particular matter, but it provides the individualizing factor, that which distinguishes different members of the same species. There is no such thing as pure matter existing by itself, but in the process of development or production one thing may be relatively to another as matter to form. So things may often be arranged in a series of grades in which each is matter to the one above and form to the one below. Thus grass would be form relatively to the inorganic materials it absorbs, the flesh of sheep form relatively to the grass, a cooked dish form relatively to the raw meat, the human body form relatively to the cooked meat, and the human mind form relatively to the body. The form is always superior to its matter; and might even be called its cause, since Aristotle insisted that in an important sense the cause of a thing was to be found in its end rather than in its origin. Its end, its form was the reason for it existing, the 'final cause'. Yet the form could not be realized in existence without the matter, and one would therefore have thought that the Aristotelian doctrine was incompatible with a future life (though Aristotle does not express himself clearly on the matter).

St. Thomas and his followers, however, think that a body is

135

supplied for the mind by miracle on the day of judgement, but they admit that in the meantime the souls of the departed, though conscious, are in an 'incomplete state'. The theory is, however, hard to reconcile with any sort of mental, conscious existence, even an incomplete one, apart from the body. Nor is it easy to see in what sense *I* shall on this theory persist after the day of judgement if I have a different body, or in what sense the new body could be said to be the same body as the old; and the Thomist philosophy seems still committed to the obscure notion of a substance over and above its attributes. Nor does the description of the relation of mind and body as that of the form to matter seem capable of being more than at best an illuminating analogy. The relation between mind (or mental state) and body is quite different from any relation of form and matter in the physical world. The mind is not the shape of the body as a statue is the shape imposed on a block of marble, and though the analogy of a tune to the instrument with which it is played is perhaps more plausible it cannot be adequate unless we are prepared to accept epiphenomenalism, which the Thomists certainly are not.

THE RELATION OF MATTER AND MIND IN THE UNIVERSE AS A WHOLE

Besides the question of the relations between the human body and the human mind there is the more general question of the relation of matter and mind in the universe as a whole to discuss. Various 'idealist' arguments stated in the chapter on Matter are relevant here, as is the philosophical case for Theism to be discussed in the last chapter of the book. An argument germane to the issues that have just been before us is to the effect that mind cannot possibly have originated from and therefore been caused by a purely material universe. This bears a certain analogy to the argument that our body and our mind are too unlike each other to interact, but is stronger. In dealing with the argument against interaction I asked how, if, as is generally admitted, we do not know anything about the internal nature of matter, we can possibly know what it can cause and what it cannot, but on this occa-

The Relation of Matter and Mind

sion there is a reply to this objection which was not available before. Those who reject *a priori* the view that mind can be produced by matter are certainly thinking of matter as unconscious and *a fortiori* without intelligence or power to act with a purpose in view, and they find it incredible that consciousness, thought, purpose could be produced by a cause which was quite devoid of these qualities. Also they may find it incredible that a world which was intrinsically valueless could by itself produce effects, mental states, which are of value. These difficulties do not arise as regards interaction between a body and a mind already in existence, except perhaps when we awake from a dreamless sleep, for in ordinary interaction the *whole* cause of a physical state is never mental or of a mental state physical. How I feel when I am pricked by a pin depends not only on the physical stimulus but on my immediately preceding mental state, e.g. on whether I was expecting the prick. It is harder to believe that consciousness should have originated from something which had no traces of the quality than that this quality in something which already has it should be merely modified by the influence of something which does not possess it. The principle that what is in the effect must have been in the cause cannot be pushed too far, since the effect certainly need not be quite like the cause, but when applied to exclude the appearance *ex nihilo* of a quite new *kind* of quality it has considerable plausibility. Some philosophers have therefore used this argument in order to support the view known as *panpsychism* according to which even inorganic matter is all the time faintly conscious. It is suggested that, just as we commonly suppose animals to have a kind of consciousness, only inferior in quality and intensity to ours, so we should suppose plants to have a lower grade of consciousness still, and inorganic matter a still lower without being totally devoid of feeling. This does not, however, remove what difficulty there is in the appearance of new kinds of qualities, for if it is hard to conceive consciousness as originating from the unconscious, it is almost as hard to conceive purpose as originating from what had no purpose and rational thought from what was completely irrational. It would therefore seem more consistent to use the argument to support theism, the view that we ultimately owe our existence to a rational and purposing mind,

137

than merely panpsychism. According to most forms of theism it is not merely that God originally created the world but that it is dependent on him for its continued existence all the time, so that he can be regarded as part (though not the whole) of the immediate cause of every event that happens, if we use 'cause' in a wide sense, as philosophers generally do, to include all the necessary conditions, and we should not have to say that even the immediate cause of the origin of a human mind at birth was wholly material. I certainly should not like to rest the case for theism on this causal argument alone, but it might help to support others.

Many thinkers have called the qualities of mind and life *emergent* properties, by which they meant that they emerge from but are not explained by what went before. This is certainly so at the level of human knowledge, but if it is merely meant that the causation of these qualities is unintelligible to us, this is the case not only as regards them but as regards all instances of causation in the physical world. The assertion of the 'emergence theory' must be viewed as mainly a denial of the principle that a new kind of quality cannot come into being, but those expositions of the theory I have read have usually left it obscure whether the emergence of the new qualities was supposed to have causes but causes which did not render them intelligible or whether it was supposed not to be caused at all.

The idealist holds matter to be dependent on mind on the ground that it is reducible to experience or that 'its esse is percipi'. This view, if accepted, leaves various alternative theories open, within idealism. (1) Berkeley makes physical objects dependent on God's mind, which enables him to reconcile his theory with the common-sense view that they are independent of human minds.

(2) The thinkers known as *absolute idealists* or *absolutists* insist that physical objects are not dependent on particular human minds but on Mind as such, while they differ from Berkeley in making this Mind not transcendent but immanent. Berkeley held that, although God created finite minds, he had a consciousness separate from theirs, but an absolutist would not regard the Absolute Mind as a centre of consciousness over and above finite minds. It would be incorrect to say that it was merely an aggre-

gate of the finite minds, for this would err both in giving the priority to finite minds and in not doing justice to the unity of the universe, which is very different from a mere aggregate like a heap of stones. On the contrary the finite minds depend for their being and whole character on their participation in the unity of the whole, the Absolute, and are so intimately related together in this whole that, viewed in the light of the Absolute, which is the right point of view, they are radically different from what they seem to be as experienced by us in their separateness. The different minds are, quite strictly speaking, one in so far as they co-operate and have qualities in common, and their thoughts, in so far as true, must be regarded as not merely similar to but as actually being the thoughts of the Absolute Mind. In so far as we think rightly, Mind as such is thinking in us; in so far as we think wrongly, it is because we are thinking merely as private individuals and therefore diverging from this on account of our individual peculiarities. So the truth about physical objects is the view which mind as such takes and from its nature must take of the objective side of experience. As for the criterion and definition of truth, both would usually be held by the thinkers in question to be coherence. Object and subject exist together and cannot be separated, though we can abstract from any peculiarities not common to mind as such, i.e. we cannot say what an object apart from all subjects or a subject who knew no objects would be like, but we can say what an object is like apart from any particular subject. We can form no idea of the physical except in terms of experience, and we must think of truth not as consisting in correspondence to something outside of and independent of thought but as immanent in the thought process itself in so far as the latter consistently fulfils its own nature. It is impossible to summarize adequately in a page one of the subtlest systems of philosophy that the world has known, but this is the best I can do. The case for it is too complicated to give here; but in so far as it depends on the contention that matter could not conceivably exist unexperienced, I have already expressed my view that the arguments for the contention are invalid and it can only be accepted, if at all, on the strength of intuitive insight. Absolute idealism is rare now, but it was on the whole the dominant school of philosophy in Germany in the first half of the nineteenth century and in Britain at the end of the century, and since climates of opinion in philosophy are liable to change and it appeals to a very important side of human nature, it may well revive some day. The tendency to absolutism in politics which sometimes accompanied it, especially in Germany, is not a necessary result of this branch of philosophy. There is nothing in the nature of reason which need require us to treat the nation state as the Absolute on earth on which the individual depends.

(3) Some idealists would just fall back on *panpsychism*. In that case physical objects do not depend for their existence on a mind to which they are objects but are themselves feeling, experiencing beings, though at a very low level. It is argued that we do not know what the internal nature of matter is, and that therefore what science tells us may well be a set of propositions about relations of units which are themselves mental; in fact if we are to form any idea of what matter is itself we can only do it in terms of feelings or mental experience generally, since this is the only thing of which we have knowledge. Further, the view accords with the arguments supporting parallelism (for whatever they are worth) and with the argument that consciousness could not have originated from unconscious matter. None of these arguments, however, seem to me at all strong. It may be that if we are to form a notion of the inner nature of matter at all, we must do it in terms of concepts derived from introspection of our psychical states, but how do we know that this notion will apply to matter? We may have no other concepts in terms of which to think it, but need its nature be limited by what we can think? Further, it may be contended that it is not true that the only objects of immediate experience are our mental states, we also experience sensa immediately and we may more plausibly conceive physical objects in terms of these.

(4) Some would just say that physical objects were mere abstractions from human experience and leave it at that. If this is put forward as a metaphysics, it differs from any other very drastically in making everything in the universe a mere function of human experience.

(5) A less dogmatic idealist will admit that our experience of physical objects does depend on something outside humanity, but

will deny that we can know anything about what that something is like. This was the view adopted by Kant, who would, although he lived later than Berkeley, be generally regarded as the founder of idealism because he had and Berkeley had not many disciples. But, when we introduce something essentially unknowable into our philosophy at all, it is difficult to avoid either making it completely superfluous or involving ourselves in implications inconsistent with its alleged unknowableness, and Kant's disciples soon abandoned his unknowable thing-in-itself altogether, accusing their master of having committed both mistakes. (5) Would in any case, not being metaphysical, be more appropriately called 'phenomenalism' than 'idealism'.

An idealist metaphysics cannot be established by purely negative arguments to the effect that we cannot prove the existence of physical objects or know what they are like. That would tell us nothing positive about the nature of the universe or the place of mind in it. To enable us to say that the universe is mental or that mind is predominant in it positive arguments are needed. These may be based on the theory of knowledge or on the contention that the esse of matter is or involves percipi. I have said a little about both kinds of argument in Chapter Four and must leave it at that. But we must remember that the vast majority of those who have given to mind the predominant place in reality have not been idealists in the philosophical sense. They have not believed that the nature of matter is such as directly to involve an experience or mind on which it depends, but for various other reasons they have believed in God and therefore believed that matter was ultimately dependent on mind or 'spirit' for its existence. 'Idealism' has been used by some philosophers so as to include all such theistic views, and 'mentalism' used instead of 'idealism' in the narrower philosophical sense, but this is not the established usage.

MEANINGS OF MATERIALISM

To turn to the opposite extreme, the term *materialism* may be understood in many different ways. (1) If it means that nothing exists but matter and material properties, then it involves behaviourism and is obviously false. (2) Towards the end of the nineteenth century it was generally used for the view also called epiphenomenalism, according to which mental events are caused entirely by bodily and have themselves no share in causing either bodily or even other mental events. (3) It is often used simply for the view that mental attributes are attributes of the body, not of a separate substance, which need not entail behaviourism or epiphenomenalism. (4) It is also used to mean simply that mind originated from matter. (5) As used by Berkeley, and by Berkeley almost alone, it stands for realism, the view that matter exists independently of being perceived or experienced. Like the 'plain man' I am a materialist in the fifth sense. Materialism in the other four senses I have already criticized. In fairness to the materialist it should be added that materialism in none of them need carry with it the implication that only what are usually called material values (roughly, those which can be bought by money) are worth seeking.

Dialectical Materialism, the philosophy of communism, calls itself materialism because it makes matter primary, but opposes itself to 'mechanistic materialism' which recognizes only the quantitative side of matter. Dialectical materialism insists on quality as well as quantity (certainly an improvement), on the essential importance of change, on the presence of contradictory attributes reconciled in a higher synthesis, and on the close connection of thought and action. But we must not assume, as do most of its supporters, that there is any logical connection between communist economics and politics on the one hand and, on the other, this communist philosophy of the universe. Communists have thought that religion encouraged conservatism and therefore tended to oppose it, but there is nothing logically inconsistent in a communist being also a theist or idealist. He could still maintain the communist political and economic theory; and conversely a man might without logical inconsistency believe in dialectical materialism and yet oppose the communist application of it to economics and politics. Dialectical materialism may therefore be considered on its own merits as a philosophy without introducing political issues, but philosophers who are not communists in politics generally think these merits small.

Chapter Seven

SPACE AND TIME

ABSOLUTE v. RELATIVE THEORY

WHILE talking of things in space and time I have not yet talked of space and time themselves as such, and I must now hasten to repair this deficiency. It should be realized, however, that the subject is far too difficult for anything faintly approaching adequate treatment to be possible in an elementary work on philosophy. The first question is whether space and time really are anything over and above the things and events in them. Space has commonly been looked on as a vast receptacle including the whole physical world, and a similar conception has been applied to time, only here, since time is always passing away, one is at a loss for a metaphor. This is known as the *absolute* theory of space and time. The view is supported by language: we do not speak of things merely as spatial but as 'in Space', not merely as temporal but as 'in Time'. We do not regard any other properties in this fashion; we do not, for instance, think of all red things as in one big 'Red', as we think of all spatial things as in one big Space. The absolute theory is, however, very hard to defend. If we ask what space is like apart from things in space or what time is like apart from events in time, we find that our concept of them seems to fade away for lack of material and become completely vacuous. We can imagine an empty space surrounded by physical things, for we can envisage the concrete things as having a relation of distance and there being no other objects between them. But can we form an idea of an empty space outside the whole physical universe and surrounding it? Further, there can from the nature of the case be no empirical evidence for the view of any ordinary kind. Such evidence would lie either in perception or in a causal argument. But we certainly never perceive absolute space and time, only things in space and time; and it is an essential part of the usual form of the doctrine that space and time cannot act as causes, so we are debarred from using a causal argument. Yet the view has been very widely accepted by philosophers as well as by the plain man. The chief reason for its acceptance by philosophers was, I think, the fact that it seemed required by physics, since without it scientists were unable to state adequately the Newtonian laws of motion. This reason has now disappeared. Modern physics itself, under the influence of Einstein's discoveries, no longer requires but is rather incompatible with an absolute view of space and time. And it is difficult to see how the scientists could be opposed here by the philosophers.

It is best then to regard space and time as simply ways of look-ing at the spatial and temporal properties and relations of things and events, not as some weird kind of entities over and above the things and events. This is known among philosophers as the *relative* theory of space and time (to be carefully distinguished from the scientific theory of 'Relativity', which besides implying the denial of absolute space and time involves a great many more specific scientific propositions about spatial and temporal relations with which we need not trouble ourselves). We are familiar in experience with spatial properties and relations such as size, shape, distance, and when we assert propositions about space as in pure geometry we are making general statements about these. We need not suppose that, when we are talking about a vacuum, we are talking about something positive, space between the boundar-ies of the vacuum; all we need understand by it is that these boundaries have a relation of distance without there being any-thing at all between. The relative theory involves the rejection of absolute points. Points are only to be regarded as abstract limits which we approach as we divide but never reach. It also involves the rejection of absolute motion. Motion becomes simply a change of position relative to other objects except in so far as the notion of force is involved. Thus, if I walk twenty miles, it is just as true to say that everything else has moved twenty miles relatively to me as that I have moved twenty miles relatively to it, except in so far as the use of the verb 'move' is meant to imply that the motion

Space and Time

is caused by the exercise of force on the part of its subject. In that case the difference is obvious: you, though sitting still, have changed your position by twenty miles relatively to me just as I have relatively to you, but you do not feel tired and I do.

BEARING ON PHILOSOPHY OF MODERN PHYSICS

It is not possible to say much here about the other philosophical bearings of modern changes in physics. To give an adequate account of them would require very high qualifications not only in philosophy but in science, and these I do not possess. Nor if I did could I say much that would not overstep the proper function of an elementary philosophical treatise of this kind and make impossible demands on my readers. An important philosophical implication alleged is that time is inseparable from space. But, as Bergson has taught us, we must draw a clear distinction between the time of physics and the time of living experience. The time of physics is time as measured in terms of space and therefore already assimilated to space. What is true of it need not be true of the time of our psychological life, time as we experience it. This is brought out still more clearly by a consideration of something else which is sometimes said, namely, that time is 'the fourth dimension'. Time may be regarded as the fourth dimension in the sense that in order to fix the position of events completely, i.e. in space and time, we need four logically independent pieces of information, just as we need three in order to fix the position of an object in space at a given time. It also may be regarded as the fourth dimension in the sense that for the purposes of graphs it can be treated like a dimension of space. We can represent in a graph, say, the increase in the depth of a river in relation to its distance from its source, and we might represent in the very same graphical form the increase in depth relative to the development of seasonal changes. The same line in a graph might be used to stand either for advance in space or for passage of time. But if we mean by speaking of it as the fourth dimension that time bears the same relation to each of the dimensions of space as they bear to each other, this is certainly not true. Two things may be the same distance apart in any of the three spatial dimensions as two other things are in any other, e.g. I can say that A is a foot above B and C a foot to the left of D on the floor, but it would be nonsense to say that A was as far away from B in one of the spatial dimensions as event C was from event D in time. The four spatial dimensions are completely homogeneous with each other in the sense that there is no intrinsic difference between the nature of a relation in one and in another. It is arbitrary which we call the length and which the breadth of an object, and it is only not arbitrary which dimension we call height because we define height relatively to the earth's surface, i.e. not because of any intrinsic difference in the relation but because we have taken a particular physical object as a standard. But it is far from arbitrary whether we say two objects are distant in space or in time, since there is an intrinsic difference between any spatial relation and the relation of before or after in time. Time also differs from space in being irreversible; we cannot move backward in time. It is therefore very wrong, at least philosophically if not scientifically, to assimilate time to space although we cannot rule out the possibility that they may fit together in some spatio-temporal system. Two things which are not at all like each other may yet be combined in a system just because being different they are needed to supplement each other, and this *may* be the case with space and time.

In general we must be very cautious about transferring direct to philosophy statements made in a science. It may well be that the statements, though useful scientifically, are only true in a 'Pickwickian' sense, i.e. a sense quite different from the literal one. This almost certainly applies to such assertions as that space is curved or that the universe is four-dimensional, and it is possible that it may apply even to the statement that physical space is non-Euclidean. It may be very difficult to decide whether one is using some expression in a Pickwickian sense, and if so in what sense. It would, however, be safer to make up our mind that Euclid's axioms and postulates probably do not apply to the physical world. This discovery bears a considerable share of the responsibility for the heightened distrust of the *a priori* to-day, but as I have remarked before it does not cast doubt on the internal *a priori* necessity of pure geometry. It remains a matter of *a priori* knowledge that if the premises (the postulates and axioms of Euclid) were true the conclusions would follow, and further we know *a priori* the negative categorical proposition that there is nothing in existence which both conforms to the premises and does not conform to the conclusions of Euclid. No *a priori* knowledge that we have, whether outside geometry or inside it, is both affirmative and categorical. We have seen earlier how *a priori* knowledge can be both hypothetical and, even practically, valuable.[1] By a combination of *a priori* hypothetical knowledge with an empirical premise we can derive an affirmative categorical conclusion. We have not the empirical premise that the physical world is Euclidean, but we have the empirical premise that it approximates to this very closely except when we are dealing with very great distances or very great velocities, and so we can make a success of applied Euclidean geometry in spite of Einstein's discoveries.

THE PROBLEMS OF INFINITY

We may now turn to a perennial philosophical problem, the problem of infinity. The trouble is that we seem driven to think of space and the physical world both as finite and as infinite, and similarly with time and events in time. They cannot be both, and they must be one or the other, yet whichever alternative we take we are subject to serious criticism from the other side. A situation where what seem to be the only two possible alternatives are both equally objectionable has been called an antinomy since Kant, who worked out four antinomies in an attempt to prove that contradictions could only be avoided by making the world in space and time 'appearance'. Antinomies arise in connection both with the alleged infinite extent and the infinite divisibility of space, time and everything in them. They have repeatedly throughout the history of philosophy been used as arguments against the reality of space and time, and therefore have been very important for metaphysics. The approach seems very negative, but it has sometimes been the starting point of an elaborate positive metaphysical

[1] Vide above, p. 46.

doctrine of what reality was like. Taking the first of the antinomies stated by Kant, it is argued that, if an infinite period of time
has elapsed[1] or an infinite series of events has occurred before the
present, an infinite series will have completed itself and this is
self-contradictory. E.g. the infinite series of events prior to noon
to-day is now over and past, it is therefore completed, though of
course the longer series of all events in time, of which it is a part,
is still continuing. But an infinite series is from the nature of the
case one which cannot be completed. To this it has been retorted
that a series may be completed at one end and yet infinite at the
other. For example, the series of negative whole numbers ends
with —1 and yet it is infinite because it has no beginning. Might
this not be the case with past events in general? This does not
seem to me, however, to remove the difficulty. For it must still be
granted that, if the series of events has no beginning, it follows
that an infinite number of events will have occurred in succession
before any given time. Similarly if time had no beginning, even
though events had, it follows that an infinite number of periods
of time of any given length will have so occurred. But whatever
has occurred is past, completed, finished. Therefore we still have
the contradiction of a completed infinite. It is true, mathematicians
do not define the infinite as what cannot be completed, but they
certainly admit that an infinite number could not conceivably be
enumerated, though they do not define the infinite in such a way
as to make this a straightforward tautology. Now to deny that an
infinite number of things could conceivably be enumerated surely
involves denying that they could all have occurred in succession,
for if they had so occurred they could conceivably have been
enumerated. If a mind had been present, it could have numbered
each event as it happened. I am not therefore satisfied that Kant's
argument has been refuted, but I must admit that most people
with whom I have discussed it seem, unlike myself, to find the
above answer a satisfactory one. There is a similar puzzle about
the infinity of the world in space and space itself.

In the last generation there have been great developments in
the philosophy of mathematics and particularly in the treatment of

[1] Kant himself does not use the argument against the infinity of time but against
the infinity of events.

the concept of infinity, but without doubting the value of these in the realm of mathematics itself, I must express doubt whether this shows it possible for an infinite number of things to exist or an infinite number of events to have occurred. We cannot argue that, because there can be infinite numbers in mathematics, an infinite number of events can happen, any more than we can argue that there might be a negative number of events because you can have negative numbers in mathematics.

If in view of the argument I have mentioned we assert the world to be finite in space and to have a beginning in time, we have to face either one of two objections according to whether we make space and past time themselves infinite or finite. If we make them infinite, then we must suppose an empty time before the world began and an empty space all round the world. This would commit us to the absolute theory of space and time according to which they have a being by themselves apart from the things in space and the events in time, and it may be doubted whether this is tolerable. Space apart from extended things and time with no change in it seem empty concepts, really meaningless. If, on the other hand, we deny the infinity not only of matter in space and events in time but of space and past time themselves, we are faced with the difficulty that we can hardly think of them as finite without thinking them as having a boundary, but to think of them as having a boundary is to think more space and time beyond the boundary. Modern physicists indeed speak of space as finite but unbounded. However this is a very difficult conception and involves the highly problematic idea of a fourth dimension to which three-dimensional space is related as the two-dimensional surface of a sphere is to space as a whole. Further, in any case it still leaves unsolved the problem of time, to which it is not applied. That the conception may be of value if taken as meaning that the mathematics of the physical world bears certain analogies to that of surfaces of three-dimensional objects I have no wish to deny.

There is also an antinomy regarding divisibility. Every part of space must be conceived as itself divisible into further spaces, and this seems to imply that every piece of matter must be similarly divisible *ad infinitum*. Now it is very hard to think of an infinite number of pieces of matter or parts of space as constituting together a finite volume. Further, the complex seems logically to presuppose the simple, yet this infinite divisibility excludes the possibility of any simple parts of matter. Electrons may be physically indivisible, but they are not logically so. Whatever size they are said to be, we can always conceive parts of them smaller than the whole, although it may be impossible for physical reasons to split them. There is a similar antinomy as regards the divisibility of time and of events in time, although Kant, curiously enough, does not use this antinomy.

Where difficulties about infinity are easiest solved is in the case of future time. Suppose somebody believed that time had a beginning but will go on for ever. He would not be obliged to suppose that a time would ever arise when anyone could say that an infinite period had elapsed, so the contradiction of an actually completed infinite need not trouble him. We may compare the case of counting: we can go on counting *ad infinitum* (not of course in practice, but in the sense that there is nothing in the nature of number to stop us), but it does not follow that it is conceivable that anybody could ever truthfully say he had counted an infinite number.

Now it seems to me that this provides the clue to the solution of all the antinomies I have mentioned,[1] although its application is somewhat more doubtful in the other cases. The type of solution I am suggesting has the authority both of Aristotle and Kant, though like the former and unlike the latter I believe it to be compatible with realism. The contradiction arose because we seemed driven to suppose something infinite and yet to suppose it completed. But what if the infinite is only potential, not actual? It would then mean not that there is an infinite number of things, but only that we could go on indefinitely.

Take first the infinity of space. It is very generally accepted nowadays, I think rightly, that space is not to be regarded as some positive entity surrounding and containing matter, but only as a sum or system of certain properties or relations of material objects. But what then can be meant by saying that space is infinite? Need it mean anything more than that, however far matter extends, it

---

[1] I do not wish to apply what I have to say here to Kant's third and fourth antinomies, which are not primarily concerned with space and time but with causality.

always might extend further. In that sense there is no contradiction in the assertion of infinity, for it does not amount to saying that there is some actual thing, space, extending infinitely, but only that we, or matter, might go further and further. In this sense we can say that space is infinite while the material world is finite. Modern scientists speak of not only matter but space as finite (though unbounded), but they can hardly be denying that there is space outside the world in my sense, since they admit the possibility—and indeed the actuality—of the world's expansion. Limits may be set to this expansion by causal laws, but not by the nature of space as such, therefore in the potential sense space may still be regarded as infinite. The world has always room to go on expanding, but the 'room' need not be held to be something actually there prior to the expansion.

Similarly, it may be suggested that matter is infinitely divisible, not in the sense that there are an infinite number of parts of it actually existing, but only in the sense that, however far we divide, there is nothing in the nature of spatial properties to prevent us from dividing further still. We could not conceivably ever be in a position to say: We have found an infinite number of parts, but only—We can go on dividing indefinitely. The problem of the infinite divisibility of time and events in time might be tackled in the same fashion.

What about the problem of past time which, as I have said, is more difficult than that of future time? It does not seem in all senses impossible that time should have had a beginning; but might we not hold that time existed before the beginning of events in the sense that, however far back the beginning goes, there is nothing in the nature of time which implies that earlier events could not have occurred? We need not in that case suppose anything actual, empty time, before the first event occurred. The solution certainly involves serious difficulties as regards the causation of the first event, but it seems that as regards this question serious difficulties must arise on any theory. An infinite regress of causes seems to me no easier a supposition than a first event which was either not caused at all or caused by some non-temporal factor.

DIFFICULTIES ABOUT MAKING TIME 'UNREAL'

As I said, these antinomies about infinity have often been used as a ground for denying the reality of space and time. It was said that they showed space and time to be self-contradictory, and what is self-contradictory could not be real. With the reality of space and time went that of everything spatial and temporal, so the whole world as we know it was reduced to mere appearance. The terms, unreal and appearances, have, however, been used in different senses. One would expect such a statement as 'Time is unreal' to mean 'All statements ascribing temporal characteristics to anything are false'. In that case all such ordinary statements as 'I had breakfast before lunch' or 'A arrived at 11 a.m.' would be just false. They would not need to be all equally false, i.e. equally removed from the truth, but they would be false. Now this is a very hard view seriously to hold, and most philosophers who denied the reality of time have avoided or evaded it. Thus Kant holds that temporal statements are true but true only of appearances. In this way he thinks he can avoid having to admit that temporal judgements are false. But I do not think his position can be consistently maintained. It is one thing to say that statements about physical things relate only to appearances, and another to say that all temporal statements do so. For what is meant by saying that something is merely an appearance? It is not to deny its existence altogether—otherwise we could not make any true affirmative statements about appearances—but to say that it exists only for our experience. Therefore to say that the self we perceive in time in introspection is an appearance is to say that we experience it in time, though it does not really exist in time, but if we can even experience it in time, something temporal is real, namely our experience. We cannot rid ourselves of anything by calling it an appearance; if it is anything at all, even only an experience, it as such still falls within the real. Experience is as real as the physical objects of the realist, if a different kind of real thing. I therefore think Kant's position an untenable compromise. If we take the arguments for the self-contradictoriness of time in earnest, we are then driven back to the first view that all our judgements about even our own experience are false in so far as they involve temporal predicates. We cannot consistently say both that they are true and that they are not true of the real but only of appearances. We must maintain frankly that we are under an illusion, not only in supposing that independent physical objects are spatial and temporal, but in supposing that we experience anything spatial and temporal at all. In that case all empirical judgements ever made are wrong in fundamental points to an enormous and incalculable degree, because time is so very much the stuff of our experience that we have not the slightest idea what our experience would be like if we took it away. If we admit that much illusion, we are very near to absolute scepticism. We should have to abandon physical science, because, if we are as subject to illusions as all that, we can have no right to put the slightest trust in those perceptions of our immediate sense-data on which, whether we take a phenomenalist or a realist view of the physical world, all our scientific conclusions outside mathematics must be ultimately based. We should have lost any basis for an idea even of our own mental life, since all our thoughts, volitions, feelings are essentially bound up with temporal change. Even if I had no reply at all to the arguments against time, it would therefore seem to me far more likely that there was some undetected flaw in the arguments than that time was unreal. It may well be that our common-sense conception of time is somewhat wrong, but its amendment cannot reasonably be carried to such a point as to make all our temporal judgements fundamentally false.

OTHER ARGUMENTS AGAINST THE REALITY OF TIME

McTaggart, a modern Cambridge philosopher, used a different kind of argument against the reality of time, and he, unlike Kant, went so far as to admit frankly that our perceptions of ourselves in introspection are illusory in so far as they involve time. He argued in this fashion.[1] Every event has the characteristics of past-

---

[1] *Nature of Existence*, vol. II, ch. 33, v. 'Broad *Examination of McTaggart's Philosophy*, vol. II, pt. I, ch. 35.

ness, presentness and futurity. Thus at noon my lunch is a future event, at 1 p.m. it is present, and at 2 p.m. it is past. But pastness, presentness and futurity are incompatible. There is a reply to this so obvious as to seem to make the argument not worth the least discussion, namely, that there would only be a contradiction if the same event were past, present and future at the same time, whereas in fact it has only been shown to be past, present and future at different times. The argument has only been stated at all by making use of the non-temporal present. What is really meant is, suppose I am speaking at 1 p.m., that my lunch *was* a future event at 12, *is* a present one now, and *will be* a past one at 2. But McTaggart rejoins that, e.g. 'an event was future' only means that at some moment of past time it is (in the non-temporal sense of 'is') future, etc. But then you have, he says, the same difficulty about the moments. Every moment is future, present and past. If we reply that the moment e.g. *is* future, and *will be* present and past, we have again to analyse this in terms of moments, thus giving an infinite regress. Dunne, an amateur philosopher whose writings have aroused a considerable interest in England in the last twenty years, uses a similar argument, but he does not think the infinite regress which results to be vicious, but on the contrary rejoices in an infinite series of times, trying to make it a ground for believ-ing in our immortality. In any case the argument seems to me easily refuted. Firstly, McTaggart does not justify his view that the pastness of events, etc. has to be defined in terms of moments. On the contrary it would seem that moments must be defined in terms of events by which they are dated. This is obviously the case if the absolute view of time, is false; but even if the latter view be true it would still follow, for on the absolute theory time is homogeneous and so there can be no means of distinguishing one part of time from another except by reference to events. Secondly, in any case moments are not present, past and future in the same sense as events. To say of an event that it is past is to say that it has happened, but moments do not happen in the same sense of 'happen'. Therefore, even if the pastness etc. had to be analysed in terms of moments, it would not follow that the pastness etc. of moments had to be analysed in terms of other moments. Thirdly, McTaggart has no right to assume that what is meant by a sentence with a temporal verb must be expressible by a sentence without one. On the contrary this is not what we should expect if time is, as seems to be the case, something quite unique.

The difficulty about time which seems most impressive to me is this. The present is all that is real. The past has ceased to exist, and the future does not yet exist. We may talk at any rate of the past as still having a sort of being, but it clearly does not exist in the same sense as the present. It is no comfort to a hungry man that he has eaten meals in the past, whereas a meal in the present would be a very distinct comfort. The present is clearly real in a sense in which nothing else is, and this is, so to speak, the most real sense of 'real'. Yet, strictly speaking, the present is only infinitesimal. If it lasted for even a thousandth of a second, by the time we had reached the second half of this tiny period the first half would not be present but past; and this would be so however much smaller we made the period in question. So it would seem to follow that the quantity of what really is is infinitesimal, which is absurd. The only solution I can suggest is that we must regard as the real present what psychologists call 'the specious present', i.e. the minimum period of which we can be conscious otherwise than as an element in a longer period, and look on the strict present as a mere mathematical abstraction like a geometrical point. An indivisible moment of time without duration cannot be regarded as a reality, still less as all the reality there is. The difficulty, however, arises that such a view seems to leave everybody with an individual time of his own and deny the common time altogether. For there is no reason to suppose that everybody's specious present has the same duration, in which case what is present for me at a given time could not be said to be present for you at the same time.

MYSTICISM AND TIME

The unreality of time has sometimes been asserted on the ground of mystical experience. If the mystic really means to say that propositions such as 'I had breakfast before lunch to-day' or

'I am awake at present' are false, we must reject his view outright. The propositions he is denying possess a certainty greater than any which even on the most favourable view we could ascribe to the assertions of mysticism. But most mystics have probably not intended to say anything of the kind. They certainly had some experience of time different from the ordinary, and seemed to themselves to be in touch with something which transcended the temporal aspect of reality in a way in which things of every day life do not; but not being a mystic myself I am unable to obtain an understanding of what they meant. Apart from mystical experience, I do not think it at all true to say, as some thinkers especially of the Hegelian school have said, that time is not of fundamental importance to any of the things we value most and therefore relatively unreal in the sense of unimportant. This may be true of mystical experience and of the love of God, but surely not of love in its human forms, moral qualities, coming to know, and human aesthetic experiences in general. Yet these are of great value on almost any ethical view. The temporal factor is of the greatest importance in all goods which depend on the overcoming of obstacles. Progress of the highest sort is a great good, but time is certainly an essential constituent element in it; and if the time order were reversed so that the better state to which we progress came before instead of after the worse state from which we start, it would be not good but bad. On the other hand there is a security, permanence and peace not to be found in the time order for which the human soul craves, but if there is a non-temporal or super-temporal reality which satisfies this craving its nature cannot be grasped by anyone but the mystic, and to get rid of time, if we could, would be to lose values as well as gain them.

ALLEGED PRECOGNITION

A serious puzzle as regards time is presented by alleged cases of 'precognition', i.e. foresight of the future, not by inference from the past based on previous experience, but by direct vision such as we have in memory. The cases in which such foresights have been verified by subsequent experience are too numerous for it to be in the least reasonable to attempt to explain them away as mere coincidences. Yet how can anybody be directly aware of the future, seeing that the future is not yet there for him to be aware of it? The occurrence of precognition has therefore led some to deny the reality of time. But before taking such a drastic step we should need to have exhausted all other possible explanations; and even in that case rather than adopt a course which would make all our experience illusory it would be preferable just to admit that with our present resources the phenomenon cannot be explained. As a matter of fact in a field of abnormal psychology where everything is still unknown we can have no idea what the possibilities might be. One suggestion I might make in this connection as my personal view. The evidence for pre-cognition is that certain people's beliefs or dreams or imaginations, call them $a_1a_2a_3$, correspond to the future events $b_1b_2b_3$ too closely for it to be reasonable to dismiss this as a mere coincidence. Now correspondence between a and b may be explained in three different kinds of way. (1) a may cause b. This does not seem to explain most cases of alleged precognition. It may indeed satisfactorily explain some, but in most such cases it is hard to suppose that the person who had the precognition, either intentionally or unintentionally, played any part in causing the event which he precognized. It is often an event which to all appearances resulted entirely from the actions of other people. (2) b may cause a. This seems outright impossible with precognition, for b, the future event, is not yet in existence. Thirdly, they may have a common cause. The putting on of winter overcoats corresponds to the falling of the leaves, but neither causes the other; they are both caused by a third circumstance, the increasing cold. Since the second explanation seems on principle impossible and the first explanation would in most cases be silly, I think we are driven to suppose that 'precognition' is mostly to be explained in some way which falls under the third heading. In most cases of alleged pre-cognition we have indeed no idea what the common cause could be, but we cannot possibly reject the suggestion on this ground. On no view have we an idea as to the causation of precognition. If it is a direct vision of the future, we have no way of explaining causally why the vision occurs with some people and not with others and on some (by no means specially important or useful) occasions and not on others. And if there is no strong positive objection to the solution, we ought to accept it rather than make the incredible supposition that the future is already present.

Chapter Eight

CAUSE

IMPORTANCE OF CONCEPT

ACONCEPTION which has played a very great part both in science and philosophy is that of cause. It is indeed sometimes said that science nowadays is able to dispense with cause, but what the people who say this have in view is some metaphysical conception of cause with which they do not agree. In one sense at least science cannot possibly dispense with cause, neither can the practical man. It is essential both to science and to practice that we should be able to go beyond what has actually been observed and make inferences from it, whether in the form of generalizations as to what usually happens or predictions as to particular facts. Now, whatever else the concept of cause involves, it involves this, that we can pass from what has happened in observed cases to what is likely to happen in cases which have not been observed, and this is absolutely necessary if we are to have any science at all or if we are to take any sensible practical steps. This has always been a difficulty for the empiricist: it cannot possibly be a merely empirical matter to predict, as science does, for we have not empirically observed the future which we predict. Not that the topic is without difficulties for the rationalist also, as we shall see shortly. However in modern philosophy it was hardly questioned till the time of Hume that we knew *a priori* the principle that every change had a cause (with the possible exception of those involving 'free will' with which we shall deal later[1]), and that this principle was a necessary presupposition of science. Even Hume did not, as he is often supposed to have done, reject it, but merely raised philosophical difficulties which he thought made it impossible to justify or defend it. The mini-

[1] Vide chap. IX.

mum sense of the principle of causation which must be accepted if we are to have science is then that the repeated occurrence of a certain kind of event under certain conditions is generally evidence which makes it likely that similar events will repeat themselves under similar conditions. Without assuming this much we can never make any scientific predictions whatever or pass from the observed to the unobserved.

REGULARITY THEORY

Let us now consider philosophical theories of what the nature of causation is or, if you prefer to put it that way, what is meant by the term 'cause'. The philosopher who is inclined to be an empiricist will be likely to adopt a view on this topic which identifies or approximates to identifying causation with regular sequence, since regular sequence is something that can be observed empirically. He will indeed have to assume one principle which he cannot justify empirically, namely, that what has succeeded a certain kind of event regularly in the past is also likely to do so in the future, but the regular sequence or 'regularity' view at any rate makes the minimum concessions to the non-empiricist. 'A causes B', if A and B stand for classes of events, will then mean that B usually or always follows A. This view is by no means identical with the common-sense view of cause, as is shown by the fact that, if it were true, there would be no more special connection between the striking of a match and the flame which followed it than between the striking of the match and an earthquake which might also occur just afterwards. It would merely be that the striking of a match is usually followed by a flame and not usually followed by earthquakes, and that would be all. We could not then say that the striking *made* the flame follow. All intrinsic necessary connection between cause and effect, all active power on the part of the cause is denied. On this view to give a cause is *toto genere* different from giving a reason, it does not in the least help to explain why the effect happened, it only tells us what preceded the effect. So it is clear that the regularity view stands in very sharp contrast to the common-sense view of causation, though this does not necessarily refute the regularity view. Despite this the latter theory, or something very like it, is distinctly popular to-day. It agrees well with the modern empiricist trend, since it makes causation something that can be empirically observed and goes as far as one can towards eliminating the *a priori*. And it is in accord with one fact about causation. Whether causation is merely regular sequence or not, it is clear that at least in the physical world we cannot see any intelligible connection between cause and effect which explains why the latter must occur if the former does so. The chemist may bring propositions such as that wood burns under more general principles about the nature of matter from which they could be deduced, but these more general propositions themselves are not of such a kind that we can see at all why they should be true, we only find that empirically in fact they are true.

But there are other respects in which the theory is less plausible. First, it presents serious difficulties when we start talking about the causation of single events. 'I caused the flame by striking the match' might be interpreted as meaning: 'Striking a match by me was followed by a flame, and an event of the second class usually does follow an event of the first.' But what about events the causation of which is much more complex such as wars and economic depressions? Nobody has succeeded in discovering a really satisfactory formulation of statements about the causes of these in terms of the regularity view. If we say that Hitler's invasion of Poland caused the second world war to break out when it did we no doubt mean that the war followed it, but the rest of what we mean is not that wars always or usually follow invasions of Poland, it is something much more specific.

Another difficulty about the regularity view is that there are cases of regular sequence which nobody would call cases of causation. For instance, the sounding of a hooter at 8 a.m. in London is regularly followed not only by men going to work at that factory in London but by men going to work at a factory in Manchester which also opens at 8 a.m. Yet everybody would say that, while the arrivals at the factory in London were caused by the hooter in that factory, the arrivals at Manchester were not.

These difficulties might possibly be met by minor amendments of the theory, others are more serious. The theory seems particularly inapplicable in the case of psychology. For instance, when I believe something for a reason, surely my mental state is really determined by the apprehension of the reason and is not merely one of a class of mental states which usually follow the apprehension of similar reasons. If that is all, the belief is not reasonable; for it to be reasonable it must not merely follow on the apprehension of the reason but be determined by the intrinsic character of the reason. Again it is surely incredible that, when I will an action, the action is not determined by my will, or that to say it is 'determined' here merely means something like 'it is a kind of action which follows most or all states of mind like my own at the time in certain specific respects'. Again for memory to be possible one would think that my present state of consciousness must be genuinely determined by, not merely follow on, the past event remembered. There can be no trusting my memory of yesterday's events if it was not really determined by the events said to have been remembered.

ENTAILMENT THEORY

All this should make one hesitate very much before accepting the regularity theory merely because it is the simplest and keeps closest to what is empirically observed. It seems that besides regularity we must introduce the notion of determination and necessity. There is a sense, it seems, in which the effect not merely does but must follow the cause, and this depends on the specific nature of the cause as such. Can we say anything more to make clearer what it is in which this necessity consists? There is another case of necessity, a clear one, which it is tempting and, I think reasonable, to take as at least an analogy. That is the necessity underlying valid inference. Where a conclusion follows logically from a premise, this must be because the fact expressed by the premise is so connected with the fact expressed by the conclusion that the former could not possibly occur without the latter occurring. This is logical necessity. The theory according to which the connection between cause and effect is the same as or very like that of logical necessity may be called the rationalist or the entailment theory of causation ('entailment' being the relation between the premises and the conclusion in an argument where the latter follows necessarily from the former or between the objective facts expressed by the premises and by the conclusion).

The entailment theory is a theory of philosophers, but it certainly is more closely akin to the common-sense view than is a purely regularity theory, and though one should not say that causation is just entailment, there is a good case for saying that it involves the entailment relation or else something very similar. It is also true of course that an effect does follow regularly its cause; the regularity theory is not mistaken in what it asserts but only in what it denies. The entailment theory was almost universal among philosophers till the nineteenth century (though they did not use that name). The first leading philosopher to question it was David Hume (1711–76), and at the time his views found little favour, though to-day the regularity theory is the one most commonly advocated.

However, it seems to me that there are two strong arguments for the entailment theory. These may be added to the arguments already given against the regularity theory, which did not by themselves suggest another theory to put in its place. The first is that we can after all make legitimate inferences from cause to effect. How could we do this if the cause did not in a very important sense entail the effect? The relation need not be exactly the same as the entailment which occurs in formal logical reasoning, but it must at least be analogous to it in the important respect that it justifies the conclusion. It would be a very odd kind of inference in which we were allowed to draw conclusions from premises which in no way entailed their conclusions. This argument gives the main, though usually unexpressed, reason why philosophers have so often believed in the rationalist (or entailment) theory of causation. I do not of course in using this argument mean to imply that a person must consciously assume the entailment theory before he can see that a particular induction is justified, only that the theory is logically presupposed if inducton is to be justified. We do not know the ultimate logical presuppositions of our thinking, at any rate till we become philosophers.

Cause

The second argument is as follows. The occurrence of regularities is in any case a fact of experience. For instance, whenever solid objects are left unattached in mid-air they fall to the ground (with certain reservations to cover aeroplanes, etc.). Now, if it were not explained in any way, it would be an incredible coincidence that this should happen so constantly. It would be like having all the trumps in one hand at bridge several times running, or more improbable even than this. But what explanation could there be except that the nature of the bodies or the nature of the physical universe as a whole somehow entailed their moving in that way? If causation merely means regular sequence, to say that A causes B gives no explanation of the regular sequence of B on A, it merely affirms that B thus succeeds. Only if the cause is a *reason* for the effect, will it explain why this repeated regularity occurs, and the facts surely cry out for an explanation, since the alternative is to leave it as a mere coincidence which would be incredibly unlikely. But how can the cause be a reason for the effect if its nature does not somehow involve the effect? In that case the latter will logically follow from, i.e. be entailed by, the former, or at least the relation will be very closely analogous to that of logical entailment.[1]

The following are the main objections brought against the entailment theory. (1) We cannot see any logical connection between cause and effect. This must be admitted as regards the physical world at least. We do not see any ultimate reason why water and not oil should put out a fire or why we should be nourished by bread and not by stones. No doubt a scientist could in a sense give reasons for these laws by explaining, e.g. that stones are too hard to digest and that bread contains nitrogenous matter in an organized form in which it is not present in stones; but the reasons of the scientist only amount either to interpolating intermediate causes so that he explains how A causes B by pointing to an intermediate link C, i.e. something which appears between A and B, or to showing that the generalization to be explained is just an

[1] Some people prefer not to use the term 'entail' of the connection between facts but only of the connection between propositions, but we cannot avoid admitting that, if two true propositions are necessarily connected, the facts for which they stand must also be necessarily connected. Whether we are to call this necessary connection between facts 'entailment' or not seems to me only a verbal question.

instance of a wider generalization itself founded on experience, e.g. that no animals can extract nutriment direct from inorganic matter. In neither case does he tell us anything which amounts to more than a statement that events of a certain kind occur under certain circumstances; he does not explain why they occur. This is made clearer by comparing the conclusions of other sciences with those of mathematics. In the latter alone do we see not merely as an empirical fact that the conclusion is true but why it must be true. No causal law about the physical world even appears to us as logically necessary like the laws of mathematics; we cannot prove any such law *a priori*, but only establish it as an empirical generalization. However the fact that we cannot see any necessary *a priori* connection behind causal laws is no proof that there is not any. Till comparatively recently most of the logically necessary connections of mathematics had not been discovered by any human being, but they no doubt held all the same in prehistoric days as much as to-day. We cannot set limits to what is in nature by our ignorance. It would be very different if we were not only unable to see any necessary connection between cause and effect but were able to see positively that there is no such connection. Some philosophers think that they can see this, and if so they are justified in ruling out the entailment theory, but in the absence of this positive insight the negative argument is only of light weight.

(2) The relation between cause and effect is in one respect at least different from that holding in any generally recognized case of necessary connection, i.e. cause and effect are not, normally at least, simultaneous, but occur at different times. This of course again does not prove that necessary causal connection cannot occur, but only somewhat lessens the plausibility of the contention that it does. But if there are good positive reasons to suppose it occurs, the fact that it is unlike what happens in other cases is no adequate ground for rejecting the reasons in question.

(3) It is objected that in cases of *a priori* reasoning we attain certainty, but in cases of causal reasoning only probability. This may, however, be explained compatibly with the entailment theory. In the first place we never know the whole cause. What common sense calls the cause is only the most striking part of a

vast complex of conditions all of which are relevant to the exact manner in which the effect occurs. But, even if the whole cause entails the whole effect, this gives no reason to suppose that a part of it, which is all we know, will do so. The best we can do is to conclude on the ground of previous experience that the factors in the cause of which we are not aware are unlikely to be of such a kind as to counteract the others and prevent the occurrence of something like the expected effect. Secondly, since we cannot see the necessary connection directly even if it is there, we are in any case bound to proceed by employing the recognized methods of induction, which can logically only yield probability not certainty. For in the absence of direct insight into it, we can only arrive at conclusions as to when it occurs indirectly by considering what regularities normally occur and inferring from those what are most likely to be the laws underlying them, as on any other view of causation.

The entailment theory is of course incompatible with the view which we earlier rejected that all logically necessary propositions are verbal or analytic in a sense which would make what is entailed part of what entails. Since the effect is a different event from and not part of the cause, the two cannot be necessarily connected unless some propositions not analytic in this sense are *a priori*. Propositions about causation may be analytic in some cases, where something has been defined in terms of its causal properties, but this cannot always be so. If we define a species of thing in terms of one causal property, it will be a synthetic proposition that members of the species have any other causal property they may possess.

So far I have spoken as if it were common ground that we could never have insight into causal entailments, but I should not be ready to admit this. It seems to me true of the physical world, not of the world of psychology. Our insight that the death of a beloved person will tend to cause grief or that insults will tend to cause annoyance does not seem to be based merely on experience. We seem also to see *a priori* that the cause will tend to produce these effects. There is surely something in the thwarting of a desire which entails a tendency to produce pain. Even apart from experience it would not be as reasonable to expect that the death of a beloved person would cause the lover to jump from joy. We must indeed admit that we can at the best only see a causal *tendency* in these cases. If A loves B now, it is not certain that he will grieve if B dies, for by the time this has happened he may have gone mad or quarrelled with B so violently as to rejoice at his death. But we can see, it seems, that the nature of love is such as to tend strongly in the direction mentioned and not in the opposite one. That we can only say what its tendency is and not predict with certainty that this will be fulfilled on a given occasion is presumably because the situation is always very complex and we cannot know that there will not be factors which counteract the tendency in question. It may further be argued that we can easily explain why we should not see entailments in the physical world even if they are really there. For, firstly it is generally held that the internal nature of matter is quite unknown to us, and how can we tell whether what is quite unknown to us does or does not entail something? In psychology alone are we immediately aware of the internal nature of the object with which we are dealing, namely mind, and here we can reasonably claim to see that certain causal entailments hold, as we have just noted. Secondly, we never are in a position to give the whole cause, and it would be the whole cause that entailed the effect, not a part of it. Incidentally it is not necessary to the entailment theory to suppose that there are any causal laws which by themselves would be self-evident even to God. It may be that any causal law depends for its evidence on the whole system to which it belongs, as many have argued to be the case even with the *a priori* propositions of mathematics. It may be that water would not freeze in the way it does in a universe where the chemical constitution of water was the same but the general world system different. The arguments I have used would be compatible even with any law we can·discover being only statistical. It has been suggested that the laws of physics do not apply to each single particle but are only statistics about the way in which most particles move, but there still must surely, it seems, be some reason in the nature of things why so many more particles move in one way than in another way.

Whether we are to maintain or reject the entailment theory depends largely on our attitude to the problem of induction,

Cause

Modern logicians generally have tried to solve the problem of the validity of induction without assuming the entailment theory of causation and generally admit that they have failed. They have not, even according to themselves, shown why we are entitled to make inductive predictions in advance of experience. The main trouble is that there is no reason why we should think that A will be followed by B in the future merely because it has been so in the past. But if we suppose that the repeated experience in the past is an indication of something in the nature of A which entails B, that will be a good reason for expecting B to follow on future occasions also, even if we do not see why the assumed entailment should hold. No detailed theory of induction has been worked out on this basis, but it is significant that modern logicians who will not admit the entailment theory of causation have (usually according to their own admission) failed to produce any rational justification of induction. Nevertheless it has seemed so odd to many philosophers that there should be a relation of logical entailment between different events that they would rather admit all our induction to be irrational than save its rationality in such a fashion. Yet we cannot really suppose it irrational to believe that if we jump from a height we shall fall; and even if we say that all induction is in some sense irrational, it will still be incumbent on us to explain the distinction between scientific inductions and those inductions which would be accepted by no sensible person. What is the difference between the two kinds if they are both irrational?

It has been said that inductive arguments, though not rational in the same way as deductive arguments, are rational in some other way. It is easy enough to say this, but difficult to grasp what this sense of 'rational' could be. Inductive arguments are after all inferences, and for an inference to be valid the conclusion must follow from the premises. But for this to be so the premises must entail the conclusion, or at the very least be connected with it by a relation closely analogous to that of logical entailment. It is difficult to escape this argument. Nor have those who try to meet the difficulty by saying that induction is rational but rational in a different sense from deduction succeeded in defining the sense in which induction is rational. They have either left it undefined or defined it in terms of practical utility. In the latter case an inductive inference is rational if it is of a kind which is practically useful. But this seems hardly to solve the problem. It is clear that in order to act in a practically useful way it is not enough to do what has proved useful in the past unless this is an indication that it is likely to be useful also in the future, and it is just as much an induction to infer that something will have good practical results in the future from the results it has had in the past as it is to infer that something will be true of future events because it has been true of past.

It seems to me therefore that there is a strong case for the entailment theory of causation. But I must admit that this is not the opinion of the majority of contemporary philosphers. It is in any case a very important issue metaphysically. One of the most fundamental differences there are in philosophy is between those who think of the world as a rationally connected system and those who regard it as a mere collection of brute facts externally related, and which side we take in this controversy will depend chiefly on whether we, consciously or unconsciously, assume the entailment view of causation or not. One of the chief issues in philosophy through the ages has been that between monism and pluralism, between those who look on the unity of things as more important and those who give a more fundamental position to their plurality; and we shall certainly regard the world as much more of a unity if we adopt than if we do not adopt the entailment view of causation. If that view is true, everything in the world will be united in a logical system, since everything is causally connected with everything else either directly or indirectly. If that view is true, everything in the world will be a unity in a very important sense, for the very nature of a thing will also involve the other things with which it is causally connected.

ACTIVITY THEORY

There is a third view of causation which is now generally known as the *activity view*. We are certainly apt to think of cause as a kind of depersonalized will, and some philosophers have thought that the key to the philosophical conception of causation lay in the notion of will. This view was taken by Berkeley. He argued that for a cause to produce something it must be 'active' and assumed that activity involved willing. He therefore contended that the only possible cause was a being possessed of will and used this as his chief argument for the existence of God, whom he, denying the material world in a realist sense, made the direct cause of everything which could not be attributed to the causation of human minds. Other philosophers, e.g. Locke, while admitting that material things could be proximate causes, insisted that, since causation ultimately involved will, the only ultimate cause must be mind or spirit. They could argue that, though a physical object once started in motion might move and otherwise affect other physical objects, it could not itself originate motion. We cannot think of a chair as getting up and moving about the room of its own accord, and if it apparently did we should feel forced to suppose either that it was moved in an unknown way by some mind external to it or that it was itself animated by some sort of rudimentary mind. In this fashion the activity view of cause has often been used as the basis for an argument to the existence of God in order to get the motion started originally. There are however forms of the activity view which would not involve such an argument. It might be held that the activity presupposed by causation was not conscious rational volition, but some kind of semi-conscious striving such as we commonly suppose to occur in the lower animals and which we might then extend in a still more rudimentary form to what we call inanimate objects. The activity theory of causation would then involve panpsychism but not necessarily theism. Or we might go further still in the direction of attenuating the idea of activity, and say what is involved in causation is a quality which we experience consciously when we will but which can exist without being experienced in any way. It might in that case occur in objects which are in the full sense inanimate and might be supposed to constitute the essence also of their totally unconscious causality.

Again, the activity view has sometimes been combined with and sometimes given as an alternative to the entailment view. In modern times Prof. Stout[1] has first argued for the entailment view and then argued that the only instances in which we can conceive

[1] *Proceedings of Aristotelian Soc. supp., vol.* XIV, pp. 46 ff.

how the cause could entail the effect are instances where will or at least some sort of conation (striving or aiming at ends) is present, not necessarily in what we call the cause itself but in or behind the whole process. This then becomes an argument either for theism or panpsychism.[1] The chief difficulty about this argument is to be sure whether it is really the case that the cause can entail the effect only if conation is present or merely that we can conceive how it could only if conation is supposed present. The cases I have mentioned in which we did seem to see causal connection directly and any other instances I could have given are cases in which conation is in some way present, but the fact that we can see causal connection only in such cases does not necessarily prove that it is only present in such cases. Others would oppose the activity view to the entailment view as providing an alternative account of the causal necessity which the regularity view errs in denying. They think of the effect as following necessarily in the sense of being forced by the cause but not in the sense of being logically entailed by it. This notion of forcing is certainly involved in the usual common-sense view of causation, but the common-sense view also involves the notion of explanation or reason, which can only be interpreted in terms of the entailment view as far as I can see. That the entailment view is, however, not a complete account of the common-sense view can easily be seen in the following way. Entailment, if it occurs, works both ways: it is just as true that the cause can be inferred from the effect as that the effect can be inferred from the cause, and so if inference presupposes entailment it will be just as true that the effect entails the cause as that the cause entails the effect. But there is certainly a sense in which we think of the cause as necessitating or determining the effect but do not think of the effect as necessitating or determining the cause. Causation is regarded as a one-sided or irreversible relation. If I hit somebody in the face and gave him a black eye, the black eye would be produced by my blow in a sense in which the black eye certainly did not produce the blow, and we think of the future as necessitated by the past in a sense in which we should never think of the past as necessitated by the

[1] V. Stout, *Mind and Matter*, bk I ch, 2-4

future. But it is impossible to give arguments to show that this element in our ordinary conception of causation applies to the real world, so the activity view must remain inadequately grounded.

It may be further asked how we form the idea of causation at all. On the regularity view the answer is simple: all that causation means is regular sequence, and it is obvious that we can observe regular sequence. On the entailment view the situation is more complex. If it can be claimed that we even occasionally see some causal entailments, we might derive our idea from those we see and then could easily apply it also in cases where we do not ourselves see an entailment but suppose there must be some cause. Or it might be held that the entailment element in our common-sense view of causation was derived from the analogy of non-causal arguments, where we do admittedly see entailments. On the activity view of causation the idea of cause is usually held to be derived from the experience of volition. It is supposed that, when we voluntarily move a part of our body, we are, at least in some cases, immediately aware of our will causing our body to move.[1] The chief objection to this is constituted by the circumstance that an act of will never moves a part of the body by direct causation, but only by means of a number of intermediate links in the nervous system. Now it is difficult to hold that we can see directly C to cause E where C does not cause E directly, but only causes an intermediate term D (a set of vibrations in the nervous system), which then produces E without our being aware of D in the least, for we have only learnt of D not through the experience of willing in ourselves but through the reports of physiologists. It is less difficult, however, to hold that we can be immediately aware of our will as cause not of physical motion but of changes in our mental states, as when we will to attend to something. If we reject the regularity view but cannot explain how our idea of what there is in causation beyond regularity is derived, we can still fall back on the theory that it is an innate idea, but we should avoid this if possible.

[1] The common objection that an act of will does not always produce motion, since we may be struck with paralysis, might be met by saying that we could still be aware in some cases of our will as at least *tending* to produce motion.

Cause

EVIDENCE OF CAUSATION

We shall leave the question of universal causation to the next chapter, where we shall discuss the problem of human freedom, which seems to many incompatible with it. That causation, whether universal or not, occurs may, I think, be established by the same arguments as we used earlier for a particular view of what causation is like, the entailment view, and the arguments might be accepted as evidence for causation by some who would not go so far as to admit that they were evidence for the entailment view. Thus it is an argument for causation that inductive inference generally presupposes some causal connections in the world if it is ever to be justified; and it is also an argument for causation that, if we did not admit any causes to account for them, we should have to regard the observed regularities, of which experience furnishes us with many, as mere coincidences, whether or not these are also arguments for a particular view of causation. For it is immensely improbable that there should be such an extraordinary run of coincidences, and it is incredible that all science and all the inductive inferences we make in ordinary practical life should be unjustified. It has been objected to the argument from coincidence, that the notion of probability or improbability already presupposes causation so that the argument becomes a vicious circle; but this seems to be refuted by the fact that the notion of probability can be applied in mathematics, where causation does not occur. But there is in any case a certain lack of ultimacy about these arguments which does not leave one quite satisfied. One would have hoped that such a fundamental principle for our reasoning and life as causation could have been established in a different way. The argument could not of course in any case possibly prove that everything had a cause, only that there were some instances of causation in the universe.

Cause

DIFFICULTIES ABOUT THE APPLICATION OF
THE PRINCIPLE OF CAUSALITY

I have already indicated that what we usually call the cause of
an event is not the cause, strictly speaking. Suppose a man killed
by being shot through the head. We should ordinarily speak of
the murderer as having caused his death by firing the pistol; but
this event only produced death indirectly by first causing a series
of intermediate events in the intervening atmosphere (stages in
the bullet's motion). At any point in this intermediate process the
bullet might have been arrested or deflected, and then death
would not have occurred. We cannot therefore strictly speak of
the firing of the pistol as the true cause. The cause would have to
be the last stage in the intermediate process in question. But what
would be the last stage? The stage at which the functioning of the
brain (or heart) was brought to a standstill? But here we have no
longer the cause of death but death itself, the effect, and since
time and any process in time is indefinitely divisible we can never
lay our hands on and specify the strictly immediate cause. Similarly, whatever happens depends partly on the environment as well
as on the more obvious cause factors. If the air had become completely unbreathable first, the shot would not have killed the man
even if the bullet had gone through his brain, because he would
have been dead already; and if the condition of the atmosphere
immediately before had been even slightly different, though he
would have still died from being shot, the condition of his body
at death and therefore the total character of the event described
as his death would have been slightly different. For to describe
his death as the effect of firing the shot as the cause is really to
make a very vague statement. It was not merely firing the shot
but firing the shot under such and such conditions which brought
about the man's death, and the effect of this total event was not
merely the man dying, but the man dying in such and such a
precise way. Death is a general description of a very large class of
different bodily events (ignoring the mental side here for the sake
of simplicity) and any difference in the condition of his body,

however slight, would be a difference in this event. (Strictly speaking, the total effect would also have to include a great many other much less striking factors besides his death which we ignore on account of their relative unimportance, e.g. the displacement of air produced by the shot.) Arguments of this kind have often led philosophers to say that the only true cause of any event is the whole previous state of the universe. Of course a momentary state is a mere abstraction, so what must be meant is some short section of the whole world process immediately preceding. Further it would be recognized that it was equally true that the effect of this whole section was not any isolable event or events but the whole subsequent world process. These conclusions might have to be modified in view of the time needed for the transmission of light, which prevents changes in the remoter bodies being part of the immediate cause, but at any rate far more than we can ever give account of would have to be included in the total cause of any event.

But that will be of little help to scientists. In order to predict or use causal arguments either for theoretical or for practical purposes we must be able to single out some parts in the whole universe from others and regard them as at least specially relevant to the effects predicted. It may be that everything had some causal connection with the death of the man, but at least we can pick out the firing of the pistol as more relevant than the ticking of the clock on the mantelpiece or millions of other things that one could name. It is said that every time we nod our head we shake all the stars, but this does not worry astronomers. The causal influence, though there, is so slight as to be practically negligible. Which events are likely to be specially relevant is largely determined by previous experience, but we are also influenced considerably by certain assumptions about causation which can only be regarded as *a priori* in character.

ADDITIONAL ASSUMPTIONS

Of these *a priori* propositions about causation commonly believed or expectations as to what kinds of events are likely to be causes we may mention the following. Distinct doubt has been cast on some in recent years. (*a*) It is assumed that mere space or time as such cannot be causes. No doubt an alteration of position in space may have very important effects. It would make a great deal of difference to my comfort if I shifted my position and sat in the fire, but then the unpleasant effects would be due not to the mere fact that I occupied a certain position in space but to my changed relation to certain objects in space, the burning coal, etc. It is assumed universally that there are no ultimate causal laws of the form—if A moves to such and such a position in absolute space so and so will happen, or the mere lapse of such and such a period of time will produce such and such effects. If a change of position in space does seem to produce effects, we always assume that there must be some physical object causing the change even if we cannot detect it; and similarly, if without any apparent physical change mere lapse of time seems to produce an effect on something, we assume that the effect is really due to a physical change which had remained undetected. This attitude may be defended on the ground that time and space are nothing in themselves, only the relations of things and events, or, even by somebody who held the absolute theory, on the ground that mere differences of position in space and time can never be causally relevant since every part of space and time is like every other except in so far as the objects and events present in the space and time are different. (*b*) A less moderate assumption than this is frequently made, namely, that no *part* of the cause can be separated by space or time from the effect except where there is an intermediate chain of causes between the two. Thus for A to affect B at a distance something must travel from A to B, and for a past event A to be even part of the cause of an event B occurring some time afterwards there must be an intermediate process of change caused by A and having as its immediate effect B. This proposition has less claim to self-evidence than (1), but has been very generally held. It has led to such unproved postulates as the ether to account for bodies at a distance in space acting on each other and the theory of brain- or mind-traces to account for memory, which would otherwise involve the direct action on a present state of a past event, i.e. the event remembered. (*c*) It has till recently generally been assumed

Cause

on *a priori* grounds that causally determined change is always continuous and does not proceed by jumps. That is, for something to increase in quantity or degree from A_1 to A_n it must pass through all the intermediate degrees or quantitative determinations, and for something to move in space from one position to another it must pass through all the intermediate spaces. But the quantum theory in physics involves the rejection of this principle.

(*d*) It is universally assumed that, other things being equal, an event is more likely to be relevant to the production of another event if it is near to that event in space and time than if it is remote. By assumption (*b*) it can indeed only be indirectly relevant if distant at all, but even indirect relevance may be very important, so (*d*) is not superfluous. The indirect causal influence of remote events is by no means wholly excluded, but in the hope of finding a cause attention is primarily directed to those events which are not remote.

(*e*) It is generally assumed that A is more likely to exercise a causal influence on B if there is some affinity in kind between A and B than if there is not. If put in the dogmatic form that the cause must be like the effect, this principle is very dubious, but it may be of greater value if put in terms of probability.

Whether these principles are strictly true or not, they have played a very important role in science and have to a large extent worked. Science depends on observation, but mere random observation would be of little use to the scientist. He must have an idea what to look for if he is to observe with effect. We are helped here by a distinction Kant drew between 'constitutive' and 'regulative' principles. The former assert that something is objectively true; the latter merely direct us to act *as if* something were true.[1] In order to find out the cause of something we need clues where to look. Then we can test by experiment or repeated observation which of the possible events suggested by the clues are likely to have been causally relevant to events of the kind we are wishing to explain. We need not assert that it is impossible

[1] This is not the only meaning Kant attaches to 'regulative' principles. He describes the proposition that God exists as 'regulative', yet he certainly regards the proposition as objectively true and one that we are entitled to believe to be objectively true. But I think it is what he generally means by 'regulative' principles when he is talking of science.

that the principles I have mentioned should be violated, but it cannot be denied that they have been found very useful in suggesting where to look for causes. It is hard to see indeed why they should have worked as well as they have if there be no objective foundation for them, but this foundation might be stated in terms of probability. We should not say dogmatically that the cause always resembles the effect, but it may still well be true that in a given case, other things being equal, it is much more likely to do so than not, and that therefore it is rational to investigate first the possible causes which resemble the effect before we investigate those which do not. And similarly with the other principles, except, I think, the first, which does seem to me definitely true *a priori*. It may well be that these principles are not universally followed in nature but are much more commonly followed than not, at least with the type of events the scientist investigates and we encounter in daily life;[1] and if so it will, other things being equal, be more probable that any particular event in question will conform to them than not. Whether this is the meaning, the ground, or the consequence of their being more probable would be disputed, but at any rate the two—more frequent occurrence and greater probability—normally go together. In deciding the causes of something it is undoubtedly not strict certainty but probability on which we have to act.

MECHANISM

The principles which thus guide men in deciding what causes what do not necessarily remain constant from age to age. A principle very generally accepted by scientists between Descartes and the present day, but now much more subject to question, is that of mechanism. This may take a more and a less extreme form. In its more extreme form it asserts that every change in the physical

---

[1] It might be objected in the case of the principle of continuity that, since according to the quantum theory, this does not hold for the electron, cases of its violation are much more numerous and indeed universal, but it is at least true that things *qua* ordinarily observable normally act in a way like that which would follow from the principle of continuity.

world could be predicted by a being with sufficient intelligence who knew the position of all the atoms at some previous time simply by applying the laws of motion. This recognizes only one kind of causation in the physical world and implies that mental events cannot cause or take part in causing any physical changes whatever. It implies, further, that none but primary qualities of matter can be real or at least have any causal efficacy. This view has been very commonly held in scientific circles, but scientists would certainly not be so dogmatic about it to-day. At a sub-atomic level it has certainly broken down, since Newton's laws of motion have had to be revised, and physicists cannot now even conceive what causal laws can determine a particular electron to take one course rather than another.[1] Yet many physiologists and biologists still believe that mechanical explanation in their sphere will ultimately prove sufficient.

In its less extreme form the principle of mechanism asserts merely that every effect can be causally explained by resolving it completely into different factors and connecting them by causal laws with different factors in the cause. To many people this has seemed self-evident or identical with the principle of causation itself, yet it makes two assumptions which are by no means obviously true. One is that, if the effect consists of factors a, b, c, and d, its characteristics can be derived simply by summing these factors. But it seems at least very doubtful whether any exhaustive account of the characteristics or states of a living organism can be given by merely putting together the character-istics or states of the different living cells which make it up or of the chemical substances of which these cells are wholly composed. It is by no means self-evident that the corresponding assumption is true even of inorganic matter. The other assumption is that the different factors, which make up the whole of an event at any moment, if the former assumption be correct, can be treated as isolable from each other. In that case there will always be a law connecting any factor in the cause, x, with y, a factor in the effect, that will hold irrespective of whatever happens to the other fac-tors, or whether they are present at all. This assumption may like-wise be doubted without absurdity. The laws may only apply with-

[1] Vide below, p. 182 ff.

in a wider system or whole and be modified according to what happens to the other factors in that whole.

This is relevant to the famous controversy between mechanism and vitalism in biology. The vitalists hold the view that a mechanistic explanation of the growth and functioning of living organisms was on principle impossible, and conceived the alternative as the postulation of some extra 'vital' factor which limits and controls the mechanism. But they have not succeeded as yet in giving any intelligible account of that factor; and it may well be that, even if the vitalists are right in asserting the impossibility in principle of a mechanical explanation, the solution does not lie in the admission of some additional non-mechanical factor, some special force of a new kind. It may lie rather in the acceptance of a kind of causation not recognized by the mechanist, a kind to which the two assumptions mentioned in the previous paragraph do not apply.

It may be said on behalf of the mechanistic principle, in its more moderate form, that it is only in so far as it be applied that we can have a really satisfactory science, but after all we need not suppose that the world is made entirely for the convenience of scientists. Even if the mechanistic principle is not true of the world altogether, it must be, at any rate in regard to the parts with which we deal, sufficiently near the truth to account for the success of science in using it. But approximate truth is not the same as absolute truth. Whether in fact organisms can be adequately dealt with on mechanical lines to the satisfaction of the biologist is a scientific not a philosophical question, but the philosopher may still do very useful work in trying to develop a clear conception of the issue between the two different kinds of causation.

There is, however, in addition, the teleological difficulty which has led to the acceptance of the argument from design.[1] The trouble is that there is much in an organism that seems capable of explanation only by purpose, yet there is no mind attached to the organism which seems capable of the elaborate planning involved. Driesch, a famous modern biologist turned philosopher, postulated in order to account for this the existence of a being

[1] Vide below, p. 225 ff.

between mind and matter which he called an 'entelechy'. But Driesch's view is open to the objection that in order to account for the purposive character of organisms in this way we should have to suppose not a being below the rank of mind, as he supposed, but one in intelligence far above the cleverest human engineer. There are more cells in a human brain than there are inhabitants of the world, and each one is far more complex than any human machine. Therefore the entelechy he posits to run the machinery of our body, our own mind not consciously doing it, would have to be far more intelligent than we are; and the same would have to apply to the entelechies even of lower animals. That such intelligent beings are present in them is difficult to credit, and it was certainly not Driesch's intention to view them in that light. His entelechies were supposed to be not super-human but sub-human.

Chapter Nine

FREEDOM

THE most intractable perhaps and certainly the most humanly important philosophical problem connected with causation is that of human freedom. The subject has been debated mainly in connection with ethics and especially with the question of responsibility. It seems a necessary condition of responsibility for our actions that these should be free, yet this seems hard to reconcile with something else that we are also strongly inclined to believe, namely, that everything is caused.

IS CAUSATION UNIVERSAL? SCIENCE AND INDETERMINISM

It must, however, at once be said that the proposition that everything is caused is not clearly self-evident in the sense in which the fundamental principles of logic are and that no proof of it has been devised which is generally acceptable to philosophers. Till recently it was generally regarded as obviously true by scientists, and the whole scientific climate favoured the belief; but now this scientific climate has changed dramatically. Scientists now often say that the movements of the electron are undetermined, and since every physical thing is composed of electrons this would ultimately make all physical motion undetermined. This, however, is going too far, at least when put forward as a dogmatic truth. It may easily be shown that science cannot prove anything to be undetermined. Science can only prove something in two ways, (1) by observation, (2) by showing that to postulate it gives the best causal explanation of observed phenomena. Now absence of causal determination is not something that can possibly

be observed, and to postulate that something was causally undetermined obviously could not give the best causal explanation
of any phenomenon. Science therefore cannot possibly establish
indeterminism. The scientist may point out that we have no means
of discovering what the causes are which determine electrons to
take one path rather than another, but he is not entitled to say
that therefore they are not determined by any causes. In fact two
at least of the greatest physicists, Einstein and Planck, are still
determinists, though they put determinism forward as a philosophic and not as a scientific opinion. On the other hand, if science
cannot prove indeterminism, neither can it prove determinism.
It cannot possibly predict every event in detail from its causes;
the sphere of detailed reliable predictions is in fact very limited.
This should be remembered by psycho-analysts, who sometimes
talk as if they had shown that our whole character was determined
by what happened in early childhood. They may be able to show
that events in early childhood are very important for character
formation, but they cannot possibly show that everything in a
man's character is determined by them. To show this they would
have to be able in a vast number of cases successfully to predict
in advance from these events in detail, e.g. how far the person
would resist each temptation. And if holders of the materialist
theory of history really mean—which I doubt whether they usually
do—that a man cannot go against his material interests or what
he takes to be his material interests, they are certainly contradicting obvious facts of experience and going beyond any evidence
which they could possibly supply. Has a rich man never voluntarily given up wealth for the general weal or a nation been moved
by nationalist fervour against what it takes to be and what really
are its material interests?

What the recent developments in science do show is that the
whole causal scheme on which we based our account of larger
objects cannot be applied to electrons and we know of none to
replace it. But that it would apply was an assumption which we
had no right to expect would be fulfilled. We cannot take for
granted that laws which are suitable for dealing with planets can
be satisfactorily applied to the tiniest and most elementary particles of matter, any more perhaps than we can take for granted,

as the mechanist often does, that the same causal laws exactly will apply to living organisms and to the inorganic molecules of which they are ultimately composed. It was worth while trying both assumptions out in order to see whether and how far they worked, but no one was ever justified in asserting dogmatically that they must always be true or even always work. All the same, the fact that the movements of electrons are not caused in the way we used to think and that we cannot think of another way does not prove that they are not caused at all. On the other hand it must be admitted that, since determinism cannot be in any case proved, the prima facie plausibility of it has been lessened by recent scientific discoveries. A generation ago scientists thought they had knowledge of causal laws which, granted a being had sufficient calculating power, would enable him to predict all subsequent physical events from earlier events. They thought they knew, at any rate in general, for the physical world how determinism could be worked out, although they did not lay sufficient stress on the fact that they had not discovered similar laws for the mental world or for the connection between the physical and mental worlds. Now even in physics, their stronghold, the determinists have had to admit that they have no longer the slightest idea how determinism could be worked out. Human ignorance as to this has no tendency to prove that determinism could not be worked out, but it is taking the recent developments rather too lightly to say that they mean merely that we do not know the causal laws by which everything physical could be predicted, they mean rather that we do not see at all even what sort of laws they could be. However, since we have no scientific knowledge of anything about matter except its 'primary qualities', which are really only external relations, our ignorance does not provide the slightest reason for thinking there cannot be such laws. What determines an electron to take one course rather than another might lie in the real qualities which appear to us as colour or other 'secondary qualities' or in some further qualities which do not appear to us in any form. It is logically impossible that matter could have no qualities but those we call primary, for the latter are really only relational properties, and relations imply something related the nature of which must be constituted by qualities which are not relational or at any rate

Freedom

not merely relational. And if they have others besides the 'primary qualities', these others may well have some causal efficacy, which we are not in a position to detect, since we are not aware of the qualities.

It is in place here to make an additional remark about the recent scientific developments. Scientists have laid down what is known as the 'principle of indeterminacy' about electrons. According to this principle the position and momentum (i.e. mass × velocity) of an electron could not both be determined exactly. The nearer we came to exactness in determining one, the more inexact an account of the other should we have to give. Now, as has often been pointed out, this indeterminacy must not be confused with indeterminism. To say that something cannot be exactly determined in the sense of specifying precisely what it is is not the same as to say that it cannot be completely determined in the sense of causally determined. 'Determined' in the first sense rather means 'determinate', and the noun 'indeterminacy' used to signify the situation is in fact derived from the adjective 'indeterminate'. It may however be contended that, if the positions of electrons are really 'indeterminate', they must be also causally undetermined, since we cannot have causes fixing exactly the position of something that cannot have an exact position to fix. Yet to talk of the electron as really having no exact position seems to come perilously near to nonsense. Surely anything in space must either occupy a certain region of space or not occupy that region? Can there be any third alternative, provided the thing in question and the region are adequately defined? The principle of indeterminacy may, however, be interpreted in two ways both of which make perfectly good sense and neither of which implies the impossibility of causal determinism. The first way of interpreting it is as meaning that there are causal laws which make it impossible for us not only at the present stage of science, but on principle and for ever, to determine accurately both the position and the momentum of an electron. These would be connected with the unique position of light. In order to observe the electrons we should have in some way to use light, and owing to the extreme smallness of electrons we could not do so without shifting the electron. We must therefore always be in regard to electrons in the same position as we should be in regard to the temperature of anything if in order to use a thermometer we had always to hold it in our hand and were unable to make any allowance for the effect of the heat of our hand. No development in the art of making more and more powerful microscopes could overcome this deficiency. But, if this is all that the principle of indeterminacy means, it does not imply that electrons cannot have an exact position or momentum, it only means at the most that there are causal laws which prevent these from ever being measured exactly. It does not even in fact show this, for it cannot exclude the possibility of their being determined by some method which no human being has ever yet thought of, or perhaps ever will think of, which would not be subject to these defects. But, secondly, the principle may be interpreted as meaning something rather more radical. It may be that the position and momentum of the electron cannot be determined, not because there are causal laws which hinder its observation, but because it is the sort of thing that cannot have an exact position or momentum. Scientists used to think of atoms as little hard balls with relatively huge gaps between them, and the same conception was at first applied to the electron; but nowadays most physicists would admit that this is just an inadequate picture of truths about the structure of matter which cannot really be pictured but only stated in mathematical form. In that case the electrons are not to be regarded as real physical things like stones, chairs, etc. It is sometimes said that the electron's position cannot be determinate because it is where its influence is and the latter extends over the whole universe in some minute degree, so that no precise limits can be set to it; but this is to give up the conception of the electron as a real physical thing and make the term a manner of speaking about causal laws.

It remains true that we cannot see even on principle how determinism could be worked out for the inorganic world, and this applies still more clearly to the realm of minds. In the first place our causal explanation of physical changes is based to a large extent on the fact that different physical things are made of and can be split up into the same elements, which can exist apart from their compounds and still act according to the same physical laws when thus separated. But there is obviously nothing corresponding to this in psychology. You cannot separate, for example, a man's anger from the rest of him and study it in isolation. Secondly, there seems no possibility of a precise measurement of mental states. This seems to exclude any method of predicting them in the least intelligible to us. If determinism is a fact it must be on principle possible to predict not only, for example, that a man will be angry on a given occasion, but exactly how angry he will be. Now we cannot predict what cannot be stated, and to state the degree of anger exactly we should need numerical terms. It is by measurement of things and subsequent application of mathematics on the basis of this that physical science makes its successful detailed predictions. Yet I do not see on principle how one could numerically measure psychological states as such, though one might measure their physiological concomitants.

But, although we may have no idea how determinism is to be worked out, we certainly have an inclination to regard it as self-evidently true. That this is so may be shown as follows. Suppose I had been in a room alone and some article were to have changed its position. Then suppose on my being asked what caused this I replied: 'Perhaps it had no cause', would not most people think me almost insane, if they believed the answer to be seriously meant? That we have the tendency I have mentioned is not incompatible with the fact that we also have a strong tendency to believe something incompatible with universal causality, namely that some events, i.e. acts of human free-will, are not caused. It is notorious that the same man may have a tendency to believe and even actually believe two incompatible propositions. And most philosophers have taken the proposition that every event is completely determined as self-evident, with or without a proviso, about which they obviously felt difficulty, in regard to human free-will. Hume won his philosophical fame by raising difficulties about this more than by any other single contribution of his, but even he admitted that he could not help believing the proposition that every event was caused. His point was not that it must be rejected, but that, though we could not help believing it, it could not be justified or defended. I think it would be correct to say that between classical times and the present generation serious doubts about the universality of causation in the inorganic world were hardly ever felt by philosophers. Considerable weight must be attached to our tendency to regard the principle of universal causation as self-evident, though it must be admitted that its self-evidence does not possess the certainty attaching to the principles of logic, and that no proof of it has been given which has won anything like general acceptance among philosophers. Yet it is very hard to believe that things could happen without causes.

It might seem as though universal causation could at least be defended as a necessary presupposition of science. Science determines what are the causes of given kinds of events by observing what events do or do not precede events of the kind in question, but it may be argued that this procedure presupposes that there is *some cause* of the event. We determine the cause by what is essentially a method of elimination, but if we conclude that C is the cause of E by eliminating the other alternatives A, B, D, this obviously presupposes that there is some cause of E. Otherwise the elimination of A, B, D as possible causes would still leave open a second possibility, namely that there was no cause of E. This is an alternative which nobody, and especially no scientist, accepts in dealing with the ordinary physical phenomena encountered by us, whatever may be his attitude in regard to the freedom of the human will or the mystery of the electron. If determinism is thus a necessary presupposition of science, this will indeed be a strong argument in its favour; but it may be replied that all science needs to presuppose is not that there is in fact some cause of every event, but the practical postulate that we ought always to look for a cause. In this way we shall have the best chance of finding what events are caused. The postulate will be justified in practice if events are mostly mainly determined by causes, even if they are not always or completely so determined.

CERTAIN PREJUDICES ABOUT DETERMINISM

No doubt the indeterminism among electrons, if such occurs, is very different from the freedom of human beings, and it is largely on moral considerations that the case for indeterminism at the human level has been based by its advocates. It is well to begin the discussion of this topic by dispelling certain prima facie objections to determinism which cannot be regarded as anything more than confusions. On being first confronted with determinism one is apt to think of it as if it meant that we were compelled to do whatever we did by something outside ourselves. That certainly would be incompatible with the minimum freedom necessary for any sort of ethics, but this is not what the determinist means. He only maintains that a man's actions are determined by his own character together with his circumstances, so that he must have done what he did, his character and circumstances being what they were. He may reply that a man's character just is the man, and it is no lack of freedom to be determined by oneself; on the contrary freedom lies in *self*-determination as opposed to determination by something else. He need not draw the practical conclusion, which has often confusedly been drawn from determinism, that it does not matter what we do because what happens is determined in any case. For, even if the future is always determined, this does not prevent our will being one of the causes which determine it, and thus it does matter what we will to do. If a father refuses to give medicine to his sick child on the ground that, if he is fated to die, the medicine will do no good, and if he is fated to recover the medicine will not be needed, he has overlooked the possibility that, even if the child's death or recovery be determined, among the causes that determine it may be just the act of the father in giving or not giving the medicine. Again determinism is not incompatible with what we call change of character. 'Character' may be used in a narrower and in a wider sense. In the former it stands for the habits according to which a man acts in a given part of his life, and in that sense of 'character' it is certainly an empirical fact that a man may change his character. But the determinist will say that he can only do so because of some more fundamental cause in his nature. All bad men would not be converted by the influence that converts any particular one; for him to be so affected he must have been the sort of man who would first go through a course of 'sowing his wild oats' and then, when he came under a certain influence, change violently. If so, that was part of his character in a wider sense, as it is part of the nature of, for example, water, to change its original properties drastically when exposed to great heat or cold.

Again determinism does not necessarily mean that the man is determined by bodily conditions only or that his physical actions are the result of exclusively mechanical causation. There are mental causes too. Nor does it mean that there is no sense of 'could' in which a man could have acted in a way different from that in which he actually did act. Clearly the determinist can distinguish between cases in which a man is physically pushed and cases in which he acts as he chooses, and he may say that free action consists in the latter. He need not say that a man who voluntarily and deliberately jumps into a river in order to save another's life is no more free than one who is precipitated into the water by the collapse of a bridge. In one case what he prefers or chooses is quite irrelevant; in the other the action is caused by his choice, and would have been different or would not have occurred at all if he had chosen differently or not made the effort of choice. The question at issue is not whether we could or could not ever have acted differently, but in what sense of 'could' we could have done so. The indeterminist sense of 'could' is an absolute one; the determinist sense is a relative one. The determinist usually holds that we could have acted differently in the sense that we should have acted differently if our choice or act of willing had been different; the indeterminist asks whether we could also have chosen differently and insists that for us to be really free it must have been possible for us also to choose differently, everything else being the same including our own nature. The determinist would say that to assert freedom in this sense was nonsense or at least incompatible with a well-established principle, that of causality.

On the other hand determinists often talk as if the indeterminist meant that causation had no part at all to play in mental life. It obviously has; and if it were not so, we could never make any of the predictions about human behaviour on which our whole practical life depends. If I did not assume that the prospect of earning money had any causal influence on human beings, it would be senseless for me even to go into a shop and try to buy something. The indeterminist need not suppose that our actions and states of mind are unaffected by causes. All he need maintain is that they are not completely determined by causes. Suppose I commit some sin, say, tell a lie. The indeterminist need not and must not deny that my action is affected by causes. However bad a man I might be, I should not have told the lie at all if I had had no motive for it, i.e. if my state of mind had not been causally affected by any desire. And external circumstances must have been such as to stimulate the desire and to bring it about that I thought that lying presented the only or most convenient way of realizing my desire. That is the work of causation. Nor need the indeterminist deny that, if I have often lied in the past, or if I have had a bad upbringing or bad friends, this will have a causal influence on my present state of mind. All he need hold is that these causes do not necessitate the lie. What he must say is that, when I sin, the causes might be just what they are and yet I might not have committed the sin; otherwise I should not be responsible for it and therefore it would not be sin. He will admit that past wrong-doing makes me more likely to sin, but he will deny that it makes this inevitable except in the rare cases when persistent indulgence in a fault such as drug-taking has reduced a man below the level of a responsible human being in respect of the fault in question. Nor need the indeterminist maintain his view as regards all human states of mind and all the aspects of mental life. All he need maintain is that we are free as regards acts of will. Those events in our life which do not involve a specific act of will may all be determined.

'Pragmatists' and 'existentialists' often maintain that not only our actions but our beliefs are or may be undetermined, but this is open to objections which do not affect a more moderate indeterminism that applies only to actions. It may be objected that, for me genuinely to believe something, my state of mind must be determined by the evidence as it appears to me. I can act against what seems to me my duty, but I cannot hold a belief against what seems to me true, though it may well through error be against what is really evident or true. 'Pragmatists' have no doubt been right in emphasizing that our beliefs are very often affected by our volitions, though I think they have carried this well beyond the point of exaggeration, but the influence is indirect, not direct. I cannot by a deliberate act of will force myself to believe something as I might deliberately force myself to do something physical; but if I want to believe something I can by an act of will avert my attention from the arguments against it while dwelling on those in its favour, or I can deliberately act as if the belief were true, and either course will be liable indirectly to produce in time a tendency genuinely to hold the belief in question. Similarly, if I like or dislike somebody, I cannot by an act of will at once make myself cease doing so and take the opposite attitude, but I may by acts of will indirectly affect my emotional attitude. Thus, if I set myself voluntarily to do good to somebody I dislike, I may come to dislike him less and perhaps even to like him. But I may quite well fail even in this indirect attempt to arouse a liking, still more a real affection, for him, and still more is it the case that there are many beliefs which no voluntary action on my part could possibly lead to my holding, however indirectly, because they go too much against my natural intellectual disposition or because they too obviously conflict with empirical facts.

It has sometimes been claimed that we can see immediately that we are free in the indeterminist sense of 'free', but this view has usually and, I think, rightly been rejected by philosophers. It is at any rate plausible to hold that we can immediately see our will to be a cause, if not of physical movements, at least of mental events; but it does not seem to me at all plausible to hold that we can see immediately that our will is not an effect.

ETHICAL ARGUMENTS

A more serious case for indeterminism is based on the argument from ethics. Again, however, the case is liable to be much overstated at any rate. The consistent determinist can still believe in ethics in the sense of believing that some states of affairs are good and some bad. That something is determined need not make it indifferent in respect of value: the fact that toothache is determined does not prevent its being an evil. Now, if some states of affairs are good and others bad, clearly actions too can be distinguished as right or wrong, at least in the sense of desirable[1] or the reverse, according as they promote good states of affairs or bad. And we can again distinguish between those actions which produce their good or bad effects through accident, so to speak, i.e. through the occurrence of unforeseen consequences, and those in which the good or bad effects are intended. The agent will be, even on the determinist view, responsible for the latter in a sense in which he is not responsible for the former, since they depend on his will. And there will still be a point in blame and even punishment on the determinist view. For, where bad effects produced by a person depend on his will, their occurrence is an indication that he is likely to produce bad effects in future also. These effects must be prevented, and experience shows that we can sometimes, though not always, modify a person's volitions by blame, punishment or threat of punishment, so that he ceases to produce the evil effects in question. An adequate reason for distinguishing acts of volition from other causes such as disease or unavoidable ignorance may be said to lie in the fact that we can only apply the above treatment to the former and not to the latter. But the indeterminist will still contend that, while some goods and evils may be determined, an action can never have the quality of *moral* goodness or of moral badness if determined. He will insist that the sense we have of remorse and shame for an act just derives its sting from the fact that we could have acted differently then, whatever our previous actions and states of mind may have been. Kant, though not himself an indeterminist, states the case against the view that all our actions are determined by previous events very effectively when he says that, even if the causes are our own past acts, we cannot alter the past *now* and so are never free *now* if this determinism is true. The indeterminists, and Kant himself, add this further argument. It is all very well to say that we are free if our actions spring from our own character, but how did we get our character? Presumably it was the result of environment and heredity. In so far as it was due to the former it was admittedly not due to ourselves, in so far as it was due to the latter, it was again not due to ourselves but ultimately to our

[1] i.e. not merely desired, but such that it is rational to desire their occurrence.

parents or God. So how can we be responsible for it and therefore the actions that spring from it? Even if we suppose that we lived in some other realm before birth, this only puts the question further back. Whenever we began to exist, our existence and original nature must on the determinist view have been brought about by some causes; and since we did not exist before, these cannot lie in us. Even if we make the fantastic supposition that we always existed and never began to exist, this only produces a sort of vicious infinite regress. Every act of mine was determined by previous causes and therefore, it may be argued, I can never be or have been free at any given time because, whatever time I take, my actions then were determined by earlier ones which I could not alter once they had been performed.

ACTION AGAINST THE STRONGEST DESIRE

An argument on which indeterminists often lay much stress is that determinism is incompatible with the apparent fact that one can act against the strongest desire. We sometimes—not nearly so often as we ought in the case of most of us, but still sometimes—perform actions of which we should say that they were not really at all what we wanted most to do at the time. These are the cases of hard choice, where it costs us an effort to do what we decide to do because in doing it we have to go against a strong desire, while if we had acted otherwise we should not have had a struggle against our desires. No doubt we should not do anything at all (except mechanically out of habit) if we had no desire to do it whatever either for its own sake or for its consequences. Even when a man sacrifices everything for conscience' sake, he clearly would not do so if he had no desire at all to do what his conscience approves. Even if he dislikes all the consequences of his action, he must have some desire to do his duty for duty's sake. Some philosophers like Kant would refuse to call this motive a desire, but even Kant has to admit that it is analogous to a desire. Now it does not seem much to matter whether we say that it is not a desire but analogous to one or say that it is a desire but admit, as we should again have to, that it is very different from other desires. The question is then not whether we can act without any desire at all, but whether we can act against the strongest desire. It might seem that, if determinism is true, we must always act according to the strongest desire; and this has been used as an argument against determinism. If the premise is right, it is a formidable one, since empirical facts certainly seem inconsistent with the view that we can never act against the strongest desire; but I think myself that the determinist may meet the objection by pointing out an ambiguity in the phrase 'strongest desire'. This phrase may mean (1) the desire which prevails, and in that case it will obviously be impossible to act against it. For, if we act against a given desire, it will *ipso facto* not be the desire which prevails with us. But in that case to say that we cannot act against the strongest desire will be merely to enunciate a verbal proposition with which everybody would agree. But (2) what 'action against the strongest desire' usually means is 'action against the desire we feel most strongly'. Now to say that we cannot act against the strongest desire in this sense is by no means a tautology, but it is by no means evident even on the determinist view that it is true. For, even if we know that our actions are always completely determined by some causes or other, this does not settle the particular causal laws by which they are determined; and it is by no means evident that the causal efficacy of a desire is in proportion to the keenness with which it is felt by us. To say that it is in proportion to this is to assert an alleged causal law, and propositions about causal laws are usually, if not always, far from evident *a priori*, at least to human beings. Certainly this one is. Further, it seems as clear that it contradicts empirical facts as does almost anything in psychology. Our only evidence for or against a psychological generalization is derived from two sources (*a*) introspection, (*b*) the behaviour and statement of others. Now on most mornings it is quite clear to introspection that, when I get out of bed, I am not yielding to the desire which I feel most strongly at the moment. It is further clear that the hypothesis that other people always act according to the desire which they feel most strongly is not adequate to explain their behaviour, e.g. to pass from a trivial to a grave instance, it is quite inadequate to explain the behaviour of martyrs who have endured tortures rather than betray what they thought to be the truth. And it is far from agreeing with vast numbers of reports of others on their own experience. It is incompatible with the well-authenticated fact of moral struggle. Though a drunkard must often feel some desire to avoid at any rate the bad effects of drunkenness, there is a very significant difference between the cases in which he acts in accordance with that desire and the cases in which he acts in accordance with the desire to drink. If he does not drink he has to 'fight' against his desire to drink, but if he drinks you never hear of him having to 'fight' against his desire to remain sober. And a special moral significance and moral worth is attached to those actions which involve fighting against the desire we feel most strongly. It may be retorted that in such a case the desire we feel less strongly is really stronger, since otherwise it would not move us to act; but what is the measure of the 'real' strength of a desire? We cannot employ a dynamometer to settle this question. The only way of measuring a desire is either by the way it feels or by its effects on action. But if we fall back on the latter method, we are really only asserting that we cannot act against the desire according to which we act. It seems to me that the plausibility of the view that we always act according to the strongest desire depends mainly on a confusion between this tautology, if 'strongest desire' is taken to mean 'the desire which prevails', and the causal proposition that we always act according to the desire which we feel most strongly. The proposition that we must always act according to the desire which prevails is evident but says nothing except that we cannot act without some desire (which may be admitted); the second proposition says something much more significant, if it be true, but is far from evident and is not supported empirically. But to say that we can act against the strongest desire is not to say that determinism is false; it is merely to say that desires do not always produce effects in proportion to their felt keenness. Our actions may still be produced by causal laws of some sort, even though this particular causal law does not universally hold of them. The fact of action against the strongest desire cannot therefore, I think, be used against determinism.

DETERMINISM AND RESPONSIBILITY

Another argument, which many indeterminists use, is connected with punishment. The determinist, as we have seen, can justify punishment on utilitarian grounds. It may deter people from committing crimes and it may possibly make the person punished less likely to repeat his offence, but most people feel that this is not an adequate account of punishment. There is also the notion of desert. We have the feeling that a man deserves to be punished just because he has done wrong and not for ulterior consequences. This has led to some very unsatisfactory and even barbarous theories of retributive punishment; but if we reject it altogether, it is difficult to see how we can defend the horror we feel at the punishment of the innocent on utilitarian grounds. Now this feeling is specially connected with the belief that the man could have acted differently. It is, for reasons which do not themselves presuppose the determinist position, a doubtful question whether a non-utilitarian view of punishment can be maintained, but it certainly is an ethical belief which we *seem* to see instinctively to be true prior to philosophical reflection.

In any case, whether we accept such a view of punishment or not, we cannot escape from the notion of a special responsibility for those actions we have done voluntarily, and at least at the common-sense level this notion is inseparably linked up with absence of causal determination. The determinist may give an account which does far more justice to ethics and even to moral responsibility than would have seemed possible for him to do at first sight, but he cannot completely reconcile his view with the ethical views of the plain man. Our decision on the issue between determinism and indeterminism will therefore depend a great deal on what view we take of 'common-sense ethics', by which I mean the ethical views that a good and rational man will seem to see himself bound to regard as true apart from specifically philosophical reflection. If the philosopher must accept such views *in toto*, he must certainly be an indeterminist. But it would be unreasonable to suppose that such common-sense views are necessarily always exactly right if only because they differ from age to age and from land to land, though on the other hand some considerable weight must be attached to such a widespread ethical belief as that about responsibility to which I have referred, and this weight will be greatly increased for a philosopher who finds that after careful philosophical reflection he cannot himself get rid of the belief. The question will then be whether determinism logically involves a sufficiently great divergence from the ethical views which we cannot help holding in our best moments to constitute a serious objection to it. It is in a way a question of degree. On the one hand we have no right to expect that the common-sense conceptions of responsibility will be exactly right; on the other we should certainly be justified in rejecting determinism if it were shown to be incompatible with any tolerable system of ethics. Determinism cannot after all be proved, and we know some ethical propositions, such as that it is wrong to ignore the interests of others, with almost as much certainty as we know anything. But is it a question of contradicting the fundamental presuppositions of ethics or of merely amending slightly a concept as difficult as that of responsibility? The determinist may contend that his view is quite compatible with responsibility in a sense in which it fulfils most of the ethical purposes required of it. Let us now see how he can develop his case.

We have already seen that, since on any view some acts produce desirable results and some undesirable, the determinist can point to a perfectly good sense in which some acts are preferable to others. Now for the production of preferable acts a good will is particularly desirable. We have seen that blame and punishment may be justified even on the determinist view as means to the production of this or at least to the improvement of a bad. Now let us understand by 'blaming' a man (morally) for an action saying or indicating that the action shows badness of will. This is by no means an unplausible definition of moral blame. We can now at once see a sense of 'could' in which it is obviously a necessary prerequisite of just moral blame that the man blamed could have acted differently. For, unless the commission or omission of the action depended at least partly on the man's will, it is obvious that the omission of it could not possibly be an indication of badness of will. It might be an indication of some other defect, e.g. physical weakness or stupidity, but it could not be an indication of the specifically moral defect, which is a defect of will. To say a man morally ought not to have done something then implies that he could have acted differently in the sense that the action would have been prevented by a difference in his will, either by his willing instead of not willing to do something or vice versa, or by his willing more strongly and persistently than he did. This gives the determinist sense of 'could': it is perfectly intelligible and can be shown to be implied by moral obligation. But, the indeterminist asks, granted that the man could have acted differently if he had willed differently, could he have willed differently? The determinist may reply that the question is an illegitimate one (on his, not of course on the indeterminist, view of responsibility). For, if we define 'could' as before, the question whether a man could have willed differently becomes: Would a difference in his will have made a difference to his will? To say that it would is a tautology. The determinist can say that it remains true that a man's will sometimes is bad, however he got it, and that to blame him morally is just to say that it is bad. Even if he just inherited it, a bad disposition of will is bad.

Is this position ethically satisfactory? An objection sometimes brought by the indeterminist is that it would be wrong to blame two men equally for committing the same offence if one had had a good home and education and the other a bad, and that this implies that in so far as the badness of a man's will is determined it is not to be regarded as blameworthy. To this the determinist may reply that at the most the argument would show not that it is not blameworthy in so far as determined but only in so far as determined by circumstances external to the agent. And he may explain and justify our attitude by saying that the same action would be indicative of much greater depravity of will if performed by a man who had had the advantages of a good home and education than if performed by somebody who had had the corresponding disadvantages. And if indicative of greater badness of will, it should even on the determinist view be blamed more.

The indeterminist may also bring this objection. Suppose the case of a man who by habitual indulgence in a drug weakens his will. At any time, however far he has developed this habit, it will be true to say that he would cease to take the drug if he willed with sufficient strength and persistence to do so. Therefore on the determinist definition of 'could' it will always be the case that he could have ceased taking the drug. It will always be true that a certain change in his will would have stopped the habit. Yet everybody would agree that a time might arrive in which his will was so affected by the bad habit that he could not give up the latter. It is impossible in practice to decide when that time has arrived with anyone, probably even for the man himself, but it does seem clear that, when once it has arrived, the man is no longer to blame for taking the drug. He is of course to blame for his previous acts of taking the drug which brought him to this hopeless pass, but once he is in such a state it does seem that he cannot be blamed for going on taking it. This seems to show that there are cases in which a person is not to blame for an act even though it is still true that a difference in his will would have led to his acting differently, and that therefore for a man to be morally blameworthy it is required not merely that he could have acted differently in the determinist sense but in some more absolute sense of 'could'. It does not seem sufficient that he should have been able to act differently if he had willed with sufficient force and persistence; what seems needed is that he should also have been able so to will.[1] To this the determinist might reply by drawing another distinction. He could say that it all depends on what prevents him from willing rightly. A hard act of will requires a very considerable degree of mental concentration. Now if the drug habit has brought the man into such a physical and psychological condition that he simply cannot attend effectively, in the same sort of sense as I could not attend effectively to my philosophical work if I had been several nights without sleep or if I had just heard that I had incurable cancer, then he is not to blame, for his action is then no longer indicative of a present bad will any more than I could be morally blamed for laziness because I failed to attend to my work under the conditions specified. But suppose the man in question defended himself as follows: 'I admit that my physiological constitution is as yet unimpaired by the drug. I

[1] C.D. Broad, *Ethics and the History of Philosophy*, p. 200.

admit that I have as much power of concentration as any normal person. My judgement is quite unclouded, so that I am perfectly aware of the harm that I am doing and how wrong it is to do it. But owing to persistent indulgence in the drug I have come to be the sort of person who prefers gratifying his desires to acting rightly, and therefore I continue taking the drug, since it is now my nature to do so. Is this to be taken as an excuse? Should he not still be blamed, not only for his past acts which have brought him to this condition, but for his subsequent continuance in the habit of taking the drug? This suggests that it is not mere determination but determination by factors other than the state of a man's will which is incompatible with moral responsibility.

It should of course be admitted by either party that there are degrees of responsibility, and that the blameworthiness of a wrong action is lessened in proportion to the strength of the temptation which led to its commission. On this account the blameworthiness of the successive actions of the drug-addict would diminish as the habit acquired a firmer hold and the craving to take the drugs became stronger. There are indeed some wrong actions, such as betraying one's friends in order to avoid the most excruciating tortures, for which we should hardly blame a man, not because we do not think them to show a defect in his state of will compared with the ideal, but because we believe that the vast majority of other men would have shown a similar or worse defect under similar conditions. We find, however, that men who have a very high ideal often blame themselves bitterly, where nobody else would dream of blaming them for such actions. We do not blame insane people; but the ground for this can hardly lie in our believing their actions to be all determined. With most insane there is no more evidence for this than there is in the case of normal man. The common attitude towards them should be based rather on our inability to decide which of their actions imply moral badness and in what degree. They may do the most atrocious things and yet be morally as good as or better than the average man. Indeed it may be a mark not of moral badness but of goodness on the part of an insane man to commit a murder; because as the result of a delusion which he cannot help having he genuinely believes it to be his duty. It would then be wrong to punish him for it, both for this reason and because there is no ground for thinking that punishment will improve his condition.

The determinist will end with a counter-attack. He will argue that it is not determinism but indeterminism which is incompatible with responsibility. It is easy enough, he will say, to see how I can be responsible for a wrong action if it follows from a bad character, i.e. from something bad in me. But in that case it will be determined; and it is more difficult to see how I can be responsible if the act is not determined by my nature, does not spring from anything in me. The determinist may therefore plausibly occupy almost exactly the reverse position to the indeterminist. The indeterminist says that I can only be morally responsible for my actions in so far as they are undetermined; the determinist retorts that I can only be responsible for my actions in so far as they are determined.

Another argument that the determinist may use is this. If we imagine a perfect being—it does not matter for the purpose of this argument whether such a being actually exists or not—his nature would have to be such that he always inevitably did what was right and therefore he would never be free at all in the sense of the indeterminist. Yet such a being would obviously be more and not less free than we are. If so, determinism cannot be incompatible with freedom.

In view of these arguments it is not hard to see why many philosophers have been satisfied with determinism. Yet we must emphasize that the principle that every event is completely determined by causes has not been proved and is not clearly self-evident. We cannot even conceive a way in which determinism could plausibly be worked out in detail for the mind;[1] and even if it be true of the material world, doubtful as this may be nowadays, mind and matter are sufficiently different for us to have no good ground for concluding by analogy that it is true of mind. It is therefore perfectly reasonable for anyone who thinks determinism hopelessly incompatible with ethics to reject it outright. If he does this, he will not be contradicting anything which we are entitled to believe with anything like the degree of certainty

---

[1] Vide above, pp. 186-7

with which we can believe some propositions of ethics. There remains, however, the question whether indeterminism is really required by ethics.

Probably the great majority of people who consider the question do not feel that determinism does full justice to the conception of moral responsibility, whether they reject determinism on that account or whether they prefer to amend their conception of responsibility. The indeterminist will, if he is wise, admit that determinism can be worked out in a way compatible with a great deal in ethics, but he will insist that on this point it breaks down. He will admit that some things may be good, e.g. happiness or knowledge, or bad, e.g. pain or ugliness, although they are determined; but he will deny that actions can be good or bad in the specifically moral sense (though they can be useful or harmful) unless they are undetermined. He will emphasize the connection between the experience of remorse and the consciousness that I might have acted differently in spite of my past habits and innate disposition and was not just badly constituted, so constituted that, my character being what it was, I could not act differently. And he will play as his strongest card the argument that, if determinism is true, my character is originally determined in its entirety not by myself but by my ancestors and that I am therefore not responsible for it. To the argument that I cannot be responsible for actions which do not spring from my character he may retort that character is not to be regarded as a positive set of qualities separable from what I do and experience. We cannot form any idea of kindness as a quality of character over and above the willing of kind acts. The indeterminist may therefore contend that a man's acts are not determined by his character, because his character is merely a name for the kind of free acts he performs. To the argument from the conception of a perfect man indeterminists would differ in their replies. Most would probably retort that such a man would indeed always do what is right but would not be constrained by his character to do so. Such indeterminists would attribute undetermined free will even to God. Others would, however, admit that such a perfect man, or at least a god, would be determined, but would say that for beings at our imperfect level freedom and so the precondition of moral value lay in indeterminism. A really perfect being might enjoy freedom in a higher sense and not need this freedom, but for us it was the only real freedom.

ATTEMPTED INTERMEDIATE SOLUTIONS

The decision between the rival claims of the determinist and the indeterminist is of course a matter where different philosophers give very different answers. As I have indicated, the issue turns largely on the degree to which we think it permissible to diverge from our common-sense instinctive ethical beliefs on the question of responsibility. But we must not suppose that the only alternatives are the acceptance of indeterminism and the admission of the view that everything we do is completely determined by preceding events. There are intermediate alternatives which have been put forward as solutions. Desperate attempts have in fact been made to arrive at a conception of psychological causation which avoids the objections of either side. These mostly take the form of contending that, although acts of will are determined, they are not determined by previous events. The advantage of such a solution lies in this circumstance. It seems, on the one hand, as if the mere fact that our action is determined by something *in us* should not be incompatible with our being free but is rather a necessary presupposition of our being free. But, on the other hand, there is the objection that, if our actions are all completely determined by past events, we are never free now because we cannot alter the past. The solution in question would be in accord with the determinist argument based on the first point and yet escape the indeterminist objection based on the second point. And certainly 'character', which is said by the determinist to determine our actions, cannot just be identified with any series of past events. But it is extraordinarily difficult, and so far has proved impossible, to work out a clear idea of this causation which is not causation by the past alone. It must, however, be pointed out in favour of the view that we seem constrained to admit on grounds quite independent of ethics that a mental state can sometimes be determined by something which is in no wise a past event. When I know something, my mental state is presumably determined by

Freedom

the fact which I know.[1] I should be by no means in the same state if I did not know it. Yet what I know is by no means always a past event. In mathematics, for example, it is not an event at all.

Another solution offered is to the effect that the problem depends on the supposition that the cause necessitates in the sense of compelling the effect, whereas it only necessitates it in the sense of justifying an inference from which the effect would necessarily follow. It is just as true that the past can be inferred from the future as that the future can be inferred from the past, it is argued, yet nobody thinks that therefore we were not free in the past because our past acts were necessitated by the future. Why therefore should one think that our future acts will not be free because necessitated by the past? But, while it is certainly impossible to prove that the past necessitates the future in any sense other than the one just mentioned, yet most philosophers find it difficult to get rid altogether of the notion of the future as being necessitated in some other sense in so far as it is determined by causation, and this solution is therefore very far from having given general satisfaction.

One solution which suggests itself to me as a possibility is this. The determinist argues that responsibility implies determination by something in the agent and so by his character; the indeterminist argues that on the determinist view a man cannot be free or responsible because his character is ultimately determined not by himself but by his ancestors or by God. Suppose we accept both arguments: then we arrive at the conclusion that a man's acts are determined by his character (together with his circumstances), but that the man's character is not completely determined by anything, each man being in some degree a genuine new beginning. In that case we seem to escape both the indeterminist and the worst determinist difficulty about responsibility. We can then hold that a man's actions follow from his character without thereby making them ultimately the product of something other than the man himself. Only we must not think of character as a set of qualities over and above the actions and states of mind in which it finds expression but rather as just a set of laws governing the latter.

[1] It may be objected that it need not be known directly, but in that case we can argue that our state of mind is determined by the facts (which likewise need not be events in time but may be logical or mathematical laws) from which we infer it.

205

Chapter Ten

MONISM v. PLURALISM. UNIVERSALS

DEGREES OF MONISM

THE issue between determinism and indeterminism is one of the issues between the type of view which is called monistic and the type which is called pluralistic in philosophy. No precise definition of these terms is possible, the difference between the two kinds of view being a matter of degree; but we may say that a monist is a person who emphasizes the element of unity in the universe more, a pluralist one who emphasizes more the element of plurality. Undoubtedly, if indeterminism is true, the world is less of a unity than if everything is rigidly determined so that nothing could be different without other things being so. And in general, since the monist will tend to emphasize the whole at the expense of the individual, the element of order at the expense of the element of spontaneity, and the pluralist will tend to lay the emphasis in the reverse direction, the latter is on the whole more likely than the former to do justice to human freedom. We cannot assume that, because a person is pluralistic in general in his philosophical outlook, he will necessarily be an indeterminist, or that because he is monistic on the whole he will necessarily be a determinist, but there is certainly a general tendency in this direction.

Only there are all sorts of degrees of monism and pluralism. The extremist kind of monism asserts that everything is just One and there is nothing more to be said about it. In that case everything practically that we experience would have to be a sort of illusion because everything is certainly not just one as it appears to us. Less extreme forms assert that everything is one substance though with different attributes (Spinoza), or a single experience (Absolute Idealism), or one logical system (the coherence theory). The pluralist maintains that the cosmos is made up of a number of

Monism v. Pluralism

disconnected entities not necessarily bound up with each other, so that they could quite well exist apart. Theism, as ordinarily believed, may be regarded as a form of monism since it admits that the world is created and controlled by a single all-powerful mind. But it stops short of more thorough-going forms of monism in that it gives human minds a kind of relative independence, holding them not to be included in, though created by and dependent on, the divine mind. The view according to which God actually includes in himself, and does not merely create, everything there is is commonly known as pantheism. Christian thought has often tended in the direction of pantheism, but before this point was reached the movement has always been condemned as unorthodox. But orthodox Christianity itself, since it asserts the absolute dependence of everything on a single omnipotent mind and a single purpose, goes very far in the direction of monism, even when this is toned down by the admission of the undetermined, though very limited, freedom of the human will. The view of 'Manichaeism' which makes the devil an independent rival of God, and not a being created by Him but fallen and allowed for God's good purposes to exercise his free-will till his own inevitable defeat, is of course much less monistic. Relatively few philosophers have adopted an at all radically pluralist view till very recent times. Leibniz (1646–1716) is often described as a pluralist because he denied that the different beings in the universe interact, but it seems to me that he would have been more appropriately described as on the whole a monist. For he supposed all other beings to have been created by a single one, God, in such a way that there was a harmony and rigid correspondence between them in a single system in which everything was determined by God's purpose down to the smallest detail. Extreme pluralism is asserted by Bertrand Russell who thinks that 'the universe is all spots and jumps, without unity, without continuity, without coherence or orderliness or any of the other properties that governesses love';[1] but in another sense in an earlier work he calls himself a monist because he puts forward the theory that there are not two irreducibly different kinds of substance, body and mind, but that everything we know is made of one kind of stuff.

[1] *The Scientific Outlook*, p. 98.

FACTORS MAKING AGAINST PLURALISM

The relative unimportance of pluralism at most periods may be ascribed to various causes: (1) To believe in one God is itself to adopt a fairly monistic view of the universe, and the belief in one God has been general in most periods we study historically. (2) What I have called the entailment theory of causation has generally, consciously or unconsciously, been assumed, and this theory carries with it a considerable degree of monism. If two things entail each other, they necessarily belong together and cannot be separated, and though everything does not itself cause and therefore entail every other particular thing, everything we know is at any rate either directly or more or less indirectly causally connected. (3) There is a natural tendency, very strong in some human beings and present in some degree in most, to regard it as intellectually, and in other ways too, more satisfying to think of the universe as a unity than as a plurality. This tendency is specially marked in many highly religious minds, and its strong development is one of the chief features which differentiate what is commonly known as mysticism from other types of religion. The great mystics have claimed that they could be immediately aware of an enormously greater unity between things than any which appears on the surface or even any which is recognized in non-mystical forms of religion. They do not claim to reach their position entirely by intellectual argument, and often regard the intellect with considerable contempt, but they still frequently use highly abstract intellectual arguments as a means of approach. The most intellectual type of mystic is represented by Spinoza (1632–77). He claims to give a strict logical proof of his philosophical doctrines, but he seems also to be laying claim to an insight which he could only attain by appreciating the force of these arguments but which, once he has attained it, is capable of carrying him beyond anything that he could prove by argument. Most mystics would not give so important a place as Spinoza does to rational proofs, but they have very commonly paved the way for their mysticism by the use of arguments which purported to disclose contradic-

Monism v. Pluralism

tions in the world of everyday life. By showing the latter world to be self-contradictory and therefore unreal, they thought they could prepare the way for the vision and acceptance of what they thought on the strength of their mystical insight to be the true reality.

The entailment theory of causation has been discussed already, and the question of theism will be discussed in the last chapter. The more general arguments used in favour of monistic views turn more than anything on the nature of relations and are on the whole too subtle for discussion in a book of this type. The monists have commonly thought that two different things could only be related if they formed a unity so that they could not ultimately be separated. From this they have drawn two alternative conclusions. Some have inferred that, since everything is related in some way to everything else, the universe as it stands must be regarded as a very closely knit unity. Others have contended that the world as we experience it is clearly not such a unity, and have concluded that relations are 'unreal', being the imperfect expression of a unity too close to be adequately described in relational terms. For such thinkers the world of daily life is appearance just because it is not a close enough unity to satisfy us intellectually and spiritually. In reply to these arguments more pluralistically inclined thinkers have drawn a sharp distinction between mere relation and logical connection. It does not seem to me that the monists have succeeded in showing that the mere fact that two things are related proves that they are connected logically so that the one could not have existed without the other or so that the existence of the relation necessarily followed from the existence of the terms. On the other hand, it is possible that something rather like the monists wish to prove might be established indirectly not from the nature of all relations as such but from the entailment theory of causation. If the cause entails the effect logically and every event is caused, every event is logically dependent on and necessitated by the rest of the universe as a whole, so that if we knew all the other facts and had sufficient intelligence, we should see that the event could not possibly have been different from what it was. And even if we combined the entailment view of causation with indeterminism, we should have at

209

any rate to admit that causality was sufficiently pervasive to make the world, not indeed a thorough-going logical system, but something very like one, though with certain gaps owing to human free will. Further, it seems much more difficult to draw a sharp distinction between the internal nature of a thing and its relations than pluralists have usually supposed. What would be left of me if you took away all my relations to everybody and everything besides myself?

PLURALISM AND PRACTICE

But, even if there are philosophical grounds for assuming that everything is logically corrected with everything else so that nothing could conceivably have been different everything else being what it is, it must be admitted that at any rate we cannot see the logical connections in question. Further, whatever the relation between different things, it must vary greatly in degree of closeness. If all the relations of a thing are relevant to it, they certainly cannot all be equally relevant. We certainly could not get on at all in practical life or in science if in making forecasts and in describing the nature of a thing we could not ignore most of them. Otherwise the complexity of the premises needed would require superhuman knowledge and superhuman intelligence, and we could make no use of them in inferences. Whatever may be the ultimate truth philosophically, practically we must be pluralists. And it does seem that the fact that we are constrained to be pluralists in practice can hardly be without any relevance to the ultimate truths even of philosophy. On the other hand we must not carry this too far. Since we have to treat things as related as well as separate, this pluralism must be tempered even in practice by a considerable degree of monism.

A word may be said here about the political influence of monism and pluralism. Monism has often, though by no means always, been associated with views which exalt the state at the expense of the invididual and do not look kindly on individual freedom in political life. This connection must not, however, be regarded as a necessary one. For it does not follow that because the individual is absolutely dependent on the universe as a whole, therefore the ties which bind him to the state compared to the ties which bind him to other human individuals or to societies other than the state should be particularly strong. We cannot, from a general proposition about the unity of everything that is, conclude that unity ought to be realized in a particular way in human life, thus deducing our politics from our metaphysics. There is nothing in the nature of things which entails that the national state is not a mere piece of political machinery but the representative of the Absolute on earth. If everything is really a close unity metaphysically, it is obvious that this unity is compatible with great disunity in the political sense, since such disunity is often an empirical fact. And I do not see how we can draw an inference from the supposed ultimate metaphysical unity as to just how much of this disunity we ought to tolerate in the political sphere. If we could, the argument would certainly tell against rather than in favour of the nation-state, since greater unity would obviously be secured by a world-state. It might, however, well be and in fact often is contended by monists that what is valuable is not abstract unity but unity in diversity, and in that case the highest unity would depend on the richest display of individual diversity. The whole would be best if it was made up of the freest individuals with the fullest life, and the individuals would be best and happiest if in such a whole they devoted themselves freely to the service of the whole. Nor need monism lead to the conclusion that there is anything in the state over and above the individual citizens. The unity on which the monist insists need not be something over and above its parts but rather constituted by its parts.

THE ARGUMENT FOR OBJECTIVE UNIVERSALS

A metaphysical argument that has probably had a great deal of influence in favour of monism is derived from the doctrine that different particulars have *universals* in common, which is held by monists to point to their essential unity on the ground that everything, having something in common with everything else, shares a part of its being with everything else. This brings one to a very common, subtle and difficult topic of philosophical controversy, which it is perhaps most appropriate to discuss here. It is strange and significant that hardly any of the words we use with the exception of those called 'proper names' stand for particular things. They stand for kinds of things, or for qualities, relations or actions, which do not exist by themselves at all. But, while one sees plenty of particular tables or particular men, one never sees a table in general or a man in general. For what then do such universal terms stand; and if they do not stand for anything in the world, what is the point of using them? This is the problem of universals.

The natural answer to the question is that they stand for what a number of particular things have in common, and it is this common element which is called by philosophers a universal. Those who accepted this suggestion were called 'realists' in the Middle Ages, and the term is still sometimes used. This usage should, however, be carefully distinguished from the sense of 'realist' in which the term stands for somebody who believes in the independent existence of physical objects. The two usages have no connection. Realism was opposed traditionally to two rival theories, Nominalism and Conceptualism. The nominalists made universals a matter of language: according to them there was nothing universal in the world but only in the language we used of it. The only universal things were words (and perhaps other signs), and they were made universal only by being used of a number of different particular objects. The conceptualists, on the other hand, regarded universals as thoughts in the human mind. They agreed with the nominalists as against the realists in refusing to give them a place in objective reality, but they insisted that they could not be merely a matter of nomenclature, which might be quite arbitrary, and concluded that they must at any rate be universal concepts in the mind that uses the words. It was for these universal concepts and not for anything external to the mind using them that the words stood.

The main (and, I think, conclusive) argument for some form of realism against these views is that, if there were no such things as objective universals, our language and thought, constantly using universals as they do, would not apply to the real world. There would be no point in calling New York, London, Paris, Philadelphia all towns, if they had nothing in common, and if they have something in common, that something is presumably an objective universal. This argument is very serious, since every sentence we use consists to a very large extent of universal terms. If these universal terms did not apply to anything beyond our language or our thoughts, how could such a sentence ever be true of the world? Our arguments all depend on connections between universals. If universals were not objectively real, how could we then prove anything at all of reality? Even if we should take a phenomenalist view of physical objects, we must surely hold that, when we make judgements in psychology, our judgements are true of something over and above the thoughts in our own mind at the time we make them. But how could they be so, if there did not exist real universal qualities to which these terms referred? If they do not exist in an independent physical world, surely they exist at least in the real men and their experiences and are not merely a sort of mental fiction in the mind of the person who uses the universal terms of other men.

The conceptualists and nominalists would usually meet this argument by asserting that a general term or concept has objective reference simply because it applies to a number of resembling particulars. We can usefully employ the word 'table' to give true propositions about the real because the objective things to which the word is applied in fact all resemble each other. But to give such an answer is to admit at least one universal, resemblance. And if we admit one, we might as well admit others. As a matter of fact it is already implicitly to admit a great number. In order to apply our different universal terms significantly we should have to distinguish different kinds of resemblances. Mere 'resemblance' is far too vague, since everything resembles everything else in some respect or other. We should have therefore to admit one kind of resemblance between things in respect of which we apply the term 'table' and others in respect of which we apply the terms 'house', 'man', 'tree', etc. For every universal term we should have to admit a different kind of resemblance. But we might just as well admit an objective universal characteristic corresponding to each term as admit all these objective resemblances. I said 'as well', but in fact it would be definitely better. For it is by no means clear that there are all these different kinds of resemblances. We cannot by inspection detect a difference between the kind of resemblance there is between two tables and the kind there is between two chairs, or between the kind that holds between two blue things and the kind that holds between two red things. But, while we cannot distinguish a vast number of different kinds of resemblances by inspecting the resemblance itself as a relation, we can easily distinguish a vast number of characteristics in respect of which different things may be said to resemble each other. We can differentiate blue and red clearly, but we cannot differentiate clearly the kind of resemblance there is between two blue things from the kind of resemblance there is between two red. While of course admitting that resemblance is a universal, we had better therefore base our theory of universals in general not primarily on different kinds of resemblance but on different kinds of qualities and other relations. I do not see how this argument can be adequately met. We must indeed grant the conceptualist that we can only be aware of universals through processes of thought, but this does not prove that they are mental or not independent of us. Incidentally, the argument has brought out one important point which is apt to be forgotten, namely, that all universals are not qualities. Some like resemblance are relations, and we must not try to reduce all relations to qualities.

We must not, however, push the above argument too far. We must not suppose that there is one and just one distinct universal in the objective world corresponding to every term with a distinct meaning used by us. We do not have words for all the distinctions in experience and in the objective world but only for a sufficient number to suit our purposes, for instance, we are far from having names for all the distinct shades of colour there are. Again, the universal terms we apply are not each applied to a class of things because those things have one single quality in common which we could point out corresponding to the word. With class terms we find rather that the members of the class are distinguished from other classes not by the possession of a single quality but by a complex of qualities and relations which vary within certain limits. There is no single quality which is the same in all men, all trees, all fish, etc., and which can constitute the definition of any of these terms. 'Rational animal' has been put forward as a definition of man, but it is quite certain that the degree and kind of rationality and animality varies greatly from man to man. And, if we, as is indeed more appropriate, add to the definition bodily form, we are confronted with the fact that all men differ in this respect also. All we can say is that we should cease to call a being a man if he differed too drastically, but we cannot determine exactly at what point it would be right to do so, any more than we can say exactly how many hairs a man has to have on his head for it to be legitimate to deny that he is bald. Again, most at least of our adjectives stand not for a single quality but for any quality of a certain kind. We may legitimately call the same thing scarlet, red, and coloured, but we must not therefore conclude that the thing has one quality, colour, another red, and another scarlet. Its colour just is its redness, and there is no quality, colour, in it besides the red. Similarly, its scarlet just is its redness, and the particular shade of red it has is scarlet. Every coloured thing possesses (under specific conditions as to light) a particular shade of colour, and everything the shade of which falls within a certain class we call scarlet, everything the shade of which falls within a certain wider class including the former we call red, etc. There are no words at all for completely specific shades of colour except perhaps 'pure white'.

THE ARGUMENT FROM THESE TO MONISM

This brings me to the argument from universals for monism. While it is true that, if our thought is to have any validity and application, the notion of universals must express an important feature of the real, I do not think we need suppose that this necessarily means that different things coming under the same universal must literally have a part of their being in common. If they have, this is indeed a strong argument for monism, since all or most things have universals in common. But to suppose that it is so is perhaps to commit the mistake of not adequately appreciating what a different sort of thing is being said when we speak of universals from what is being said when we speak of particulars. This is shown by the fact that, while it would be complete nonsense to speak of the same particular thing as existing both in China and America, if we were referring to an individual entity, it is by no means nonsense to speak of the same universal as existing in both places. When we admit the objectivity of universals, we must not think of the universal as a part of a particular, that would be to make it itself a particular. Universals do not even exist in the sense in which particulars do, and we must not think of the assertion of them as though it expressed the discovery of a new kind of existent, but rather as a more illuminating way of talking about and so looking on particulars.

Yet the argument I have given for realism remains valid as showing that there must be an objective foundation for our universal judgements and our use of universal terms in the nature of the particular. Particulars are not just unqualified particulars, and in respect of their qualities and relations some particulars are like other particulars. This likeness and their possession of these qualities or relations are objective facts if anything is so. Indeed, if we took away all facts about universals we should thereby take away all facts about particulars also. Particulars are nothing apart from their qualities and relations.

PSYCHOLOGICAL PROBLEM HOW WE CAN THINK OF UNIVERSALS

I have not yet referred to what is perhaps the best-known discussion of the problem of universals, that by Berkeley.[1] The latter's account has often been regarded as necessarily implying a denial of objective universals, and was possibly so regarded even by himself, but I think this mistaken. We should distinguish carefully two problems about universals, the problem of their objective being and the problem of what we are doing when we think of them. It was the latter and not the former question that Berkeley was discussing, a question of psychology and not a question of metaphysics. What he said in answer to the psychological question was that we can only think of universals by using a particular image to stand for a class of particulars. In support of this he

[1] *Principles*, Intro.

Universals

pointed to the obvious fact that we cannot have, for example, an image of a triangle which is neither scalene, isosceles nor equilateral or is all these at once, or of a man who is no particular size; and his may well be a true doctrine psychologically. But it does not necessarily carry with it the conclusion that universals are not objectively real. They are not particulars, but for us to grasp them they may still have to be represented by particulars. As a matter of fact Berkeley's account already presupposes the objective reality of universals, whether he realized it or not. For there is no point in using a particular image to stand for a class of particulars unless the members of this class have the same or similar attributes, and these attributes, or the relations of resemblance between them, or rather both, are universals. Where Berkeley is in difficulty is in regard to those universals, such as figure commonly in philosophy, which being non-sensible cannot adequately be imaged. We may, however, still hold the doctrine that we cannot think without the help of particular sensuous images, provided we recognize that the rôle of such images is commonly played by words. Words are themselves sensuous images, whether we picture them as written or as spoken, but they differ from the images of which Berkeley was thinking in that they are usually not in the least like the objects they represent. They are therefore a very useful device for thinking of things which could not or could not conveniently be imaged. Whether we can think without any images at all is a disputed question among psychologists; but even if we cannot, this does not debar us from thinking of what, like God or the laws of logic, we cannot image in the sense of constructing a sensible likeness of it in our mind. For, instead of an image which is actually like the object of thought, we can use one, a word, which is not like it but can still stand for it in our thinking. Without using either words or other images it is at least hard, and perhaps quite impossible, to carry on a definite train of thought of any length, and many people commonly think in words even of sensible objects instead of imaging the latter. We must, however, be on our guard against a confusion here. We must not, because we cannot or can hardly think without using words or other images, suppose that thinking consists merely in having images. If so, there would be no distinction between saying to oneself a set of nonsense syllables and thinking out an abstract argument which we understood. In both cases the only images are words. What else there is in our mind it is one of the hardest tasks of psychology to describe, but we are perfectly well aware that there is something. For we are conscious not only of uttering or imaging but of understanding the words. Even when we use images other than words, as Berkeley himself realizes, we do not apply the whole content of the images but can abstract at least in the sense of attending to some features of the image and ignoring others. Thus in proving a proposition about all triangles we may have a mental image of a triangle which is equilateral or use such a triangle as an illustration on a blackboard, and we can do this quite well without implying that all triangles are equilateral. In such cases we are clearly therefore attending to the figure in our mind or on the board only as triangular and not as equilateral. It is a well-known fact that I can see a physical object without attending to all its characteristics, and I may do the same with an image. The important thing is that I must not assume in the proof any property, such as equilaterality, which is not common to all triangles. If I do, my proof will not be valid for all triangles.

The necessity of universals for thought is one of the reasons why a purely empiricist psychology is untenable. In order to arrive at any propositions at all we have not merely to accept what is given in sense-experience but to abstract from it universals. No proposition can just assert a particular state without ascribing to it qualities or relations, i.e. universals.

UNIVERSALS OUTSIDE THE EXISTENT WORLD

We must then recognize universals as having being at least in the particulars which are instances of them. Are we, with some distinguished philosophers, to go further and say they have also a being in themselves over and above the particulars in which they are exemplified? One of the chief differences between Plato and Aristotle was that the former gave an affirmative, the latter a negative answer to this question. The distinction is expressed technically by saying that Aristotle believed only in *universalia in re*,

Universals

Plato in *universalia ante rem*. The chief argument for the Platonic view is that we can intelligently assert and even know the truth of hypothetical propositions which do not apply to anything actually existing. The question then arises what they are true of. For them to be true they must be true of something. But there are no existent facts of which they are true, they say not what actually is but only what would be a fact if something were the case which is not. This leads to the conclusion that they are true simply of relations of universals, and that the universals have therefore a being even without being realized in particulars. For, if they had not, how could anything be true of them? Further, with *a priori* propositions, even when in fact they apply to existents, their truth is surely logically independent of whether anything to which they apply exists or not. That two million plus two million equals four million would surely be true even if the total number of things in the universe were less than four million. That $2+2=4$ cannot just mean that every existent $2+2=4$. It must mean too that there is something in the nature of twoness which entails this, and that would be the case even if there were no actual instances of two and never had been or would be any. It is a fundamental and generally accepted doctrine of modern logic that an *a priori* proposition cannot be affirmative existential, i.e. assert the existence of something, and that no affirmative existential proposition can be deduced from it alone. But if the truth of an *a priori* proposition were dependent on the existence of particulars to which it applied, it would be affirmative existential in character, i.e. assert or imply the existence of the particulars in question. But if the truth of such propositions does not depend on whether anything exists of which they are true, on what does it depend? Surely they must then be true of universals which are not realized in the world of particulars but are still real and objective?

The difficulty about this view is that it is difficult to attach any meaning to the assertion that universals have a being apart from particulars. They clearly do not exist in the sense in which particulars do; we do not encounter universal men in space and time, only individual men. So if we accept the above argument, we have to make a distinction and say 'they have being without existing' or 'they do not exist but they subsist'. But it is not at all clear whether we can attach any meaning to subsisting or having being without existing. When we have subtracted the notion of existence from being, there seems to be nothing left. Or, if there is any meaning in the statement at all, it seems to reduce itself to a mere restatement in technical terminology of the reasons given for holding it true. If this is so, to say, for example, that perfect goodness subsists is simply to say that some affirmative propositions about perfect goodness are true, whether anything perfectly good exists or not, and this does not solve but merely states the problem. The fact may be admitted, but to invent technical terms to describe it does not tell us how it can be a fact, and that was what we wanted to know. So I cannot say that I find the alleged solution satisfactory. If we could be sure that 'subsist' had a clear meaning apart from 'exist' it would be all right, but as it is it seems to be like a cheap verbal dodge. On the other hand I do not know how to answer the arguments for subsistence. I do not think that anything approaching a solution has been found yet for this problem about universals. It must be admitted, however, that in saying this I am presupposing something which I hold to be true but which many philosophers would reject, namely that the truth of a proposition consists in or depends on its relation to objective facts distinct from any proposition. The argument presupposed that, for propositions about universals to be true, there must be universals independent of the propositions, the truth of the latter consisting in a relation to these. This assumption would not be universally accepted by philosophers. A person who defined truth as coherence between judgements would not make it, nor would some pragmatists. Further, it would be less difficult to maintain such views about hypothetical propositions than it would be to put them forward as a general theory of all truth. But I should not myself accept such a solution, partly because I find it very hard to believe that hypothetical propositions are true only in a quite different sense of 'true' from that in which categorical propositions are true, and partly because I do not think it escapes all, though I think it escapes some, of the objections to the coherence or pragmatist theories of truth.

Chapter Eleven

GOD

WE have left to the last the philosophical question
of most extreme importance, both theoretically
and practically, namely that of the existence of
God. By 'God' I shall understand in this chapter
a supreme mind regarded as either omnipotent or at least more
powerful than anything else and supremely good and wise. It is
not within the scope of a purely philosophical work to discuss the
claims of revelation on which belief in God and his attributes has
so often been based, but philosophers have also formulated a great
number of *arguments* for the existence of God.

THE ONTOLOGICAL ARGUMENT

To start with the most dubious and least valuable of these, the
ontological argument claims to prove the existence of God by a
mere consideration of our idea of him. God is defined as the most
perfect being or as a being containing all positive attributes.[1] It is
then argued that existence is a 'perfection' or a positive attribute,
and that therefore, if we are to avoid contradicting ourselves, we
must grant the existence of God. The most important of the
objections to the argument is to the effect that existence is not a
'perfection' or an attribute. To say that something exists is to
assert a proposition of a very different kind from what we assert
when we ascribe any ordinary attribute to a thing. It is not to
increase the concept of the thing by adding a new characteristic,
but merely to affirm that the concept is realized in fact. This is

---

[1] 'Positive' (1) enables us to exclude evil attributes on the ground that they are
negative, (2) implies the infinity of God, for there would be an element of negativity
in him if he possessed any attribute in any limited degree, i.e. superior degrees would
be denied of him.

God

one of the cases where we are apt to be misled by language. Because 'cats exist' and 'cats sleep', or 'cats are existent' and 'cats are carnivorous', are sentences of the same grammatical form, people are liable to suppose that they also express the same form of proposition, but this is not the case. To say that cats are carnivorous is to ascribe an additional quality to beings already presupposed as existing; to say that cats are existent is to say that propositions ascribing to something the properties which constitute the definition of a cat are sometimes true. The distinction is still more obvious in the negative case. If 'dragons are not existent animals' were a proposition of the same form as 'lions are not herbivorous animals', to say that dragons are not existent would already be to presuppose their existence. A lion has to exist in order to have the negative property of not being herbivorous, but in order to be non-existent a dragon need not first exist.[1] 'Dragons are non-existent' means that nothing has the properties commonly implied by the word 'dragon'.

It has sometimes been said that 'the ontological proof' is just an imperfect formulation of a principle which no one can help admitting and which is a necessary presupposition of all knowledge. This is the principle that what we really must think must be true of reality. ('Must' here is the logical, not the psychological must.) If we did not assume this principle, we should never be entitled to accept something as a fact because it satisfies our best intellectual criteria, and therefore we should have no ground for asserting anything at all. Even experience would not help us, since any proposition contradicting experience might well be true if the law of contradiction were not assumed to be objectively valid. This, however, is so very different from what the ontological proof as formulated by its older exponents says that it should not be called by the same name. And in any case the principle that what we must think must be true of reality could only be used to establish the existence of God if we already had reached the conclusion that we must think this, i.e. had already justified the view that God exists (or seen it to be self-evident).

[1] We can of course say that dragons are not herbivorous if we are merely making a statement about the content of fictitious stories of dragons.

222

God

THE FIRST CAUSE ARGUMENT

The *cosmological* or first cause argument is of greater importance. The greatest thinker of the Middle Ages, St. Thomas Aquinas (*circ*. 1225–74), while rejecting the ontological argument, made the cosmological the main intellectual basis of his own theism, and in this respect he has been followed by Roman Catholic orthodoxy. To this day it is often regarded in such circles as proving with mathematical certainty the existence of God. It has, however, also played a very large part in Protestant thought; and an argument accepted in different forms by such varied philosophers of the highest eminence as Aristotle, St. Thomas, Descartes, Locke, Leibniz, and many modern thinkers certainly ought not to be despised. The argument is briefly to the effect that we require a reason to account for the world and this ultimate reason must be of such a kind as itself not to require a further reason to account for it. It is then argued that God is the only kind of being who could be conceived as self-sufficient and so as not requiring a cause beyond himself but being his own reason. The argument has an appeal because we are inclined to demand a reason for things, and the notion of a first cause is the only alternative to the notion of an infinite regress, which is very difficult and seems even self-contradictory. Further, if any being is to be conceived as necessarily existing and so not needing a cause outside itself, it is most plausible to conceive God as occupying this position. But the argument certainly makes assumptions which may be questioned. It assumes the principle of causation in a form in which the cause is held to give a reason for the effect, a doctrine with which I have sympathy but which would probably be rejected by the majority of modern philosophers outside the Roman Catholic Church. Further, it may be doubted whether we can apply to the world as a whole the causal principle which is valid within the world; and if we say that the causal principle thus applied is only analogous to the latter the argument is weakened. Finally, and this I think the most serious point, it is exceedingly difficult to see how anything could be its own reasons. To be this it would seem that it must exist necessarily *a priori*. Now we can well see how it can be necessary *a priori* that something, p, should be true if something else, q, is, or again how it can be necessary *a priori* that something self-contradictory should not exist, but it is quite another matter to see how it could be *a priori* necessary in the logical sense that something should positively exist. What contradiction could there be in its not existing?[1] In the mere blank of non-existence there can be nothing to contradict. I do not say that it can be seen to be absolutely impossible that a being could be its own logical reason, but I at least have not the faintest notion how this could be. The advocates of the cosmological proof might, however, contend that God was necessary in some non-logical sense, which is somewhat less unplausible though still quite incomprehensible to us.

Can the cosmological argument, clearly invalid as a complete proof, be stated in a form which retains some probability value? It may still be argued that the world will at least be more rational if it is as the theist pictures it than if it is not, and that it is more reasonable to suppose that the world is rational than to suppose that it is irrational. Even the latter point would be contradicted by many modern thinkers, but though we cannot prove the view they reject to be true, we should at least note that it is the view which is presupposed by science, often unconsciously, in its own sphere. For, as we have seen, practically no scientific propositions can be established by strict demonstration and/or observation alone. Science could not advance at all if it did not assume some criterion beyond experience and the laws of logic and mathematics. What is this criterion? It seems to be coherence in a rational system. We have rejected the view that this is the only criterion, but it is certainly one criterion of truth. For of two hypotheses equally in accord with the empirical facts, scientists will always prefer the one which makes the universe more of a rational system to the one which does not. Science does this even though neither hypothesis is capable of rationalizing the universe completely or even of giving a complete ultimate explanation of the phenomena in question. It is sufficient that the hypothesis adopted brings us a step nearer to the ideal of a fully coherent, rationally explicable world. Now theism cannot indeed completely rational-

---

[1] It is one of the objections to the ontological proof that it claims to find a contradiction in God not existing.

God

ize the universe till it can show how God can be his own cause,
or how it is that he does not need a cause, and till it can also overcome the problem of evil completely, but it does come nearer to
rationalizing it than does any other view. The usual modern
philosophical views opposed to theism do not try to give any
rational explanation of the world at all, but just take it as a brute
fact not to be explained, and it must certainly be admitted that
we come at least nearer to a rational explanation if we regard the
course of the world as determined by purpose and value than if
we do not. So it may be argued that according to the scientific
principle that we should accept the hypothesis which brings the
universe nearest to a coherent rational system theism should be
accepted by us. The strong point of the cosmological argument is
that after all it does remain incredible that the physical universe
should just have happened, even if it be reduced to the juxta-
position of some trillions of electrons. It calls out for some further
explanation of some kind.

THE ARGUMENT FROM DESIGN

The *teleological argument* or the *argument from design* is the argument from the adaptation of the living bodies of organisms to
their ends and the ends of their species. This is certainly very
wonderful: there are thousands of millions of cells in our brain
knit together in a system which works; twenty or thirty different
muscles are involved even in such a simple act as a sneeze;
directly a wound is inflicted or germs enter an animal's body all
sorts of protective mechanisms are set up, different cells are so
cunningly arranged that, if we cut off the tail of one of the lower
animals, a new one is grown, and the very same cells can develop
according to what is needed into a tail or into a leg. Such intricate
arrangements seem to require an intelligent purposing mind to
explain them. It may be objected that, even if such an argument
shows wisdom in God, it does not show goodness and is therefore of little value. The reply may be made that it is incredible that
a mind who is so much superior to us in intelligence as to have
designed the whole universe should not be at least as good as the

225

best men and should not, to put it at its lowest, care for his off-spring at least as well as a decent human father and much more wisely because of his superior knowledge and intellect. Still it must be admitted that the argument could not at its best establish all that the theist would ordinarily wish to establish. It might show that the designer was very powerful, but it could not show him to be omnipotent or even to have created the world as opposed to manufacturing it out of given material; it might make it probable that he was good, but it could not possibly prove him perfect. And of course the more unpleasant features of the struggle for existence in nature are far from supporting the hypothesis of a good God.

But does the argument justify any conclusion at all? It has been objected that it does not on the following ground. It is an argument from analogy, it is said, to this effect: animal bodies are like machines, a machine has a designer, therefore animal bodies have a designer. But the strength of an argument from analogy depends on the likeness between what is compared. Now animal bodies are really not very like machines, and God is certainly not very like a man. Therefore the argument from analogy based on our experience of men designing machines has not enough strength to give much probability to its conclusion. This criticism, I think, would be valid if the argument from design were really in the main an argument from analogy,[1] but I do not think it is. The force of the argument lies not in the analogy, but in the extraordinary intricacy with which the details of a living body are adapted to serve its own interests, an intricacy far too great to be regarded as merely a coincidence. Suppose we saw pebbles on the shore arranged in such a way as to make an elaborate machine. It is theoretically possible that they might have come to occupy such positions by mere chance, but it is fantastically unlikely, and we should feel no hesitation in jumping to the conclusion that they had been thus deposited not by the tide but by some intelligent agent. Yet the body of the simplest living creature is a more complex machine than the most complex ever devised by a human engineer.

Before the theory of evolution was accepted the only reply to

[1] Hume's criticisms of it in the famous *Dialogues concerning Natural Religion* depend mainly on the assumption that it is such an argument.

this argument was to say that in an infinite time there is room for an infinite number of possible combinations, and therefore it is not, even apart from a designing mind, improbable that there should be worlds or stages in the development of worlds which display great apparent purposiveness. If a monkey played with a typewriter at random, it is most unlikely that it would produce an intelligible book; but granted a sufficient number of billions of years to live and keep playing, the creature would probably eventually produce quite by accident a great number. For the number of possible combinations of twenty-six letters in successions of words is finite, though enormously large, and therefore given a sufficiently long time it is actually probable that any particular one would be reached. This may easily be applied to the occurrence of adaptations in nature. Out of all the possible combinations of things very few would display marked adaptation; but if the number of ingredients of the universe is finite the number of their combinations is also finite, and therefore it is only probable that, given an infinite time, some worlds or some stages in a world process should appear highly purposeful, though they are only the result of a chance combination of atoms. The plausibility of this reply is diminished when we reflect what our attitude would be to somebody who, when playing bridge, had thirteen spades in his hand several times running—according to the laws of probability an enormously less improbable coincidence than would be an unpurposed universe with so much design unaccounted for—and then used such an argument to meet the charge of cheating. Our attitude to his reply would surely hardly be changed even if we believed that people had been playing bridge for an infinite time. If only we were satisfied that matter had existed and gone on changing for ever, would we conclude that the existence of leaves or pebbles on the ground in such positions as to make an intelligible book no longer provided evidence making it probable that somebody had deliberately arranged them? Surely not. And, if not, why should the supposition that matter had gone on changing for ever really upset the argument from design? Of course the appearance of design *may be* fortuitous; the argument from design never claims to give certainty but only probability. But, granted the universe as we have it, is it not a much less improbable hypothesis that it should really have been designed than that it should constitute one of the fantastically rare stages which showed design in an infinite series of chance universes? Further, that matter has been changing for an infinite time is a gratuitous assumption and one not favoured by modern science.[1]

But now the theory of evolution claims to give an alternative explanation of the adaptation of organisms that removes the improbability of which we have complained. Once granted the existence of some organisms their offspring would not all be exactly similar. Some would necessarily be somewhat better equipped than others for surviving and producing offspring in their turn, and their characteristics would therefore tend to be more widely transmitted. When we take vast numbers into account, this will mean that a larger and larger proportion of the species will have had relatively favourable variations transmitted to them by their parents, while unfavourable variations will tend to die out. Thus from small beginnings accumulated all the extraordinarily elaborate mechanism which now serves the purpose of living creatures.

There can be no question for a properly informed person of denying the evolution theory, but only of considering whether it is adequate by itself to explain the striking appearance of design. If it is not, it may perfectly well be combined with the metaphysical hypothesis that a mind has designed and controls the universe. Evolution will then be just the way in which God's design works out. Now in reply to the purely evolutionary explanation it has been said that for evolution to get started at all some organisms must have already appeared. Otherwise the production of offspring and their survival or death in the struggle for existence would not have come into question at all. But even the simplest living organism is a machine very much more com-

[1] Strictly speaking, what is required by those who put forward the objection in question to the argument from design is not necessarily that matter should have been changing for an infinite time but only for a sufficiently long, though finite, time. But the length of time allowed by modern science for the development of the earth and indeed for that of the whole universe does not in the faintest degree approach what would be needed to make the appearance of organized beings as a result of mere random combinations of atoms anything less than monstrously improbable.

plex than a motor car. Therefore, if it would be absurd to suppose inorganic matter coming together fortuitously of itself to form a motor car, it would be even more absurd to suppose it thus coming together to form an organism, so without design the evolutionary process would never get started at all. Nor, even granting that this miracle had occurred, could the evolutionists claim that they had been altogether successful in removing the antecedent improbability of such an extensive adaptation as is in fact shown by experience. It has been urged that, since we may go wrong in a vast number of ways for one in which we may go right, the probability of favourable variations is very much less than that of unfavourable; that in order to produce the effect on survival required a variation would have to be large, but if it were large it would usually lessen rather than increase the chance of survival, unless balanced by other variations the occurrence of which simultaneously with the first would be much more improbable still; and that the odds are very great against either a large number of animals in a species having the variations together by chance or their spreading from a single animal through the species by natural selection. The arguments suggest that, so to speak, to weight the chances we require a purpose, which we should not need, however, to think of as intervening at odd moments but as controlling the whole process. The establishment of the evolution theory no doubt lessens the great improbability of the adaptations having occurred without this, but the original improbability is so vast as to be able to survive a great deal of lessening, and it does not remove it.

Some thinkers would regard it as adequate to postulate an unconscious purpose to explain design, but it is extraordinarily difficult to see what such a thing as an unconscious purpose could be. In one sense indeed I can understand such a phrase. 'Unconscious' might mean 'unintrospected' or 'unintrospectible', and then the purpose would be one which occurred in a mind that did think on the matter but did not self-consciously notice its thinking. But this sense will not do here, for it already presupposes a mind. To talk of a purpose which is not present in any mind at all seems to me as unintelligible as it would be to talk of rectangles which had no extension. The argument from design has therefore

God

to my mind considerable, though not, by itself at least, conclusive force. It is also strange that there should be so much beauty in the world, that there should have resulted from an unconscious unintelligent world beings who could form the theory that the world was due to chance or frame moral ideals in the light of which they could condemn it. It might be suggested that a mind designed the organic without designing the inorganic, but the connection between organic and inorganic and the unity of the world in general are too close to make this a plausible view.

The counter argument from evil is of course formidable, but I shall defer discussion of it to a later stage in the chapter, as it is rather an argument against theism in general than a specific objection to the argument from design. I must, however, make two remarks here. First, it is almost a commonplace that the very large amount of apparent waste in nature is a strong prima facie argument against the world having been designed by a good and wise being. But is there really much 'wasted'? A herring may produce hundreds of thousands or millions of eggs for one fish that arrives at maturity, but most of the eggs which come to grief serve as food for other animals. We do not look on the eggs we eat at breakfast, when we can get them, as 'wasted', though the hen might well do so. It is certainly very strange that a good God should have designed a world in which the living beings can only maintain their life by devouring each other, but this is part of the general problem of evil and not a specific problem of waste in nature. Secondly, the occurrence of elaborate adaptations to ends is a very much stronger argument for the presence of an intelligence than its apparent absence in a good many instances is against it. A dog would see no purpose whatever in my present activity, but he would not therefore have adequate grounds for concluding that I had no intelligence. If there is a God, it is only to be expected *a priori* that in regard to a great deal of his work we should be in the same position as the dog is in regard to ours, and therefore the fact that we are in this position is no argument that there is no God. The occurrence of events requiring intelligence to explain them is positive evidence for the presence of intelligence, but the absence of results we think worth while in particular cases is very slight evidence indeed on the other side where we are debating the existence of a being whose intelligence, if he exists, we must in any case assume to be as much above ours as the maker of the whole world would have to be. The existence of positive evil of course presents a greater difficulty to the theist.

OTHER ARGUMENTS FOR GOD

Besides the specific argument from design there is a general argument which on the whole impresses me more strongly. When I consider the physical world as a whole, its order, its beauty, its system strongly suggest that it is a product of mind, or at any rate that the least inadequate category for interpreting it is mind. It displays the characteristics which we expect in and regard as essentially connected with a high-grade mind and its products. And in particular the characteristic of beauty has made very many feel as though they saw through it not only the wisdom but the supreme goodness of God.

The cosmological argument and the argument from design have often been supplemented or even replaced by other arguments based on the nature of causation. Two I have already mentioned, namely, the argument that causation involves will[1] and the argument that it is incredible that conscious rational mind should have originated from unconscious irrational matter.[2] The latter seems to depend mainly on the assumption that the effect cannot possess quite new kinds of properties which are not present in the cause. A stronger argument seems to me to be that it is exceedingly difficult to see how we can be entitled to have faith in our intellectual processes at all if they originally spring from unconscious matter alone. The case seems clearest if we start by thinking of the epiphenomenalist. According to him the only cause of a mental event is a physical change in the brain. In that case we do not believe anything because we have good reasons for it, but only because something has changed in our brain. It would follow that all our beliefs were unjustified, and this has already been used

---

[1] *Vide* above p. 170,   [2] *Vide* above, pp. 136–8.

by me as an objection to epiphenomenalism. Most opponents of theism are, however, not epiphenomenalists. They believe that mental processes can play a part in causing other mental, and even bodily, processes. But, if they believe that these, even *ultimately*, originate solely from an unconscious, or at least (even if pan-psychism be true) an unintelligent, matter incapable of purposes and itself not directed or created by a purposing mind, it may be argued that they are only putting the difficulty further back. Have we any guarantee that we are so constructed that our mental processes are any more likely to be right than wrong if they were the result originally of mere unpurposed accidents?[1] For us to be entitled to accept any of the results of our thought on any subject, must we not therefore assume that our mental processes, and the bodily ones on which they depend, are originated for a purpose and a purpose we can trust? It may thus be contended that a certain faith is needed even to be a scientist or a critical philosopher; we must trust the universe so far as to believe that it has not made us such as to be irretrievably misled in our thought by the nature of our minds or bodies, and is it consistent to assume this in the sphere of thought without also assuming that it is in general trustworthy? If we must, in order to escape complete scepticism, treat the universe as if it were made with a good purpose at least as regards our thinking, is this not an argument for taking up the attitude that its purpose is also conducive to the fulfilment of the best moral ideals that can be conceived? The pre-supposition of this argument is simply that we cannot be thorough-going sceptics. It will not appeal to anybody who is prepared to adopt the position of complete scepticism about everything; but is there such a person? Even confirmed agnostics about religion and metaphysics are very far from being complete sceptics about science or about their sense-experience, yet even this much departure from scepticism involves assumptions as to the validity of their mental processes which are hard to square with their beliefs as to the

---

[1] Someone might reply that a species of beings whose faculties are not so constructed that they could find out truths about the world or at least act as if they had found them out would soon become extinct; but this reply like any other argument must already presuppose the reliability of our mental processes and therefore cannot be used to justify trust in the latter without a vicious circle.

origin of the latter. Nor does it seem an adequate reply to the argument merely to assert agnosticism as to the ultimate origin of the human mind. If we are not entitled to say anything more than that, are we entitled to trust our minds at all, since we have *ex hypothesi* no justification for thinking that they have been constructed for the purpose of attaining any truth? We cannot argue that they may be trusted merely because trusting them has worked, because we can only decide whether they have worked or not by using our minds and therefore by already trusting them. (The argument is not of course intended to imply that God created each man's mind specially at birth, only that the whole world-process on which we depend is subject to divine guidance.)

If the view about matter known as idealism is accepted on general philosophical grounds, it may be used to provide an additional argument for the existence of God, as it was by Berkeley. The idealist, having by means of his arguments reached the conclusion that matter necessarily involves mind, may then argue that we must believe it to be independent of human minds and must therefore suppose a super-human mind on which it depends for its existence. The conclusion is based on two premises one or the other of which has been accepted by the great majority of philosophers. The great majority of philosophers have either been idealists so far as to believe that matter logically implies mind or realists so far as to believe that matter is independent of our minds. Nor are the two premises, though not usually combined, in themselves incompatible with each other. The difficulty is to establish the first premise by arguments which will not refute the second. For most of the arguments used by idealists are of such a character as to show, if valid at all, not merely that physical objects imply dependence on some mind or other, but that they imply dependence on the human mind or are mere abstractions from human experience, or at least that, if they exist independently of us, we are not justified in making any assertions about them. An idealism based on such arguments could not consistently be used as a ground for theism. There are, however, some idealist arguments which do not have this effect and the idealist who was also a theist might rely on those.

God

MORAL ARGUMENTS. ETHICS AND RELIGION

Turning to *moral arguments* for the existence of God, we must remark at the start that such arguments necessarily presuppose certain views as to ethics. If we regard ethical propositions as simply statements about what emotions and mental reactions human beings have as a matter of fact under given conditions, I do not see how we can possibly use ethics as a basis of any valid argument for the existence of God. Still less can we do so if we regard our ethical words as merely expressing the speaker's emotions and not anything objectively true at all. To put this in technical terms, any ethical argument for the existence of God must presuppose a theory of ethics which is not 'naturalist' or 'subjectivist', i.e. which regards ethical words neither as expressing concepts analysable simply in terms of a natural science such as psychology or biology nor as simply expressions of the state of the speaker as an individual without objective validity. It is a precondition for using ethics as a ground for theism that we should neither regard it as merely a branch of psychology nor adopt a sceptical view of its claim to objective validity. Whether a naturalist or subjectivist view of ethics should be taken is a question for the special branch of philosophy known as ethics or moral philosophy, a study of which is not included in the purpose of this book; and I can only say here that it seems to me quite clear on purely ethical grounds, that no such views should be adopted. This decision is independent of their metaphysical repercussions.

The main objections to naturalism in general may be summed up as follows: (1) It is clear that no ethical proposition is simply equivalent to a collection of psychological statistics. To say that all or most people's reactions to something are favourable is not to say that it is good or right. (2) The goodness or badness of anything which is' good or bad follows *necessarily* from its nature, but the attitude of human beings to it might quite conceivably be different from what it is. (3) Whatever empirical property, e.g. being desired or liked, is put forward as a definition of 'good' or 'obligatory', it is clear that the question whether anything that is good (or obligatory) has that property is not merely a question of definition but a question of fact, goodness and the property still appearing as different concepts and not as synonyms. (4) The naturalist definitions leave out the essential nature of obligation. The 'ought' is different from the 'is'.

The subjectivist view that ethical judgements are merely expressions of the speaker's own attitude is open to similar objections and also to others peculiar to itself. Thus, if the view were true, no two persons would ever mean the same thing when they made an ethical judgement, nor would even the same person mean the same thing at different times. Further, if I judged something to be good and you judged it to be bad, our judgements would not be logically incompatible; and when I judged, e.g. that Hitler acted badly, I should not be talking about Hitler at all but only about my own psychology. Nor could ethical judgements be even supported by arguments (except perhaps ones which had the effect of disclosing new facts about the speaker's psychology).

Granting then that our ethical judgements have objective validity and are neither mere expressions of the speaker's subjective attitude nor purely factual statements about men's attitudes in general, can we use them as the basis of a good argument for the existence of God? We must not suppose that we can have no ethics without a theology or that a man cannot do right unless he believes in God. The latter proposition is contradicted by empirical facts; and the former is incompatible with our ability to see the truth of ethical propositions without presupposing theological. We can surely see that it is bad, e.g. to inflict pain unnecessarily by merely considering the question on its own merits without first having to presuppose the existence of God. Further, we could only rationally deduce ethics from theology by first deciding what actions were right and then assuming that God, being good, would wish us to do those actions, and such a line of argument obviously presupposes that we already have a conception of ethics. Even those who accept their theology solely on the strength of revelation as Christians can have little justification for doing so if they do not first assume at least that Christ is good, and this would already presuppose our possession of ethical criteria which enable us to realize independently of theology that He is good.

God

But it does not follow from this that we may not be justified in drawing theological conclusions from our ethics. Because ethics cannot be derived from theology, it does not follow that theology, or a large part of it, cannot be derived from ethics; and many attempts have been made in this direction. The best known is that of Kant. The latter's argument, shorn of excrescences, is to this effect. We are bound by the essential nature of morality to form an ideal of a supreme good which cannot be completely realized in this life. Further, since we are dependent not only on our own efforts but on the co-operation of nature, we must suppose, if the ideal is to be capable of realization at all, not only that we survive bodily death but that nature is controlled in such a way as to subserve the ideal in a future life or lives, as well as in this. This we can only conceive if we think of the world as controlled by a morally perfect being having adequate power and wisdom to adjust it to the supreme end, i.e. if we accept the belief in God. The belief in God is therefore vindicated for Kant because without it we should have to regard the moral law as sending us on a wild-goose chase, i.e. commanding us to seek what could never be achieved. This argument cannot be regarded as logically conclusive but has some probability value. Kant himself in a later work, and many other thinkers, have argued from the existence of the moral law to a law-giver, God. This argument has also been used: The moral law is objective. In what, then, does it reside? Certainly not in the physical world. Nor only in the minds of men. An ethical proposition such as that it is better to forgive one's enemies than to hate them might be true even at a time when no human being realized its truth at all. Yet it is impossible to see what else the moral law could reside in but a mind. Therefore we must postulate a super-human mind. Such arguments have the advantage, if valid, of directly establishing not only the existence, but the perfect goodness of the supreme mind. A being in whom the whole moral law resided could hardly fail to be perfectly good. Apart from its realization in such a mind the moral law would be merely a hypothetical fact to the effect that if we did so and so it would be right, and it may be argued that such a mere hypothetical non-existent abstraction could not have the authority we know in our hearts it has. I do not think we can

God

regard any of these arguments as logically conclusive, but they do at least give some support to their conclusion.

The supreme authority of the moral law is certainly best explained if it can be thought of as bound up with the essential structure, the fundamental groundwork of the real, thus implying that this is spiritual. On the other hand we must not think of it as being the arbitrary product of God's will. It is incredible that even God could make the wanton infliction of pain good by willing it, any more than he could make $2+2$ equal to 5, whether we think of the moral law as something independent of God which limits him or (a more usual religious conception) as immanent in God. In the latter case he still could not violate or alter it, because he would thereby be contradicting his own nature.

The connection between ethics and religion is close, though the former is certainly possible without a conscious belief in the latter. Indeed the attitude of any man, in so far as he is good, to the moral law is significantly like the attitude of the religious man to God. To both is ascribed an absolute and unconditional authority and a sanctity which transcends any other values. It may be argued that, if we do not worship God, we must worship the moral law and that is unworshippable because it is a mere abstraction. On the other hand to reject ethics because one could not believe in the existence of God would in any case be unjustified, because, while some ethical propositions such as that we ought to consider other people's happiness as well as our own are about as certain as anything can be, we cannot give nearly *that degree* of certainty to the belief that ethics entails God. If two beliefs which we are inclined to accept are incompatible we must accept the more certain, and therefore if we decide theism to be false we must reject the view that ethics entails theism rather than the view that some ethical propositions are true.

It is sometimes said that God might be good and yet not act according to our ethical standards. But there are only two alternatives here: either our ethical propositions are false, or a good being, in so far as he is good, must act in accord with them, though he may also act in accord with others which we do not know. No doubt some ethical propositions commonly believed are false or partly false, but *in so far as* our ethical propositions are true, to say that a good God might still not act in accordance with them is like saying that for a perfectly wise God $5+7$ might not be equal to 12. If anything is evident in ethics, it is that love and benevolence are better than hate and indifference, and therefore we may be quite confident that a good God will love and concern Himself closely with the welfare of the beings dependent on Him. The argument is: God is good, goodness entails love, therefore God loves.

In order to appreciate the strength of the theistic case it is not sufficient to look at each argument separately. We need also to consider their cumulative force. It would often be admitted even in religious circles that each argument, considered by itself, stopped far short of cogent proof, and yet held that the arguments taken all together constituted a very strong case indeed. While it would of course be impossible to estimate the probability given by such arguments mathematically, we may illustrate by this means how probability can be increased by different converging lines of argument. Suppose an argument which by itself only made its conclusion twice as probable as not, i.e. gave it a probability of $\frac{2}{3}$. Suppose four more, independent arguments which had the same effect. Then the probability of the conclusion being false relatively to the arguments taken together would be only $(\frac{1}{3})^5$, i.e., $\frac{1}{243}$.

THE 'ARGUMENT FROM RELIGIOUS EXPERIENCE'

It may be very much doubted, however, whether all these arguments would inspire a real faith in God, though they might lead someone to intellectual assent to his existence as a probable hypothesis, unless the man's heart were touched by some experience not the result wholly of argument or even describable fully in intellectual terms. This brings one to the so-called *argument from religious experience*, on which in Protestant philosophical circles the main stress is now usually laid. It is, strictly speaking, however not an argument but a claim to intuitive awareness, at least in any form in which it deserves very much attention philosophically. The mere existence of religious emotion could hardly

of itself constitute a valid ground for asserting the existence of
God, but what is meant by the appeal to religious experience is
usually the claim in states where this religious emotion is present
to have a direct apprehension, not based on inference, of the
existence and to some extent the nature of God. There is a clear
difference between a religious emotion and a religious belief, as
there is between, e.g. a mere feeling of happiness and a belief that
something good has happened or is going to happen; and there is
no doubt that both religious emotion and religious belief are
present in very many cases where the belief is not founded mainly
on argument, even on bad arguments. The only question is
whether one is justified in accepting as true such an intuitive belief
apart from the arguments, i.e. in regarding it as a genuine intuition. We have seen that we cannot dispense with intuition in our
theory of knowledge,[1] so the mere fact that the claim is an appeal
to intuition does not discredit it. It has, however, been objected
that the assertion of an intuitive conviction can be of no help in a
discussion on the ground that, if I have the conviction already,
I do not need to be convinced of it, while, if I do not have it, the
mere statement of the fact that somebody else has it will be no
ground for my accepting it apart from any argument he may give.
But suppose this situation: A man has a confused and rather feeble
intuitive conviction of God. He is aware that what seems to him a
reliable intuition may not really be so, and he would certainly not
be justified in placing any considerable faith in the intuition if he
thought himself to be the only person who had it. But if he finds
that it is very widespread and possessed in a stronger and clearer
degree by very many men who in other respects quite especially
deserve the titles of good, wise and great, this may well justify
him in trusting it. This is a very common situation, I think, as
regards religious intuition. We must not suppose this intuition
to be limited to a few great mystics; it is in some (though a much
lesser) degree possessed by the plain man who says 'I cannot
prove, but I feel there is a God', when in saying this he is really
sincere. By 'feel' he does not mean 'has an emotion'. It would
not make sense to say 'I have an emotion that'. The word is only

---

[1] *Vide* above, p. 48.

a synonym for 'believe' or at least for some particular way of believing. The fact that very many people have an intuition is indeed hardly likely to convince anyone who has no glimmering of it himself, but even such a person will be unreasonable if he takes it for granted that those who have it are necessarily wrong because he has not got it himself. He may well be relatively to them in the same position as a tone-deaf man is relatively to a musician, though it must be admitted that you can hardly expect him to accept its truth merely on their authority. But if a person has the conviction in a weaker degree, he may justifiably confirm it, that is, hold the probability of its truth to have been strengthened, by appealing to the authority of those who have it in a higher degree. Intuitive religious conviction has been so widespread and such a dominating factor in the thought of many, we might indeed say 'most', who were in other respects obviously among the greatest and best of mankind, and so much the basis throughout history of a whole extraordinarily persistent, fertile and fundamental side of life and thought as to constitute a strong prima facie case for the view that there is at least a great deal in it.

In very many cases the intuitive conviction is attained or maintained after a very prolonged meditation on the question and exercises a tremendous transforming influence on the believer's whole life and conduct. It further seems to him 'to make sense' not only of his own life but of the whole universe. Those who have had it very strongly have been able to make it the basis of a serenity and goodness which in many cases might be described as almost superhuman, and for vast multitudes the worthwhileness of life and the ability to bear misfortune worthily and to live unselfishly have seemed to depend, for themselves at least, on the experience in question. We must not indeed think of religious intuition as consisting in the seeing of certain definite clear-cut propositions to be self-evident as in logic. Such a claim would be very hard to defend. What presents itself to intuition must rather be regarded as something confused needing further clarification and analysis. The content of a genuine intuition may also be mixed up with other elements which have really been accepted on the strength of authority and, perhaps fallacious, reasoning. Only in such ways can we account for the differences between intuitions.

We must also of course insist that the intuitive faculty requires training and is capable of development.

Religious beliefs are after all only in the same position as other fundamental beliefs in not being strictly provable. By 'fundamental belief' I mean a belief presupposed by a whole important department of human thought. When we consider belief in memory, in an external world, in minds other than one's own, in induction, in ethics, we are driven back to something which we either cannot prove at all or at least cannot prove in a way which wins general agreement among philosophers, yet we continue unflinchingly to hold the beliefs. It is doubtful whether it is possible to give a more plausible case for the reliability of induction or for the existence of the physical world than it is for the existence of God, only the ability to cognize God is less widely distributed or at least less widely developed than the ability to cognize the physical world and see the validity of inductive inferences.

The main positive objections to the claims of religious intuition are made by dogmatic empiricists who assert that knowledge is limited to sense-experience, but as we have seen[1] this dogma cannot be proved. There must be some intuition if there is to be inference at all, and there is no way of determining by *a priori* argument in what fields intuition is or is not possible. Any argument against it must therefore be an empirical generalization, which would need to be of this form: No veridical cognition of class A occurs. Veridical religious intuition, if it occurred, would be a veridical cognition of class A. Therefore it does not occur. But the major premise cannot be established as a universal generalization without first assuming that religious intuition is not veridical, so the argument begs the question unless the major premise means merely that no veridical cognition of class A *other than religious intuition* occurs. In that case it becomes only an argument from analogy to the effect that religious intuition is so very different from any other cases of cognition which can be regarded as veridical that its claims to be veridical should be dismissed. But if the religious man is right, we have every reason to expect that religious cognition will be different from any other kinds of

[1] *Vide* above, pp. 39-42

cognition, since its object and the relation of its object to us are so very different. He himself usually most strongly emphasizes the difference when he speaks about it. So the argument must be regarded as a very weak one, even if it could be shown that there are no other authenticated cases of cognition in the least analogous to religious intuition.

It is, however, objected that apparent religious intuition can be explained by psychology. All beliefs must have psychological causes and so can be explained psychologically—I do not think there is room for undetermined free-will in the sphere of belief at any rate—so it depends on the nature of the explanation whether it shows the belief to be unjustified. Now no doubt the causal explanations given by e.g. anti-religious Freudians are of such a kind that we can say that any belief caused in such a way would be unjustified, and in general we may say that a belief due simply to a desire to hold the belief must be unjustified for the person who thus holds it. But the psychologist can have no means of proving that the beliefs are due to the causes he suggests. He can only point out certain factors which might lead people to hold a religious belief even if it were false. The most he can say is that the religious man *may* have been prejudiced by his desires, not prove that he has been, and the risk of being thus prejudiced by one's desires is present in the case of any argument which leads to a pleasant belief (and by one's fears in any argument which leads to an unpleasant one). We are not obliged to abandon all arguments which lead to such conclusions because we *may* have been prejudiced, though we ought to do our level best not to be prejudiced. The same applies to apparent intuitions. And the theist can retort that, if there are some factors which would make a man likely to hold a belief in God even if it were false, there are others which would make him likely to reject the belief even if it were true. For (1) prima facie appearances are very much against it. There is a complete absence of direct evidence for it in everyday experience, and whatever our ultimate decision as to the problem of evil, there can be no doubt that prima facie the existence of evil, at least on the scale on which it does exist, *seems* completely inconsistent with the creation and control of the world by a perfectly good omnipotent God. (2) We are most of our life absorbed in everyday concerns of this world which make it very difficult for us to get away from them sufficiently to concentrate our full energies on an attempt to 'find religion', and relatively few people have the zeal to do that. Few, if any, who have done it have ultimately failed in the attempt, and a person who has not tried is certainly not justified in taking for granted that those who have made the effort are deluded in the view that they have succeeded. So if the atheist can explain how people can be theists even if theism is false, the theist can explain rather more plausibly how people can be atheists or agnostics even if theism is true and capable of discovery by intuition.

So the religious man, provided he has faced the difficulties and retains his intuitive conviction unimpaired after having honestly asked himself whether it may not be merely due to his desire to believe, need not be much worried by the doubts of the psychologist, unless indeed he insists on claiming absolute certainty for the belief in God, which would in any case be unreasonable. He may be wrong, but he need not have an uneasy feeling that he is a fool for holding the belief. A study of theory of knowledge can show that we cannot expect to prove everything and that it is legitimate to have a faith in intuitions if certain conditions are fulfilled, especially if we also do our best to use our powers of inference about the subject. To a man who knows the belief from the inside, so to speak, the psychological explanations offered will probably appear just puerile and absurd.

We may add that it is by no means such a simple task as might be thought to explain religion by a reference to wish fulfilment. Religious beliefs are by no means always pleasant to the person who holds them or is on the verge of doing so. The acceptance of religious beliefs has often exposed those who adopted them to terrible persecution, it has often intensified their sense of sin till this became agonizing, it has inspired the dread of hell. I do not wish for a moment to countenance the morbid exaggerated sense of sin or the belief in eternal hell which have been far too often prevalent in religious circles, but am merely citing these to show that we cannot explain religious conviction simply by the desire to believe what is pleasant, because the beliefs have often been acutely painful. People who have undergone religious conversion have commonly represented themselves as fighting against the new belief for a long time till they adopted it. The psychologist is of course not beaten yet; he may have a theory to account for the beliefs indirectly as, e.g. masochistic, but he can only do so by making his explanation highly elaborate and far-fetched, and the more complex he makes his explanation the less probable it becomes. The position would be much more favourable for him if the religious beliefs people adopted were uniformly such as would naturally be most pleasant to them and made no unwelcome demands on them. No doubt in the case of a particular person the belief in God may be explained by the desire to believe and the belief is then unjustified for the person in question. But that this is so with all intuitive religious beliefs is a very far-reaching assumption which cannot possibly be proved or even supported by arguments, the most that can be maintained is that it is *possible* that they should have been so caused. This is all that I can say about the question in general: no doubt we should find a good deal more to criticize if there were space to go into the particular explanations given in detail.

But of course great caution is necessary in accepting ostensible religious intuitions as giving the exact truth. It is difficult to separate intuition from what is due to authority or to argument; and although we are not entitled therefore to dismiss all intuition, the differences between beliefs held intuitively by different people in different religions may well be explained on these grounds. However the fact that a person is already familiar with a certain doctrine need not exclude the possibility of his being able later to verify it by an intuitive insight which he did not have when he was first taught it, and in many cases the experience has led a man to embrace views which he never held before.

What, then, does religious intuition establish, if anything? We must clearly be very doubtful about it when it is put forward as a justification for believing without argument the peculiar doctrines of particular sects. But when we are concerned with the most fundamental beliefs of religion the position is different, and a good intuitive basis can be claimed for at least two such religious beliefs. The first is the belief in the fundamental goodness of reality, by which I mean that goodness somehow preponderates, not that some things are not bad. This belief is essential to religion in the sense that without it a religious attitude to reality could not be justifiable. For religion is an attitude either to reality as a whole or to the fundamental principle or being on which reality is based, and it could not be desirable—still less, as religion holds, the supreme good—to enter into a relation of communion or worship with what was not good. The value claimed for their experience by religious people is inseparably bound up with the value of its object. What I have said here is not necessarily contradicted by religions which stress the badness of this world, because they have asserted or suggested the supreme goodness of a more ultimate reality behind this bad world. Buddhism, despite its alleged pessimism, regards everything as morally governed by the law of justice or Kharma, and believes in a 'Nirvana' which most scholars now think usually means not annihilation but a supremely good positive state. This rather than the evil phenomenal world represents for the Buddhist ultimate reality, and this most or all human beings will eventually attain.

The second belief to which I refer is that in a personal God, or at least a God who is best conceived as personal relatively to us. It certainly cannot be contended that all deeply religious men have believed in such a God, but it may be contended that the religious attitude essentially involves emotions and states of mind which have only a point and sense as directed towards a being conceived as having attributes which we can only think of as personal. I am referring to love, adoration, gratitude, devotion. These are all parts of the normal religious attitude to God, and they are all states of mind which imply essentially as their object a being having at least consciousness and the capacity for deliberate benevolence. This does not of course mean that a man like Spinoza who had no place for the doctrine of the personality of God was not religious, only that he was inconsistent in adopting an attitude which was not in accord with his metaphysics. (Similarly I should not call, e.g. Eddington a bad scientist because I disagreed with his theory as to the philosophical assumptions necessary for science. I should only say that his science was inconsistent with his philosophy.) To the belief in a personal God it is, however, objected that God must be conceived as so much

God

above us that we cannot reasonably apply to him such a category as personality, involving.as it does, in the only forms in which we know it, limitations incompatible with deity. The difficulty about this is that, if we do not think of God in personal terms, there is no higher category in terms of which we can think Him, and so we shall not be able to form any conception of Him at all, or else think of Him as a sort of non-conscious force, which will be to make Him sub-personal rather than super-personal. We may say at least that to think of God in personal terms is the least mis-leading way we have of thinking of Him, and that to accord with religious intuition God must in some form possess all that is of value in the essential attributes of personality, though they may of course be combined with other attributes which are quite beyond our power of comprehension. In the direction of ascribing personality to God even Christian orthodox theology does not go further than this. Perhaps the difference is one less of kind than of degree of emphasis, for the mystic who believes in an impersonal God would surely admit that the analogy of personality had some value, though it was not to be taken literally, and most Christian theologians would presumably admit that it is rash to say that personality in God is to be conceived as more than analogous to personality in ourselves. In addition to the beliefs I have men-tioned there seems to be an awareness of a quality of 'holiness' quite unique and irreducible to other values.

In describing these beliefs as fundamental to religion I do not mean that people could not psychologically take up a religious attitude without holding them. People can commit all sorts of inconsistencies. What I mean is that such an attitude would be irrational and unfitting in the sense in which it is irrational and unfitting to praise what is bad or to be angry with an inanimate thing. Some people contend that the value of religion lies solely in the psychological states it engenders and their moral effects, and that these might remain whatever one's metaphysical beliefs; but it may be retorted that, if the objective beliefs are unjustified, to advocate such a religion is equivalent to urging one to live in a fool's paradise. It is hardly possible and is certainly not worthy of a rational being to maintain a lasting emotional state of con-fidence in the universe if he recognizes that the confidence is without any objective foundation, and it should surely be for the religious man a great sin to go on worshipping what he recognizes to be unworthy of worship.

Of the two beliefs I have mentioned the first is commonly inferred by Christians from the second, but has by very many people especially in the East been held without it. It is necessary if the sense of peace and security characteristic of the religious life are to be maintained and is the most important element in the intuition of the mystic. The second belief will entail the first if we think of God as morally good and dominating the world to such an extent as at least to secure the ultimate triumph of good over evil, and this is of course the usual view of the theist. Indeed most theists would go further and say that God must be conceived as completely omnipotent if the religious consciousness is to attain satisfaction. God seems to be intuited not only as good but as absolutely supreme.

THE PROBLEM OF EVIL

But it is objected that the existence of a good and omnipotent God is incompatible with the fact of evil. Such an objection could not indeed at the worst disprove the existence of God, because God might be conceived as limited by external obstacles of some kind so that he could not prevent the evil, but such a conception of God is in any form in which it has yet been put forward very unsatisfying to the religious mind and would only be acquiesced in if absolutely necessary. It does in fact seem to conflict with religious intuition. It is not therefore a matter for surprise that strenuous attempts have been made to suggest some solution of the problem which would preserve God's omnipotence. A course adopted sometimes has been to declare evil unreal, but if this solution means what it says it is clearly intolerable. For it contradicts either our most certain judgements of introspection or our most certain judgements of ethics. If we say that we did not really feel the pain we thought we felt or commit the sins we thought we committed, then we are contradicting some of our most certain judgements of introspection and memory. If we say that we really felt the pain and really committed the sins but that these are not really evil, we are contradicting the most certain judgements of ethics.

A more common and less unpromising solution is to say that much evil is necessary for the attainment of a greater good. This might be thought to imply a limitation of the omnipotence of God, but when philosophers have attributed omnipotence to Him they have usually not meant that He could do things which were logically impossible such as make $2+2$ equal 5 or create a being who was both a man and not a man in the same sense of 'man'. Certainly, if God is omnipotent in this sense, the problem of evil is insoluble. In that case we can never argue that the creation of a world containing evil is justified as a means to a greater good. For a god who was omnipotent in that sense could have produced the good without the evil even if the former necessarily depended on the latter. But it seems pretty clear that such a conception of God's omnipotence is self-contradictory in any case. If we suppose the existence of a power to do self-contradictory things we are already postulating something self-contradictory. But what has usually been meant by calling God omnipotent is not that He could do anything whatever, but that He could do anything which was not logically impossible and that he was not limited by anything outside Himself. God might well be omnipotent in this sense and yet be incapable of producing some kinds of goods without some evil. Similarly He might be omnipotent in this sense and yet be incapable of producing certain goods without incurring the *possibility* of evil.

The last sentence brings one to a very widely adopted solution of part of the problem of evil. It is said that, if man is to be a moral being, he must have freedom and this freedom implies the absence of complete determination even by God. But in so far as man has undetermined freedom, there can from the nature of the case be no guarantee against his abusing the freedom. If there were, he would be determined to do right, and not undetermined. God could not therefore prevent men from sinning without taking away their freedom and thus destroying most of what is of value in them. This enables one to avoid admitting that God is the author of sin. He merely permits it, as He must if man is to have the freedom to act morally. Even if indeterminism is accepted, this will however hardly solve the whole problem, since there are many evils which cannot be traced to the abuse of human free-will.

In order to deal with these evils we must therefore fall back on the supposition that the actual occurrence of certain evils and not merely their possibility is justified because it is necessary for the production of good,[1] and this will be for a determinist the only way of solution for all evils. Now it is a fact that there are many kinds of good, including some, perhaps all, of the highest we know, which could not be attained without the occurrence of evil. How could there be moral good without temptation and obstacles and therefore without some evil, at least in the form of pain and thwarting? How could there be courage without pain, difficulties and danger? How could there be love of the highest kind we know if there were never the slightest occasion for sympathy and self-sacrifice? Not all the goods we know but very many involve for their realization evil. And a world which involved these latter goods might well be better than a world which did not in spite of the attendant evil. We must have evil to conquer if we are to have the very great good of conquering it. There may be other kinds of love and virtue such as superhuman beings might be conceived as enjoying which do not involve any evil, but if so they will be different in kind from ours, and the more different kinds of good the better. That might even supply an explanation for the theist why God created us, namely, there is something that we can do which even God could not do of Himself without us, i.e produce the kind of goods which involve evil. And if the evil is really necessary for their production and does not outweigh their goodness, this would justify the production of evil. The theist need not indeed suppose that God specially intervened to produce each evil as a means to a greater good. He need only suppose that it is to the good that there should be some evils of a certain kind and some general laws relating to them, even though by accidental interplay or the badness of men these may sometimes yield a particular evil which does not carry with it a corresponding good. This solution would not deny the reality of evil.

[1] Unless we are prepared to ascribe free will, e.g. to disease germs and volcanoes.

God

Evil is there to be conquered; for it to be a real conquest of real value we must have real evil. Nor should the solution discourage us from fighting against evil, for evil can only be a means to the good if fought against and conquered.

It must be added, however, that, in view of the magnitude and distribution of the evil in the world, such a solution of the problem of evil cannot be regarded as in the least degree plausible unless there is survival of bodily death. If we take this life alone, it is surely incredible that the world can have been produced by a perfectly good and omnipotent God. This is a strong argument for a future life if we accept theism, and I cannot see any theoretical objection to postulating such a life. Another argument is that we must conceive of a really good God as loving the personalities He creates, and if He loves them how could He allow their annhilation?

The evil in this world is undoubtedly terribly great, but we cannot possibly know how great the evils are which are needed for the attainment of the best. The greatest goods of character are realized in combating the greatest evils. Nor is it fair to expect the theist to show how each particular evil is conducive to the good; even if his view is true, it is not to be expected that a human being could possibly see this about each particular evil with the limited knowledge at his disposal. Some people find the suffering of the innocent the greatest problem, but a universe in which happiness was always in exact proportion to goodness would hardly be one conducive to disinterested action, nor would a good man, in so far as he was really good, grudge equal happiness to others less good than himself.[1] The belief in an omnipotent and perfect God cannot therefore be dismissed as necessarily impossible because of the problem of evil.

A great many other problems arise in connection with the concept of God which have been much discussed in the past by

---

[1] The suffering of animals raises special difficulties because animals are not usually regarded as capable of morality, and therefore requiring freedom, nor as immortal; but, if we cannot solve the problem, it is one of those problems of which we can say that, even if there be a solution, we could not expect to see it. For we do not know what an animal's experience is like and so cannot see whether there are not any goods in an animal's life, besides mere pleasure, to which the pain might be a necessary means.

theologians and philosophers. Such discussions must in general not be deprecated but encouraged: it is one of the finest occupations of man to form as clear an idea of the fundamental reality as we can. But in discussing them the theist must always remember that God is far above any ideas of Him we can form. In order to avoid excessive dogmatism there is needed some conception such as that of analogical senses put forward by St. Thomas Aquinas or that of regulative ideas put forward by Kant. The former held that, because God was a being of quite a different nature from ours, no concept could be applied to him in the same sense as it could to us but only in an 'analogical' sense; the latter insisted that we could never have 'constitutive' but only 'regulative' ideas of God, meaning that we could not form clear definite concepts of God as we could of scientific objects but only highly inadequate and formal ones, and could not prove the applicability even of those in any strict sense of 'prove'. The working out of both these doctrines by the philosophers in question is liable to much criticism in detail, but something of the kind is certainly needed in order to make clear the limitations of any human concepts of God.

Philosophy of religion is not religion, but if I am right the former can be used to defend the latter. Philosophy can be employed, if not to prove conclusively the fundamental truths of religion, at any rate to work them out, to defend them against attack, and to use them to make a fairly coherent picture of the universe thus providing a partial justification. If so, none can deny the great practical importance of philosophy, even if we are careful not to identify religion with the theoretic acceptance of certain dogmas and are not prepared to go so far as those who assert that only a return of religion can save civilization from complete collapse. At the same time religion and philosophy must both be regarded as something more than means to social good. If we are not prepared to respect them each in their own right, then we shall not discover the truths which they contain nor will they ever acquire the full utility of which they are capable. The best results are not obtained by those who are always thinking of utility and aim too directly at results.

BIBLIOGRAPHY

CHAPTER II

B. RUSSELL, *Problems of Philosophy*, ch. v–xi (London, Home University Library).

J. LOCKE, *An Essay on the Human Understanding*, bks. i and iv.(Princeton University Press, and London, Humphrey Milford).

A. N. WHITEHEAD, *The Function of Reason* (Princeton University Press, and London, Humphrey Milford).

On verification principle:

A. J. AYER, *Language, Truth and Logic* (London, Gollancz).

J. WISDOM, 'Metaphysics and Verification' in *Mind*, vol. XLVII, p. 452 ff.

On intuition:

R. I. AARON, *The Nature of Knowing* (London, Williams & Norgate).

A. C. EWING, *Reason and Intuition* (London, Humphrey Milford).

For more advanced work:

Readings in Philosophical Analysis, ed. H. Feigl and W. Sellars (N.Y., Appleton Century-Croft).

B. BLANSHARD, *The Nature of Thought*, vol. II, ch. 28–30 (London, Allen & Unwin).

C. D. BROAD, 'Are there Synthetic *a priori* Truths?' *Proceedings of Aristotelian Society Supp.* vol. XV.

M. R. COHEN, *Reason and Nature* (Rahway, N.J., Quinn & Boden Co., and London, Kegan Paul).

H. W. B. JOSEPH, *An Introduction to Logic* (Oxford University Press, England).

C. I. LEWIS, *An Analysis of Knowledge and Valuation* (La Salle and London, Open Court Publishing Co.).

J. R. WEINBERG, *An Examination of Logical Positivism* (London, Kegan Paul, and New York, Harcourt, Brace & Co.).

CHAPTER III

W. P. MONTAGUE, *The Ways of Knowing*, pt. i (New York, Macmillan Co., and London, Allen & Unwin).

Bibliography

B. RUSSELL, *The Problems of Philosophy*, ch. 12, 13 (Home University Library).

On pragmatism:

W. JAMES, *Pragmatism* (New York, Longmans Green).

C. S. PEIRCE, *Collected Papers*, V (Harvard University Press).

R. B. PERRY, *Present Philosophical Tendencies*, ch. 9 (New York, Longmans Green).

For more advanced study on coherence:

A. C. EWING, *Idealism*, ch. 5 (London, Methuen).

BOSANQUET, *Implication and Linear Inference* (London, Macmillan).

BRADLEY, *Essays on Truth and Reality* (Oxford University Press).

B. BLANSHARD, *The Nature of Thought*, vol. II, ch. 25–7.

CHAPTER IV

BERKELEY, *Principles of Human Knowledge* and *Three Dialogues between Hylas and Philonous*.

C. D. BROAD, *Perception, Physics and Reality*, ch. 1, 3, 4 (Cambridge University Press, England).

J. LAIRD, *A Study in Realism* (Cambridge University Press, England).

G. E. MOORE in *Contemporary British Philosophy*, 2nd series, ed. J. H. Muirhead (New York, Macmillan Co., and London, Allen & Unwin).

B. RUSSELL, *Our Knowledge of the External World*, Lects. 3 and 4 (London, Allen & Unwin).

G. F. STOUT, *Mind and Matter*, bks. 3 and 4 (Cambridge University Press, England).

For more advanced study:

H. H. PRICE, *Perception* (London, Methuen).

C. D. BROAD, *Scientific Thought*, pt. II (London, Kegan Paul; New York, Harcourt, Brace & Co.).

The New Realism, ed. E. B. Holt (New York, Macmillan Co.).

A. O. LOVEJOY, *The Revolt against Dualism* (New York, Norton).

CHAPTERS V and VI

In general:

J. LAIRD, *Problems of the Self* (London, Macmillan).

H. H. PRICE, 'On Knowledge of Other Minds', in *Proceedings of Aristotelian Society*, vol. XXXII, and in *Philosophy*, vol. XIII.

J. WISDOM, *Mind and Matter*, pt. I (Cambridge University Press, England).

Bibliography

For more advanced study:

G. F. STOUT, *Manual of Psychology* (London, University Tutorial Press).

J. WARD, *Psychological Principles* (Cambridge University Press, England).

B. RUSSELL, *The Analysis of Mind* (London, Allen & Unwin, New York, Macmillan Co.).

C. D. BROAD, *The Mind and its Place in Nature*, (London, Kegan Paul).

F. R. TENNANT, *The Soul and its Faculties*, ch. 5, 6 (Cambridge University Press).

G. RYLE. *The Concept of Mind*, (Oxford University Press).

CHAPTER VII

B. RUSSELL, *Our Knowledge of the External World*, Lects. 5–7 (London, Allen & Unwin).

M. F. CLEUGH, *Time* (London, Methuen).

For more advanced study:

KANT, *Critique of Pure Reason*, chap. on Antinomy.

C. D.'BROAD, *Scientific Thought* (London, Kegan Paul; New York, Harcourt, Brace & Co.).

CHAPTER VIII

HUME, *Treatise*, bk. 1, pt. 3 (London, Allen & Unwin).

B. RUSSELL, *Our Knowledge of the External World*, Lect. 8 (London, Allen & Unwin).

C. D. BROAD, *Perception, Physics and Reality*, ch. 2 (Cambridge University Press, England).

A. C. EWING, *Idealism*, ch. IV, sect. 3 (London, Methuen).

Proceedings of Aristotelian Society Supp., vol. XIV, articles by G. F. Stout and C. D. Broad.

B. BLANSHARD, *The Nature of Thought*, vol. II, pp. 495–513.

CHAPTER IX

W. JAMES, 'The Dilemma of Determinism' in *The Will to Believe* (New York, Longmans Green).

H. RASHDALL, *Theory of Good and Evil*, vol. II, bk. 3, ch. 3 (Oxford University Press, England).

R. E. HOBART, 'Free Will as involving Determination' in *Mind*, vol. XLIII, p. 1 ff.

Bibliography

W. D. Ross, *Foundations of Ethics*, ch. x (Oxford University Press, England).

C. A. Campbell, *Scepticism and Construction*, ch. iv, v (London, Allen & Unwin).

A. E. Taylor in *Contemporary British Philosophy*, 2nd series, ed. J. H. Muirhead (London, Allen & Unwin).

CHAPTER X

Berkeley on universals, *Principles*, Introduction.

Plato, *Republic*, vi, 503–vii, 521.

Bertrand Russell, *Problems of Philosophy*, ch. 9, 10 (Home University Library).

R. I. Aaron, *Our Knowledge of Universals* (London, Humphrey Milford).

H. H. Price, *Thinking and Representation* (London, Cumberlege).

On relations from pluralistic point of view:

W. James, *Essays in Radical Empiricism*.

From moderately monistic:

B. Blanshard, *The Nature of Thought*, vol. ii, ch. 21, 22.

CHAPTER XI

Butler, *Analogy*.

Hume, *Dialogues concerning Natural Religion*.

Kant in *Watson's Selections*, pp. 195–222 and 289–349.

Lotze, *Outlines of the Philosophy of Religion*.

J. M. E. McTaggart, *Some Dogmas of Religion* (London, Arnold).

H. H. Farmer, *Towards Belief in God* (London, S.C.M. Press).

A. E. Taylor, *Does God Exist?* (London, Macmillan).

W. R. Wright, *A Student's Philosophy of Religion* (New York, Macmillan).

E. S. Brightman, *A Philosophy of Religion* (New York, Prentice-Hall).

E. A. Burtt, *Types of Religious Philosophy* (New York, Harper).

For more advanced reading:

Thomas Aquinas, *Summa contra Gentiles*, bks. i, iii.

A. N. Whitehead, *Religion in the Making* (New York, Macmillan).

G. F. Stout, *God and Nature*, (Cambridge University Press).

Index

Index

Index

Index

Index

bearing of its modern development on philosophy, 81, 97, 145–7, 149, 167, 182–6

and phenomenalism, 73, 91

presuppositions of, 159–60, 163, 175–80, 188, 210, 224

Secondary: primary qualities, 77–8, 85–7, 95, 184

Self-identity, 112–18

Sense data or sensa, 69 ff., 86–7, 89

v. Given, the

Sense-experience, 44–5, 60 ff., 69

as criterion of truth and meaning, 39 ff., 72 ff.

innate ideas, 42–4

sensing: sensa, 75–6, 103

v. Perception

Socrates, 24

Solipsism, 119–22

Space, 129–30, 143–51, 176

Spencer, Herbert, 18

Spinoza, 206, 208, 245

Stout, G. F., on cause, 170–1

Structure: content, 85–6, 116

Subjectivism, in ethics, 235

Subsistent entities, 219–20

Substance: of physical objects, 95 ff.

of self, 112–18

body and mind same substance? 129–33

idea of, 44

Survival, of bodily death, 116–17, 133–5, 236, 250

Syllogism, 29

Synthetic *a priori* propositions, 33 ff., 166

Teleology, in organisms, 180–1 225 ff.

Telepathy, 120

Thomas Aquinas, views of body: mind, 135–6

on God, 251

Time, 19, ch. VII *passim*, 176

Truth, ch. III *passim*

Unconscious, the, 109–11

Universals, 211 ff.

Use, of philosophy, 10 ff., 24–5, 251

Values, 156, 249

v. Ethics

Value Theory, 17

Verification principle, 39–42

Vitalism: mechanism, 180–1

War, 14

Whitehead, on importance of philosophy, 12, 14

Will, and cause, 162, 172

freedom of, 189 ff.

Wisdom, practical, and philosophy, 24